Different Lives in One
A Collection of Memories

Different Lives in One
A Collection of Memories

John M. Moody

Copyright © by John M. Moody

Different Lives in One, A Collection of Memories
First Edition – 2019, May 10th Revisions

Paperback   ISBN 13: 9781093419580

All rights reserved. This book or its parts may not be copied or disseminated in any form or by any means, either electronically or mechanically, including through photocopies, recordings, or through data storage and retrieval systems without the written permission of the copyright owner.

This is a work of non-fiction. Every effort has been made to show all people and events herein as truthfully as possible. In some cases names of individuals have been left incomplete on purpose even though these lines are not meant to offend anyone.

This work is available from Amazon.com and Amazon Europe.

This book is dedicated to Mary Ann with the hope that the lines it contains will help her to gain knowledge and wisdom.

Forward

  I presently work at Grayson College in Denison, Texas, as a writing lab instructor. (Not an exciting way to start a book, right?) On January 24, 2018, Stella Thompson, my friend and immediate supervisor, all at once told me (and I paraphrase), "John, you know so many interesting stories, why don't you write them down?"
  As a writer of adventure fiction who has been involved in a fair share of real-life adventures, I have been writing down some of these stories for years, but not in the way Stella meant. I've included parts of my true adventures as details in my novels. She wanted the non-fiction accounts, not the fictional versions. For this reason, I am now undertaking a completely new endeavor. I have never before tried to assemble a collection of true tales of this sort for public consumption.
  It wasn't the first time I considered Stella's suggestion. I've been thinking about it for years, but I was usually doing something else—mostly writing fiction. A couple of years ago I even made a start of it. I wrote down a few stories about my mother and father—details of their lives I thought were pretty interesting. I've related some of my included tales to my wife, Belkis; she even participated in many of them. I've also told some of them to our daughter, Mary Ann; I sometimes told them as bedtime stories to possibly shape her life, much as my parent's stories helped me to shape mine. And I have to admit, I'm not getting any younger. As in the words of a song by one of my favorite musical groups, the Moody Blues, "Time waits for no one …"
  In fact, I feel obligated to publish them for several reasons. The Greeks, the Irish, and other peoples around the world during early

times used to maintain traditions of passing along stories, songs, and other information by word of mouth. It's great they did it over the years; otherwise, some really good stories might have been lost forever. Even so, it's a dangerous practice when it comes to our present and future generations being able to remember things *exactly* as they've been told. Too often when a link is severed, the information is lost forever. We have access to a number of ancient works today only because someone eventually wrote them down. But how many other works are gone forever?

I often recall a scene from the movie *Blade Runner* (Warner Bros., 1982) between Harrison Ford and Rutger Hauer when the "replicant" (an artificial human) spares the "blade runner's" life and promptly begins to describe some of the marvelous things he has seen over his short lifespan—all of which will be lost when he dies. And then he dies, taking with him those memories. This idea is much like I hope to avoid by writing things down and having them published.

With the electronic age upon us, human's also have a tendency to "lose" data either by accident, through neglect, or on purpose—as news stories have lately shown in cases where top-level government information that should have been saved electronically has "disappeared" or was "wiped" from existence, never to be seen again. What if the same thing happened to the US Constitution? Could an unexpected EM pulse near a cloud farm in Iceland permanently delete a group of authors' works? This random thought also serves as a stimulus for me to set a text down in print, but it will also be available electronically for wider distribution. In this way I can have the best of both worlds.

Mostly, though, I hope to give my daughter and her descendants (if any) access to my stories in the future by writing them down. And by publishing them, others can read them, too, because this collection of tales holds a little something for just about everyone.

I have included stories about ancestors and family. I am related to remarkable sets of genes. But fundamentally, these are *my* memories. Therefore, I have been an active participant in most of these tales. I include stories from my early youth while living in Oak Cliff south of Dallas, Texas, and in Denison, Texas, and tales from school, collage, and university days. I worked on a railroad signal gang one summer during college. After graduation, I worked in a petroleum services lab for a number of years. This allowed me to see and even to reside in some pretty interesting locations. While living in Venezuela, I became involved with a university biology museum as its curator of paleontology. As a result, our team discovered some remarkable and important fossils. After I returned to the US, I worked in several aspects of education. I also better developed my writing skills. I wrote novels—quite a few of them. This has now allowed me to put together this collection of tales so Mary Ann, Stella, and others might enjoy them—and possibly learn from them. And while doing all this, other phases of my life continued to happen outside these realms.

As I made my first list of the subjects to include, I realized how much my past has shaped my present. Most especially when I reviewed the first draft, it showed how often my actual experiences ended up as parts of my fictional stories; I point out both where and how they ended up in my books.

However, I want this to be generally a "happy book." Life is too short for people to dwell on sadness. You may be disappointed if you seek the deep, nitty-gritty scandals and juicy, gossipy details of modern personal accounts because I have left most of those out. At the same time, some of what I did was quite adventurous—even dangerous at times.

You know, it's sort of funny; I've just realized I am ending my introduction much like I ended my first novel, *Journey from Mezet*. In this one, the main character named Marc has just set down on paper a story about his journey "so that the truth, as I know it, will be written." And just the same as Marc's grandfather urged him to do, I am sharing with others what I have learned during my own journey through life up to now.

The title of this book comes from the idea that I've lived my life in diverse stages almost as separate lives. For example, I lived a different life during my school years than I did as a working adult; in turn, that life ended up quite different from my years working as a paleontologist at a museum, and so forth. These lives occasionally overlapped or ran parallel to one another. Some join together like links in a chain. Others divided or united along different tangents. I even use information from one life during others, such as when I shared bits and pieces of them fictionally, or when I gathered knowledge as a child to use as an adult. Even so, I still view them distinctly—different, but still part of a whole.

Students of history tell us we need to know our past so we can learn from our mistakes. In my case maybe this didn't happen all the time, but at least I've tried to build toward a future based on the past. Another of my purposes in relating these stories is so people who read them will enjoy them, but I would feel especially pleased if people will also learn something from what I write.

> John M. Moody
> Denison, Texas

The Lives of Ancestors

A Few Real Characters ... in More Ways than One

Early, Miscellaneous Names

I hope the first part of this book won't bore readers other than my daughter, but I feel it's necessary to set the scene. I am, after all, made from what my ancestors have given me.

Aunt Rosalie (Rosalie Moody), whom I will describe in more detail later, was a big fan of genealogy. She was the first person I ever knew who actually kept up with such things, and according to her, my father's side of the family had roots from England dating back at least to the 1600s where one of my ancestors had been a town mayor. Rosalie also once told my mother (with me listening in at a young age) that somewhere in our distant past we had royal French blood. She based the information on the use of a fleur-de-lis on an ancestral crest, which she claimed meant we have a regal French ancestor. I never saw her information, and I feel pretty sure her research is now lost. She also claimed we have ancestors from Holland. I haven't tried one of those DNA tests yet to see what it might say, but maybe someday I'll confirm her data.

My mother, Mary Moody, whom I will also discuss later, actually did a lot of genealogical research in her later life, and she turned up a number of interesting family details. In contrast to Aunt Rosalie's case, I still have access to my mother's valuable notes.

One detail she discovered was an ancestor named Sir George Yeardley (1588 –1627) who after being shipwrecked on Bermuda, first arrived at Jamestown Colony in 1610. He apparently traveled to and from the colony more than once, returning to England one time where the King of England—James I at the time—knighted him just before he was appointed as one of Virginia's first governors (about 1618). He served as governor more than once up until his death. According to reports, he was a popular leader. One source even claimed that *his* early ancestor was a baron who witnessed the signing of the *Magna Carta* in 1215.

My mother also noted English ancestors with family names of Thorogood from London (born 1440), Mason from London (born 1566), and Rhett from Brentwood, Essex (born 1666), among many others and their American descendants.

The Rhett name had more recent family members in Mississippi and in other locations, and probably still does. My grandmother on my father's side was a Rhett. Another one in particular was a more distant relation, Alicia Rhett (1915 - 2014), who played India Wilkes in the 1939 Selznick International Pictures film *Gone With the Wind*.

My mother also turned up ancestors from Ireland named Barnwell and Carberry from Dublin—dating from around 1700, Rutledge from County Tyrone, who migrated from Ireland in 1738, and George Cathey—also from Ireland, born in 1736—who later served as a captain in the American Revolution (on the American side). In my novel, *Many Shades of Green*, two of the characters meet in Ireland because one of them is researching his Irish roots.

My mother encountered Scottish ancestors named Nimmo and Morehead. She also found Welch ancestors named Pollard from Ways, Wales. I found the names in some of her notes and photocopies, and I think she knew what she was doing when she listed them.

The Early Moodys

Throughout my life, I've naturally heard mostly about the Moody line from my father's side. Before I came along, five people named John M. Moody extended along a line of descendants, with the fifth being my father. One of these was a child who died at a young age, but his parents had another son, whom they also named John M. Moody. Some of these Moodys are buried at Friendship Cemetery in Columbus, Mississippi, and I remember visiting their gravesites a few

Different Lives in One

years ago. And I'll say another thing; it looks pretty strange to see my name on several tombstones, even if I'm not buried under any of them.

I learned from one of my aunts that someone in the family located the portraits on canvas of the original John M. Moody and his wife. As I understand it, these paintings were in poor condition, but they were later restored. My Aunt Emily sent me photos of the restorations, and they look pretty nice. I have also seen photos of some of the later Moodys, including some wives and my grandfather on my father's side when he was a boy. I never got to know him because he died when my father was quite young. Aunt Emily also sent a silver baby spoon to Mary Ann that once belonged to him (approximately 1880). I've always thought it was interesting to view old photographs of most anyone and any place, but it's especially nice to be able to look ancestors in the eyes.

According to one of my distant cousins who has also done extensive family research, one of these men named John M. Moody was killed in a duel at a fairly advanced age (about 68). It is said he was the last man to ever be killed in a duel in North Carolina.

From what I understand, the Moodys lived mostly in Virginia, North Carolina, and Mississippi until my mother and father moved to Texas (where I was born) following World War II.

Family Heroes Who Wore Dresses

Some of my ancestors were military men. They include (according to my mother) a British Naval Commander named Shelton. My father was also an army veteran, whom I will describe in more detail later. However, some of my ancestors were women who distinguished themselves during war time.

As a boy, my family used to return to Mississippi to visit grandparents. My grandmother on my mother's side (Mrs. J. L. Meador, whom I called Ganny – also to be described later) had a framed photo hanging on the wall of the living room. It showed a statue of a woman.

At a young age, I never felt especially curious, but when I got older, I learned that the monument had been built in honor of my great, great, great, great, great, great, great grandmother, Kerenhappuch Turner (1692 – 1807). (Oh, by the way, that's *seven* "greats.") During

John M. Moody

the American Revolution, she traveled 300 miles on horseback after learning that one of her sons had been wounded in battle. When she found him, she nursed him back to health by inventing a device (a wooden bucket with holes in it to drip cool water) that helped her son to break his fever. It is for this reason that this monument now sits in Gillford Court House Battleground National Park in North Carolina. As people might notice from the dates next to her name, she lived to be about 115 years old. It is said she danced the first dance at a ball given in honor of her hundredth birthday. The photo of her monument now hangs on the wall at our home, having come into our family following my grandmother's passing.

Ganny also told another story about a heroic woman ancestor. It took place during the American Civil War, although I'm not a direct descendent. Her name was Alice Thompson. I believe she would have been my grandmother's aunt, and at the time of the story, she was only 17 years old.

According to Ganny's tale, which has previously been published in Tennessee historical accounts, the Battle of Thompson's Station, Tennessee, was in progress on March 5, 1863. As a slightly older girl, she had taken refuge in a half basement of a neighbor's farm known as Homestead Manor as Federal soldiers entered the town. According to one account, she was the only member of her family in the cellar at the time, but there were others with her, including the family that lived in the house. She and the others monitored the fighting taking place. (In my grandmother's version of the story, she watched through a crack between slanted cellar doors.)

Early during the battle one of the Confederate officers was shot and killed. Without an officer to direct them, the Confederates were in disarray, and they soon began to lose their position. Then Alice watched from her hiding place as a man from an Arkansas regiment carrying the Confederate flag was also struck by a bullet and fell, dropping the flag.

As a patriotic young girl from The South, she promptly opened the basement door and ran out to raise the flag, waving it over her head. All at once one of the soldiers noticed and called out to the others that a woman carried their flag, and they began to surround her in order to protector her. One account claims a cannon shell hit the ground not far away, but it only threw dirt on her.

Remarkably, the nucleus of solders protecting the woman with the flag became a rallying point, and from there, the Confederate soldiers soon took the advantage, eventually winning the skirmish. Even the Federal officers later praised her bravery.

After the battle, she also helped some of the wounded soldiers who were carried into the house. One account says she used pieces of her dress to make bandages. Not long afterward, she married one of the soldiers, David Dungan, who was apparently impressed by her actions. Sadly, however, she only lived until the age of 23.

Lately, some people have been saying that monuments commemorating Confederate personalities and events should all be removed and destroyed because they are symbols of racism. Even so, I still believe that no matter what side of the conflict a person supported, bravery in the face of death should still be recognized.

Thompson of Thompson's Station

Another direct ancestor, my great, great grandfather on my mother's side, was Dr. Elijah Thompson (1805 – 1871). He must have been a real "go-getter," a man who did a lot of things. He studied medicine in Franklin, Tennessee, under another doctor and received his medical degree in 1830. Later, he served as a medical surgeon for the Confederate Army during the American Civil War. He speculated in cotton and succeeded in it, making money. He served in the House of the Tennessee General Assembly during two terms. He helped to build the rail line for the Tennessee and Alabama Railroad between Columbia and Nashville. Much later, this line became part of the Louisville and Nashville Railroad, which eventually ended up as part of CSX.

Elijah Thompson married three times, but he only had children (10 of them within about 12 years) with his second wife, Mary Ann Riley Thompson, who died about 1853. One of their daughters was Alice Thompson, "the Heroine of Thompson's Station" mentioned earlier. Another was my great aunt, Mickey Thompson, whom I will describe later. Still another was my great grandmother, Mary Emma Thompson Laws, whom I will include in the next section. Most importantly, Dr. Thompson inherited land from his father, John Thompson, and in 1853 he deeded some of the land to create the town of Thompson's Station, Tennessee, which is located along the rail line he helped to create. The town of Thompson's Station is still an active community.

Real-Life Book Characters

In my romantic adventure novel *Return to Nowhere*, part of my story concerns a young woman named Sarah Elizabeth Bell who travels with her family from central Tennessee toward the north as her father seeks a better life. I included my great grandparents, Dr. H. A. Laws, and his wife, Mary Emma Laws, in the story as I imagined them from old photos and from the stories my grandmother and my mother used to tell about them. Some of the things they did over the years sound pretty extraordinary from today's standpoint. Not only did my information come from family stories; I have confirmed some of it from my grandfather's newspaper obituary. I discovered a clipping a few years ago, and I also found the information repeated in other sources.

I am fortunate that through the encouragement of my mother, Ganny in her later life started to write down facts and stories. My mother once told her to keep a notebook handy, and whenever she thought of something the family might like to know, she should write it down. I guess by writing my book, I am also fulfilling the wishes of those who came before me. I have photocopies of Ganny's handwritten pages to study as I relate some of this information.

Hiram Laws was born on November 10, 1850. His father was Colonel John Laws, and his mother was the colonel's second wife, a widow named Mary Cathey Bishop (Laws). Hiram was the youngest, and his mother died when he was only two years old.

When John Laws, senior, married a third time to another widow named Frances Allen Dazey (Laws) following his second wife's death, she became a good mother to all the children, from what my grandmother says.

Hiram had five brothers and sisters, including an elder brother, also named John Laws. This brother served as Register of Deeds in Orange County, Tennessee, for about 63 years until he died at the age of 93 in 1913. I'd like to be working at 93, too. He had four half-brothers and sisters through Frances Laws, too, not all of them of direct blood because she entered the marriage with two children already.

The doctors described Hiram as having "sore eyes," for which they were unable to help him. For this reason, he didn't attend regular school at all. According to my grandmother, this caused him to get into "a lot of mischief." His father gave him a "yellow" mule, which he loved quite a lot. He also seemed to like people, and whenever he heard about any kind of gathering, such as a dance or a camp meeting, he rode his mule to the event. However, when he was about 16, someone gave him some whiskey, and he rode his mule into a general store, shooting up the place. The store had tin buckets hanging from the rafters throughout the establishment, and he shot a hole through each one. His father had to pay for the damages, which I suppose was the way they kept him out of jail.

The Presbyterians in town for a time were holding revival meetings at their church, and because of the gathered crowd, Hiram also attended. The preacher invited everyone who wanted to become a Christian to come down and sit in the front seats where someone would talk to them. Hiram went to sit in front, but he must have had a pretty poor reputation because no one would talk to him. The church meetings went on for ten days, and each time he attended, he sat in front. Still, no one would talk to him until the last night when the preacher urged someone to talk to the boy. Finally, his brother-in-law, who attended the church, sat and talked to him, but according to my grandmother, Hiram didn't "feel satisfied." He went outside to where he had tied his mule to a stump, but he felt lost.

Finally, he knelt down beside the stump and prayed for God to save his soul. All at once, he said he felt "as light as a feather." He jumped up and cried out, "I'm saved!"

It was late by then, and people who heard him began to light their lanterns to see who was yelling, but when they saw him, they only said, "That's just Hiram Laws," and they went back to sleep. He claimed he had to live like a good Christian for six months before anyone noticed the difference.

In some way, Hiram's eyes got better, and he finally attended a boy's school at the age of 18. He must have done well in only a short time because he went on to further his education. He also became a medical doctor and a certified preacher.

Medical Practice

After Hiram Laws completed his basic education, he attended the University of Nashville Medical School. He ended up graduating with a medical degree in 1873. (Just imagine; here is a man who first went to formal school at the age of 18 who is now a practicing physician at 23.) Based on my grandmother's writings, he began to practice medicine in Thompson's Station. Unfortunately, he had to wait for several months before he treated his first patient. Finally, a woman who had tried several doctors previously asked him to see her. She got better and told everyone. This was the time his practice really got started.

Hiram Meets Mary Emma

By living in Thompson's Station and practicing medicine there, he eventually met more people. At different times, he ended up dating three of Elijah Thompson's daughters before he finally fell in love with Mary Thompson.

Mary Emma Thompson was born in 1852. She had seven brothers and sisters, most of whom I know of only by names, except for Mickey. (I'll describe more about Mickey a little further on.) Two of Mary's sisters, Sophie and Alice (the same one from the battle), had died before my grandmother got to know them.

After a while, Hiram's medical practice didn't seem to be doing particularly well, so he decided to leave Thompson's Station and travel to Fort Smith, Arkansas. A few months later, he returned to Thompson's Station and went to visit Mary to ask her to marry him. He asked her on a Sunday night and thought she might tell him they could be married in the spring. However she responded, "I can't possibly get ready before Wednesday night."

Mary and her sisters wore about the same size dresses, and Sophie and Mickey gave Mary their best clothes as wedding presents on such short notice because soon after the wedding, the newlyweds went to live in Fort Smith. After a while, however, Mary became homesick, so she traveled alone back to Thompson's Station for a visit.

While she was with her family, Hiram became ill with "swamp fever" and also ended up returning to Thompson's Station. Apparently, he was in pretty bad shape, and a doctor came to examine him. The doctor informed Mary that Hiram "wouldn't live through the night." Hiram heard the doctor and thought to himself, *I'll show that doctor!* Slowly, he began to improve. He once told my grandmother that if he hadn't heard the doctor talking to Mary, he might have simply "laid there and died."

After his death, Elijah Thompson's land was broken up and sold in parcels by some of the family. Hiram purchased 125 acres with the Elijah Thompson home upon it, where he and Mary could live. Mickey Thompson didn't want to sell her portion of the Thompson estate, so she ended up living with Hiram and Mary in part of the house. Her part of the estate was to be united with the property of Hiram and Mary upon her death, but she outlived them both.

My great grandparents had four children, including Daisy Laws, who died as a child, my grandmother, Ganny (Mary Frances. Laws [later Meador], Hiram Laws, junior, who also became a doctor, and Ewell Laws, who after receiving a diploma from a business college, traveled to Panama at an early age to seek his fortune. Great Uncle Ewell became a planter near Boquette, he married, he raised children, and he stayed there the rest of his life.

As it turned out, Hiram and Mary never returned to Fort Smith. They remained in Thompson's Station for the rest of their lives. Hiram continued to practice medicine for about 20 years, but he later gave it up due to poor health. Even so, he lived for at least 35 years afterward. He also became a licensed preacher in 1884 and was instrumental in organizing the Thompson's Station United Methodist Church.

Always There to Help

My grandmother wrote down in her notebook how her mother was a good neighbor in her community, a person who was willing to step in to help whenever needed. She describes Mary as a "quiet soul." I sometimes think of the old adage "opposites attract" when I read about my great grandmother in comparison to my great grandfather.

Mary could sew well. On occasion, wealthier family members passed along hand-me-down dresses for her to use. She usually took them apart and used the material to make smaller dresses for her daughters. My grandmother described the garments as being "pretty."

One story written about her describes how a woman in town died of meningitis. From my research, I've learned that for bacterial meningitis, about 90 percent of cases were fatal at the time, and it could be passed readily through close contact. The undertaker simply delivered a coffin to the home, but at the time, they didn't prepare a body for burial. It was up the family or friends. In this particular case, no one wanted to go to the house to help the family—no one except Mary.

She went to the house and helped the family to bathe and dress the body, and place it in the coffin. At the end of the day, she returned home, but she wouldn't let anyone get near her. She had someone bring fresh clothes and two washtubs of hot water to a place behind "the coal shed." Then she removed her clothes, placing them in one of the tubs while using the other tub for bathing, "hair and all." Later, everyone in town admired her for helping the family.

Civil War Relics - Collecting must run in the family.

My mother often spoke of my great grandfather collecting Civil War relics. On the family farm as he plowed the fields around the house, he often picked up items that had been lost, shot, or discarded during the Battle of Thompson's Station, part of which had taken place right there around the house. One of my uncles also spoke of picking up "Minié balls" that washed out along the dirt road between the main road and the house.

My mother once decided that during one of our trips to Mississippi we would drive Ganny to Tennessee to visit in person with remaining family members. Besides my mother and Ganny, my two sisters and I went along. (I think I was about eleven years old at the time, but I remember a lot about the trip, which I later ended up using to some extent in my novels.) It also gave Ganny a chance to tell us stories and let us see some of the places she remembered. She even pointed out where graves of ancestors stood, and I saw the headstone on my great, great grandfather—although I was too young at the time for the event to really impress me.

After we passed the old home place, where the house where Ganny grew up no longer stood, we traveled to Franklin, Tennessee, which is located only a few miles north of Thompson's Station. Great grandfather's collections were on loan to a military academy there, and they were on display. I got to see them, and it was a pretty impressive collection filling a small room with glass displays along the walls. I saw cannon balls, bullets, bayonets, and other items. Among the items, they even had on display a complete Confederate officer's uniform, which my mother believed belonged to a great uncle who served in the war.

At the time, arrangements were being made to donate the entire collection to the State of Tennessee, and I believe this is where the items eventually ended up. I wonder if the collection is still on display somewhere or if they simply stored it away in boxes.

When I look back at my great grandfather, I see something of me in him. He enjoyed collecting interesting items, and I do, too.

"Hey, you shot my house with a cannon!"

The home where Hiram and Mary Laws lived was a rather large place that was built by Elijah Thompson. At some date after my great grandfather and great grandmother returned from Arkansas—as described earlier—Hiram bought his deceased father-in-law's house.

On a wall near the ceiling—I believe my mother said in the dining room—the house had a hole in it. During the Battle of Thompson's Station, some careless gunner from one army or the other fired a cannon, which hit the house and created the hole.

It might have been a solid iron shot that perforated the wood. If it had been an explosive shell, it thankfully didn't explode.

For some reason, Elijah Thompson never fixed the hole. Hiram Laws never fixed it, either. He proudly pointed it out to visitors, and my mother remembered seeing it as a young girl. The only modification Hiram made at some later date was to place a section of window screen across the hole, so when the doors were closed, they could keep out the flies.

I also mention Hiram pointing out this cannon ball hole in July of 1899 to travelers in my book *Return to Nowhere*.

John M. Moody

Helping Travelers along the Road

Speaking of travelers, in my novel, *Return to Nowhere*, as I previously described, I have created a scenario involving several of my ancestors. The family of Sarah Bell, one of the principal female protagonists, is traveling on foot and by wagon in the summer of 1899 along the road north of Thompson's Station. They reach a spot as evening approaches where a woman is standing beside the road near the entrance to a property. She invites the family to come to her house for dinner and to rest there for the night. Soon her husband, a doctor, also comes out to greet them. This is precisely how Mary and Hiram Laws helped total strangers through acts of Christian charity.

As evening approached, they stood near the road and invited travelers into their home. They fed them dinner at night, provided them with places to sleep, and fed them breakfast in the morning to see them on their way, well rested and with full stomachs.

According to what I've read and heard, they did the same thing for years and years, especially during the years when people traveled by horse, by wagon, or on foot. They never accepted payment. Much of the action I describe in my book was a true scenario as far as I could determine, only I've added my fictional characters interacting with my ancestors during what I imagined as a typical encounter. I wrote my book more than six years ago, and ever since then, there is nothing in my tale I care to change based on anything I read afterward.

An Old Picture in an Even Older Frame

In my grandmother's house, a framed picture hung in the living room. I now have this same picture hanging in our house. It measure about 12 inches tall by 18 inches wide. In the background, it shows a large, frame house with a porch and three chimneys at widely-spaced locations. A rather old couple stands in the foreground. The man, who stands on the right, has a full, white beard. He wears a dark coat and boots with his trousers tucked into the tops. A dark, brimmed hat is tilted confidently toward the right. He stands in a somewhat casual pose.

In contrast, the woman on the left appears ill at ease. She is somewhat plump and wears a dress with a bell-shaped, full skirt that covers her legs completely. She seems to have a rather serious expression on her face, as if she has been unexpectedly drawn away from her daily chores. This picture is actually a large-format photograph that has been "colorized." The following is an interesting story about this photo and how it was taken.

Late one afternoon, as usual, Hiram and Mary helped a young man they encountered along the road by inviting him to their house for the evening. He turned out to be a traveling photographer. The next morning after breakfast when they were about to send him on his way, he talked them into posing in front of their house for his camera, but then he charged them a dollar. My great grandfather mostly figured the man needed the dollar more than him and imagined they would never hear from him again.

A few weeks later, they received a package, which contained the photograph, complete with color tinting in blue for the sky. When they received it, they wanted to hang it on the wall, but they didn't have a frame. Then Hiram had the idea of using an old frame that once belonging to his father-in-law. It was a good fit, and this photo still resides in the same frame—the frame that once held Elijah Thompson's shaving mirror, the one he used each day while at home. This information comes from my mother and my grandmother.

Each time I look at this photo, I feel moved by how the traveling photographer captured this moment in time. Most of the photos I've seen of my family during this time period, which I figure to be around 1910, were taken in studios. When they went in for these studio poses, they wore their "Sunday best." However, this photo captures how Hiram and Mary appeared on most any regular day. This was the image I tried to create for my novel.

The "Old Gun"

Along the main road below the hill where Hiram and Mary Laws lived, an "old gun" once stood. I heard about it a number of times as a boy. My mother used to call it a cannon, and I always wanted to see it. When I asked what happened to it, they told me it had been stolen.

During that trip of several days through Tennessee in the summer of 1964, we stopped briefly along the road north of

Thompson's Station. Ganny and my mother said it was the hill where my grandmother's childhood home once stood. The old house had been torn down many years earlier. All I could see higher up was a dirt road leading to a clump of trees at the top of the hill.

Then my mother announced, "That's where the old gun once stood," pointing out a cement slab. I stepped out of the car to take a closer look.

I discovered that the "old gun" wasn't a cannon after all. I saw what I realized even at eleven years old was part of the stand of an old machinegun. Someone had taken a hacksaw and cut off the feet of the stand near the cement in order to steal the gun quickly, leaving only four metal stumps embedded in the cement.

Later, I found confirmation in an old photo album. One of the shots shows my great grandfather as an old man (pre-1929). He stood beside a young child, maybe my mother, next to a Maxim machinegun, the kind the Germans used during World War I. These are large, heavy, water-cooled guns that had to be mounted on large, elaborate bases or stands made of steel. The feet of this gun's base had been mounted in a cement slab measuring about the same size as the overall gun. The chances are it was a gun captured during World War I, which someone either gave to Hiram or he purchased, and he had it mounted as a curious display for passersby. (In my mind, someone gave it to him, knowing the kind of person he was.)

If anyone knows of a Maxim machinegun that either has the feet cut off the base or has been repaired to replace the feet, now you know where it came from. It's stolen property.

Books and Bookcase

As a young boy, my great grandfather's bookcase sat in a corner of the living room at Ganny's home in Mississippi. The bookcase consists of a table with a very tall set of glass shelves resting directly on top as a separate piece. However, the lower part of the shelves includes a fold-down, dark purple writing pad that hides a set of small drawers and cubbyholes. It looks like it might have been a tall writing desk where the legs were broken off, and to fix it, my great grandfather merely set it on a table.

As a boy, I was always fascinated with the treasures this desk contained. Later in life my grandmother let me look through the items there. They included papers and some other curious items I'll soon describe.

The bookcase also held an interesting set of books at the time. They were a complete set of *Confederate Military History* (1899). When I was about 14, my grandmother gave them to me. Some of the books contain notes made by my great grandfather, which he had marked in penciled in the margins. He had an interesting habit of indicating important information in the text by drawing tiny hands with index fingers pointing to certain passages. Many of the noted lines concern brave actions by soldiers and sometimes atrocities. At least once he marked a spot and added a note showing that an officer mentioned was a relative. Hiram Laws placed a sticker inside the cover of each volume with his name on it, along with the lines, "Friend, you promised to return this book."

The cubbyholes of the cabinet were stuffed full of documents. I found old letters, newspaper clippings, and old notebooks. One notebook lists supplies purchased for a trip to Texas before it was a state, but about all it lists are the item and the prices paid, if I remember correctly.

One of the documents I discovered is a land deed printed and signed on a piece of parchment for one square mile of Dallas County, Texas. I have no idea why it was there because it doesn't have any family names on it. The only scenario to come to mind is the fact that, according to my mother, Hiram sometimes loaned money to people, and perhaps the deed served as collateral. I suppose the loan was never paid back, and I doubt my great grandfather ever followed up on being the new owner of a square mile of empty prairie in faraway Texas. It was surely sold later for nonpayment of property taxes. If the deed happened to still be valid, the owner would be a multi-millionaire. Even so, the document, itself, probably holds a little historical value, not to mention having on it the signature of the Governor of Texas in 1855, Elisha M. Pease.

I found an old, metal token. It is marked "H.A. LAWS.M.D. THOMPSON.STA.TENN." It is similar to the ones people can still make at tourist attractions where they stamp the outer border using letters and numbers of their choosing. The modern versions have a five-pointed star in the center, but this one has a six-pointed star.

Another interesting item from a cubbyhole with no explanation was a type of small gunpowder flask for a muzzle-loading gun. It is shaped similar to a cylinder, although it is oval shaped in cross-section. At one end it has a spring lever for a person to press in order to pour a measure of black powder into the muzzle of a gun, probably some sort of pistol. When I first found it as a boy, it still contained a small amount of black powder. Next to the powder container, a swing-away tab allows access to a compartment where lead bullets can be stored. On the base, another compartment with a swing-away lid hides a small area where some sort of wadding or cloth patches could be kept to place between the bullet and the powder. It was made in England. The bullet compartment contained a lead Minié ball when I discovered it. The exterior is no longer in good condition, and it appears to be quite old. This might represent one of the relics from his collection that for some reason he kept apart from the others in his bookcase. If so, it didn't go with the rest of the collection. I guess I'll never know for sure.

Great Aunt Mickey

My mother's "Aunt Mickey" was Mary Laws' sister, also a daughter of Elijah Thompson. When I mentioned earlier that Hiram Laws dated three of the Thompson daughters before he fell in love with Mary, Mickey was one of the three. A photo of her as a young woman, which came to me through my mother from my grandmother, hangs in our house. She appears rather pretty.

Mickey never married, but she ended up raising quite a few children in one of the most important ways—she was a school teacher. I've seen photos of her posing in front of the Thompson's Station school along with all the school's children lined up. She continued to teach school until she was simply too old to do it anymore.

She was also a pretty good artist. A large, oil-painted portrait, which shows a young girl of about eight or ten years old standing next to a seated baby, used to hang in Ganny's dining room. The older girl is Daisy Laws, the eldest child of Hiram and Mary, who died at only eleven years old. My grandmother is the baby in the painting. My niece now has this portrait. It was painted by Mickey Thompson based on an early photo. I've seen the original photo, which shows not two but three children, one of them a young boy (my great uncle, Uncle Ewell, I believe). For some reason, Mickey chose to exclude the boy from the painting.

When my mother visited her grandparents during the summer along with her mother (on occasions between about 1921 and 1929), her Aunt Mickey still lived in the house with Hiram and Mary. My grandmother wrote in her notes that the woman always wore black dresses, but most of the time during the summer she remained in her room. As far as I can tell, she was the last person of our family to live in the old Thompson house, passing away in 1936.

Great Aunt Rebecca

My mother and grandmother spoke often of Rebecca. My mother thought of her as an aunt, and my grandmother thought of her as a sister, but she wasn't a blood relation. At some time when my grandmother was young while growing up as a Laws daughter, Rebecca and a sister came to live in their home. I don't know the full details, but apparently the girls' mother died, and for some reason, the girls' father was no longer able take care of them. The Laws family agreed to raise them in their home along with their own children. I don't know if any formal agreement was in place, or if it was just another act of Christian charity arranged by members of the church or the community. Early on they were referred to as "the foster sisters," but my grandmother soon loved them as if they were blood relations.

During that same trip to Tennessee in 1964, my mother drove my grandmother to visit Rebecca and her husband Harvey on their farm north of Duck Creek in central Tennessee. Rebecca and Harvey had children and grandchildren who were all very nice to us. We remained for a couple of days, and I had fun. I played with some boys who lived there. They showed me the trick of how to tell if an electric fence is electrified or not without touching it by placing a long leaf of green grass on it to feel only a slight current flow instead of a painful shock. I found Native American artifacts in their corn field. I watched the older men of the family stack hay bales (before the big hay rolls were in use), and I learned the reason why hay bales should never be stacked in a hay loft if the hay is still green. (It can lead to combustion due to excessive heat build-up.) On one afternoon, I helped to pick corn so we could eat it as corn on the cob the same night. I've heard the expression "from the farm to the table," but this was an extreme, first-hand case for me.

This might have been the last time my grandmother and Rebecca ever got together in person, although I believe they corresponded regularly for years afterward.

It was a great side trip during this journey to Tennessee. At the time, I had no idea how much this journey of only several days into "The Volunteer State" would influence me in my later life. Thinking back on those few days, I ended up gathering a lot of information about my family and about Tennessee that I later used in various aspects of my writing.

Family Lives

The Ones I Remember and a Few I Still Know

Ganny and Pawpaw

The grandmother I've been referring to up to now is Mary Frances Laws Meador (Mrs. J. L. Meador), the daughter of Hiram and Mary Emma Laws. I always called her Ganny, and her husband (my grandfather, Joshua Louis Meador) sometimes called her Fanny. She was born in 1883.

Ganny had long, dark red hair (auburn?), but she tended to wear it most of the time in a bun or gathered up using hair pins for nearly her entire life. Even when she was old, she still had long, red hair, and as a young child, I remember occasionally seeing her brushing it before she went to bed at night.

Joshua Louis Meador, whom I called Pawpaw, was born in 1886. As readers can see, my grandmother was three years older than my grandfather. Friends called him Louis, and although I never saw him at a young age, he seemed to have light colored hair as a youth.

When my grandfather entered college, my grandmother was already there. During the family tour of Tennessee, my mother drove us to see Ruskin Cave, about 40 miles west of Nashville, so Ganny could see once more where she met Pawpaw. They met at Ruskin Cave College.

This location has quite a history. Before the college existed, the place had been the site of a socialist colony for several years. Up until 1899, some of the activities taking place there remind me of California in the late 1960s, including the "free love" movement. I wove some of the stories into the plot of my novel, *Return to Nowhere*.

At the time of our visit, a large building stood not far from the road. From the best I can determine, this building still stands. A large cave entered a cliff face behind the building, which we could see from where we parked. We walked inside the building, and Ganny pointed to a staircase. She described being near the top, beginning to descend. Pawpaw entered the building for the first time with a friend and future classmate. The friend drew my grandfather's attention to my grandmother and said, kiddingly, "Hey, Louis, there's your woman." At the time, Ganny was a first-year teacher at the college while Pawpaw was a beginning student. In any case, three years later when my grandfather graduated, they got married.

Ganny once told a tale about exploring the depths of Ruskin Cave with a group of students. They had to carry a kerosene lantern for light. When they reached some point pretty far underground, the young man carrying the lantern extinguished the light and said, "Okay, boys, now you can kiss your girlfriends." Everyone had a laugh until they realized the person with the lantern wasn't carrying any matches to light it again. They were stuck there for quite a while until a search party found them. I also mention this story in *Return to Nowhere*.

Ganny and Pawpaw had three children, which were my uncle, Laws Meador, my uncle, Josh Meador, and my mother, Mary Meador (Moody).

Hidden Riches

Not long after Ganny and Pawpaw were married, Pawpaw came down with a serious illness, causing a high fever. They needed some money for doctor's bills and other expenses, and during Pawpaw's delirium, he described to Ganny a place under a house where some money was hidden. I was never sure of the house's location at the time I heard the story, but apparently it was a place Ganny knew and could reach. I understood it was a place different from where they lived at the time. Anyway, she reached the place and crawled under the house. In the indicated spot, sure enough, she found some coins. She gathered them up and took them to the bank, but as soon as she set them on the teller's counter with a thud, he announced,

"Counterfeit." The coins weren't "tempered," and the teller recognized they weren't authentic because they didn't "ring" when she set them down. When Pawpaw got better, she asked him about the coins. He said he had no idea about them and couldn't recall telling her about them. The mystery was never solved.

A Man of Numbers

Pawpaw found work at the Columbus and Greenville Railroad as an accountant. He always had work when others were being laid off during the Great Depression because in both good and bad times, a business such as a railroad always needed an accountant to tell them just how good or bad they were doing. He was working out of Columbus, Mississippi, in the 1920s, but I understand he had to travel on occasion.

My mother described him as being quite good with basic math. She recalled him simply run his finger down a long list of multi-digit numbers and giving the correct total as soon as he reached the bottom.

A Nice Place to Visit

Nearly every year during my early youth, my family traveled to Columbus, Mississippi, to visit my grandparents (both sides of the family) for two weeks. Most often we went during the summer, but I recall going once during the Christmas season. We might have gone more than once, but if so, I was too young to remember. Not only did Ganny and Pawpaw live in Columbus, my grandmother on my father's side and many other family members lived in the area. We always stayed the entire time with Ganny and Pawpaw.

Because of their prosperity, Ganny and Pawpaw built their house in the 1920s, and they both lived there for almost the rest of their lives. I always remember it being painted gray with white trim.

It faced a large, white, pre-Civil War, plantation-style house that was marked with a date on a small sign on the street in front. This house looked impressive, with two-story, fluted columns on two sides facing a street corner.

My grandparent's home sat on high ground above the street, so a person had to climb a lot of cement stairs even before reaching the wooden stairs to climb onto the front porch. The front porch had a view straight across toward the big, white house because the other house sat lower on the same hill. This front porch was wide and L-shaped. Green-painted, bentwood chairs (including rocking chairs) stood there where people could sit in the evenings during the summer when the temperatures cooled down and when the mosquitos weren't too bad.

A two-person porch swing hung on the east side of the porch. My mother and father used to sit there when they were dating, and I recall fond memories of sitting sideways on the swing during the summer while reading comic books or *Mad Magazine*, with a cold glass of iced tea or Coca-Cola sitting just below on the porch at perfect arm's length. Occasionally, someone fixed me popcorn as well. As I read, I flexed my toes against the chains supporting the swing, and the suspended chair rocked gently sideways, creating a slight breeze as I read comic after comic.

The house always impressed me as being pretty large, although it was merely a single story and only had two true bedrooms. The living room had a nice fireplace, but I only saw it in use during our wintertime visit. (Pawpaw made sure that no fire burned in the fireplace on Christmas Eve.) I've already described some of the items that hung from the walls there, but an oil painting of a group of grazing sheep hung over the fireplace. It was painted by my uncle, Joshua Meador, whom I will describe in more detail further on.

A set of glass doors separated the living room from the dining room, but they were almost always open. The dining room table was quite special. It was of the type that expands on either end by pulling leaves out one at a time from underneath. The canvas painted by Mickey Laws of my grandmother as a baby with her sister Daisy hung on a wall of the dining room. The dining room also held a large sideboard with a mirror, and a small, antique, glass-fronted bookcase stood in a corner. We always ate on original, multi-colored Fiesta dinnerware. I especially remember the spherical salt and pepper shakers. A tight roll of paper replaced a lost stopper on one shaker.

A small room they called a pantry stood between the dining room and the kitchen, separated from the dining room by a large, swinging door with no window through it. When people were preparing the dining room table for a meal, they used to shout "Comin' through!" so as not to smack someone approaching from the other side.

The kitchen wasn't especially large, but it had a deep, porcelain-covered, cast iron sink. A small table stood on the north side next a window with a view looking out onto a screened-in back porch and the back yard beyond the screen. I recall Ganny sitting at the table while cutting green beans or okra. A battered aluminum dipper with a black-painted, wooden handle hung next to the sink, and anyone who wanted a drink used to take down this dipper to run water from the faucet for sipping. Everyone used the same utensil, and we never thought about spreading germs. This now hangs in our kitchen, but my family uses glasses from a cupboard when getting a drink of water.

A hallway ran from the east end of the living room all the way to the back porch. A bedroom my mother used stood off this hallway toward the front of the house. Further back, a bathroom sat about midway down the hall near the entrance to my grandparent's room. It held a cast-iron bathtub supported by feet, and the water valve handles were of white porcelain. A large room they called a "sleeping porch" connected to their bedroom, and when I was young, this is where all the visiting kids slept. A side door connected the sleeping porch to the back porch. A small horseshoe was attached to the upper doorframe.

Near the back door of the porch, a small, brass bell hung from a holder attached to the outer wall. A short, double chain hung down from the cast iron clapper. This served as the back doorbell, and when local farmers stopped by on Saturdays to sell their produce, they always rang this bell to call Ganny's attention.

As a child, Ganny and Pawpaw's yard was a great place to play because of the gardens, the irregular landscape, and the areas full of trails and steps. It provided a lot of places that stimulated adventure. The always-shady back yard was full of large pecan trees. The tree bark had been pecked in places by woodpeckers. I used to crack pecans from the trees to eat for a healthy snack, and I still like pecans to this day, cracking them after they fall from trees that presently hang over our yard. A grape arbor stood on the west side of my grandparent's back yard, and the scuppernong grapes when in season were a golden color. A single car garage sat toward the back of this part of the yard, but the property continued uphill, again by way of a few cement stepping stones embedded into the slope.

When my grandparents bought the property, they acquired the entire east side of the block. (Another large, plantation-style home sat up the hill toward the west, but most of that property had years earlier been sub-divided for homes covering the rest of the block. The large house itself had been converted into apartments.) My grandparents' original idea was to reserve plots of land so each of their three children could build houses behind theirs, but only one of my uncles, Uncle Laws, used the property on the far northeast corner to build his home at a later date. After crossing the back yard heading north, a large vegetable garden sat on the plot of land up the hill before reaching my aunt and uncle's house. When I was young, my grandmother often sent me up to the garden in the morning to cut okra to fry for lunch.

The house was a fun place for a young boy to spend a couple of weeks during summers, and I always looked forward to my trips to Mississippi.

A New Car Each Year

Pawpaw always bought a new Packard as soon as a new year's model went on the market, whether he needed a car or not. I saw a photo of him standing next to one of his cars (a black one) in the early 1930s when my mother was a young girl. As I said, he had a prosperous job, and he simply preferred to update his cars frequently. As I understand it, people waited in line for the opportunity to buy a J. L. Meador used Packard because he had merely "broken them in" by the time he decided to sell. When Packards were no longer made, however, he stopped buying cars. His last one, a maroon one with a large swan as its hood ornament, still sat in the garage after he died, but Uncle Laws continued to use it for years off and on to keep it running.

A Likable Character

I don't remember a lot about Pawpaw. I was pretty young when he died, and our family didn't see them except for about once a year. He was friendly and likeable to most everyone. I have a photo showing him reading a story book to me as a very young child. He liked birds and animals, and he enjoyed keeping up with the weather using a special barometer that hung on the back porch of their home. He was a long-time member of the Kiwanis Club. He liked fishing, too. Soon after my family moved from Dallas to Denison around 1959, my grandparents came to Denison to visit our new home. My mother arranged to take him pole fishing near the end of Preston Peninsula on Lake Texoma, and that was the first time I recall going fishing. Back in Mississippi, he used to fry fish and hushpuppies over a wood fire in a large, iron kettle at a certain spot in the back yard. When not in use, I remember the kettle resting up-side down near the entrance to the porch. It had a brass water sprinkler hanging from one of the cast iron feet, reminding me as a child of a deep-sea diver's helmet. This kettle now hangs by a pair of chains in our back yard, mounted there by my parents in a decorative, metal stand.

My grandfather died of a sudden, massive heart attack on July 11, 1963. I remember traveling to Mississippi earlier in the summer than expected to attend his funeral. It was my first funeral.

I recall Ganny calmly standing beside the open casket at the funeral home's chapel while she slightly rearranged Pawpaw's hair. She remarked that he never wore it the way the mortician fixed it. I guess the first time I ever saw my father cry was during the service.

On the way to the gravesite, my mother mentioned that Pawpaw always liked watching the weather, and maybe God had plans for him along those lines. It was a day with plenty of tall, white, fluffy clouds, and after her statement, I imagined it would be interesting to look up and see him peeking down at me from behind one of them.

Ganny told my mother that soon after Pawpaw died she had a dream where he spoke to her saying not to worry about him because he was all right.

Ganny's Later Life

In her later years, Ganny tried to stay busy. She often participated in church activities at the Presbyterian Church in Columbus. When we used to visit her after Pawpaw passed away, she enjoyed tell stories about ancestors, and I have already described the trip when my mother drove us to Tennessee—the time I learn so much I didn't really know I learned.

John M. Moody

I recall several times when my mother encouraged Ganny to write down stories in a notebook when she remembered them, and I've already passed along some of those. Once, my mother even took a tape recorder and recorded Ganny's voice as she told some of these stories. This tape is still around, but I'm not sure where it is at the time of this writing. It might be stored in the family safety deposit box.

Ganny continued to live in the same house as she grew older. She participated in a Meals-on-Wheels type of program for a while, and she also used a small toaster oven to prepare meals. And of course, her son (my Uncle Laws with his wife, Aunt Eloise) checked on her frequently.

She told one story I recall about falling in her house. I guess she was about 80 at the time. I believe she said she had on her robe, and it somehow got caught when she passed through a doorway, causing her to lose her balance and fall in the hall toward the front of the house. She felt she wasn't hurt, but she couldn't stand up. She crawled little by little into the living room, hoping she might be able to pull herself up into one of the chairs. The front door had a lot of glass, and all at once a postman stepped onto her porch to deliver her mail. He saw her on the floor and tried the front door. Ganny had left it unlocked. Without coming inside, the man asked if she was all right, and she explained the problem. The postman felt too afraid to help her up, believing she might have suffered injuries she didn't recognize, but he was able to contact my Uncle Laws in some manner. Even so, the postman waited until everything was okay before continuing on his route. Ganny sustained a bruise, but she was otherwise fine.

Ganny ended up living by herself in the same house until she was 100 years old. I was living in Maracaibo, Venezuela, at the time (1983), but I called her that day. My mother was there, and they were having a big party for her.

After that, Ganny decided she needed someone to help take care of her. She moved into a rest home, and her house was eventually sold. Much of her furniture was divided between Uncle Laws' side of the family and my mother's side. This is how our family ended up with so many pieces of furniture and other items that still bring back memories. According to my mother, Ganny seemed to be happy in her new place, and she began to make friends right away.

During a routine medical exam, a doctor discovered a tumor with an open sore on Ganny's chest. He left it up to her if she wanted to have the operation to remove it or not because it was apparently somewhat minor. Because there was a chance the open sore might produce "an offensive odor," Ganny decided to go ahead and have the operation. The procedure was performed, and the tumor was successfully removed. Ganny seemed to be recovering from it just fine, but only a few days later, the rest home personnel discovered she had died in her sleep overnight. I guess if someone has to go, that's the best way after living a long, full life.

Mama Moody

I don't know much of the early life of my paternal grandmother, who my family called Mama Moody (Julia Rhett Moody), except for what people told me and wrote about her years later. She was born in 1883. When she was married to my grandfather, John M. Moody IV, the family apparently lived in Columbus, Mississippi, for a while. My family once drove past a house where my father was born when we learned from Mama Moody that it would soon be torn down. I was pretty young at the time, but I think my mother took a photo of it.

Later, my father's family moved to the country a few miles out of Columbus. My grandfather served as a clerk of some sort, but he died fairly young of "blood poisoning," which developed through a sore on his nose. His death occurred when my father was about 12 years old, and it placed a great hardship on the rest of the family. After his death, the family moved back into town.

The house where they came to live in town had been a log cabin, which was moved from out in the country to its present location, but rooms were added over the years. As I understand it, the center room, which the family used as a somewhat narrow living room, had once been a "dog trot," an open breezeway running from front to back through the entire house. The space was enclosed long before I first saw it. The house is still located not far from the Tombigbee River, but it has been remodeled in front to such an extent, I hardly recognize it now. The place once had a special marker on the street to identify the year the cabin was originally built (1830, I think).

Trips to Columbus during the summer allowed both my parents to visit their living parents and other family members. Most often, we stayed in town for two weeks—the amount of time my father had for vacation each year. On a trip from Denison to Columbus, we normally drove straight through. The trip was 545 miles, and it usually took about 11 and a half hours. When we arrived late in the afternoon after traveling all day, we always stopped at Mama Moody's house before continuing across town to my other grandparent's house (later, Ganny's house) where we always stayed throughout our visit because that house had more room.

Mama Moody was always sweet to my sisters and me as grandchildren, but she always seemed rather old to me whenever we visited, I think my impression came because her health wasn't good during the time I knew her. She ate a restricted diet and sometimes had trouble getting around the house. My Aunt Rosalie lived with her and took care of her, and another aunt, Julia, also visited fairly often. Mama Moody seemed to live a simple life in her later years.

I recall my grandmother sitting in the same spot on a sofa in the living room most of the time, and she read paperback novels. Her favorite books were from Earl Stanley Gardner's "Perry Mason" series. Later, however, she began to lose her vision, making it difficult for her to do one of the things she seemed to enjoy most. This was previous to the use of audio book files or even books on tape.

I once recall her allowing me to rummage through a bookcase in the living room while the family sat there and visited. I found a fantastic, illustrated set of Dante's *Divine Comedy*. When she saw my fascination for it, she gave it to me. I still have it. Based on an inscription inside, it might have been a gift from an old boyfriend at a time before she met my grandfather.

When I was in college in 1973, my mother called to say Mama Moody had died. Because of my studies, they didn't take me with them to the funeral. She is buried in Friendship Cemetery in Columbus among the other Moodys.

A Collection of Aunts, Uncles, and Cousins

Aunt Emily or Emily Givans, my father's sister, has been my closest link to the past for many years. I've kept in touch with her by phone whenever I could, and she has kept me informed concerning the activities of my cousins who have remained so distant I can barely remember what they look like. Aunt Emily married Uncle Jay, who has now passed away. Uncle Jay worked for *National Geographic* magazine, and for many years my family received subscriptions sent monthly to our home. (I learned a lot about geography from these.) Emily and Jay had two children, Jean and Charles, but I only hear news from them second-hand because they live halfway across the country.

I also remember Aunt Julia, Julia Broyles. She was another of my father's sisters. She was married to Uncle Jim, but he died when I was young. Aunt Julia lived on a farm south of Starkville, Mississippi, and when I went to visit, it was a lot of fun to play with my four cousins, Julia's children. She sometimes took me fishing on a pond on their land, and I caught the largest catfish I ever caught there. Aunt Julia died in 1995.

Cousin Jim, Julia's only son, was the oldest. He had platinum-blond hair, and he was physically fit. He had a friendly disposition, and as a boy much older than me, he always treated me nicely when our family went to visit. He later became a fireman, and I have a couple of interesting stories to tell about him.

When Jim was young, he drove a Volkswagen *Carmen Gia*. One summer when he came to visit, we mounted a 1955 Chevy hood ornament onto the hood of his car. It looked like a small airplane. We had fun doing it. If anyone ever encounters a *Carmen Gia* with such an alteration, it might be our handiwork.

On one of his trips to Texas, he had to pass an agriculture control station at the Mississippi River bridge near Greenville. The state at the time was trying to prevent the spread of insects that might be harmful to crops by asking motorists if they carry unprocessed plants, fruits, or vegetables. When my cousin pulled up, he said the man asked him, "Have you got any plants?" My cousin responded, "No, but I have a trunk load of boll weevils." The inspector didn't see the humor, but he let my cousin continue his journey.

Years later, I car-pooled fairly regularly to get to work in Dallas. I hadn't seen my cousin in at least 10 years. All at once, our car passed a fire station, and I spotted my cousin's platinum-blond hair as he stood outside talking to some other men. Remarkably, he had been working at that fire station for months. All that time I had been passing his place of work twice a day without knowing it. Unfortunately, Jim also passed away a number of years ago. He died rather young. I felt extremely sad to hear the news.

Aunt Julia had three daughters, Judy, Jan, and Jane, and I played with them during visits to the farm or when they came to Columbus to see us while we were on vacation. Judy was older, so she usually got together with my sisters. I played mostly with Jan and Jane. Jan was the nearest to my age.

Once while on their farm, Jan, Jane, and I went exploring. When we dropped into a gulley, I spotted the largest black snake I had ever seen, and we all ran away. Looking back, I doubt it was harmful.

One of the writers of my local writing group told me she meeting my cousin Jane at a Texas renaissance faire. She just happened to figure out Jane was my cousin through their conversation. It's a small world, but I'm sorry to say I haven't visited with my cousins much since I became an adult.

I mentioned Aunt Rosalie—Rosalie Moody—at the beginning of this book as being the first person I knew with an interested in family genealogy. She was another of my father's sisters. She never married. She worked for years to support the rest of the family, and she stayed at home later in life to take care of Mama Moody. Aunt Rosalie died in 1997.

My uncle, Laws Meador, was one of my mother's older brothers. I don't know a lot about him. He apparently lived in Columbus most of his life, but at some time during his early life, he work at a radio station in Savanna, Georgia. This is where he met his wife, my Aunt Eloise, who also worked at the radio station, perhaps as a secretary. I can always remember them living on the high end of the block north of Ganny and Pawpaw in a house they built on land Ganny and Pawpaw bought specifically for this purpose. They built themselves a pretty nice place. It had a den with glass windows facing the northeastern corner of the block. They could look out onto that portion of the world, rain or shine, and it was a cozy, comfortable room.

During the times I remember him best, Uncle Laws owned and operated a printing business near the center of town. He used to print personalized envelopes and stationary for my father. I always thought it was interesting to visit his shop to watch the printing presses running and to see the type trays full of individual letters—a characteristic of printing businesses dating back to Gutenberg.

When Pawpaw died, I had a birthday coming up, and my mother hadn't had time to buy me a gift because of our unexpected trip to Mississippi. She gave me a dollar so I could go into a variety store to pick out a toy. I selected a plastic patrol boat. It came with some toy sailors. It had a price of 99 cents, but when I went to the counter to pay, the clerk said I didn't have enough money. I didn't understand. That was the moment I learned about sales tax. The boat actually cost $1.04 with tax.

Just then, Uncle Laws happened to step into the store. His print shop sat only a block away, and he apparently entered the store fairly often. He saw me and figured out the problem. From his pocket, he came up with the four cents I needed. I walked out with my boat, and I always appreciated him coming to the rescue at the nick of time.

Uncle Laws smoked a lot, and it took a toll on his health. I recall him during his later years walking down from his house to visit us at night during our visits. He arrived practically out of breath. I'm not totally sure, but I believe that smoking eventually led to his death.

I remember Aunt Eloise's pleasant Georgian accent, which she held onto until the last time I saw her when I guess she was in her 90s. Laws and Eloise were always nice to me and my sisters when we went to visit.

They had two daughters named Marsha and Mary Laws (my cousins). They were very close in ages to my sisters, and I guess they became close for this reason. Unfortunately, Laws and Eloise didn't have a son my age, so as the youngest of the family, I tended to want to play with them, especially with my sister Frances and Mary Laws, who were closest to my age. Instead, they preferred to go off by themselves to talk about boys.

During one visit, however, they set up a treasure hunt for me, and at the end of a set of clues, I discovered that Mary Laws had given me all her old comic books (*Little Lulu*, *Archie*, *Mickey Mouse*, and others) and copies of *Mad Magazine*. During this visit, they successfully kept me occupied as I went to read for days at a time on the porch swing. I think I still have some of these comics in storage.

Uncle Laws liked radios. He was an amateur radio enthusiast. I've never heard how he got started, but it was apparently when he was pretty young. At an early age he built his own crystal radios when starting out, and he used to grind his own quartz crystals when building them. In his later life, he had a room in his house full of ham radio equipment, and he used to talk to people all around the world during the 1950s and 1960s. They used to exchange printed cards through the mail showing their call signs, and I recall he had files full of these cards.

One time he discovered randomly that a neighbor who lived only a block away from our house in Denison was also a ham radio enthusiast, and in some way we arranged to talk to my uncle in Columbus by radio one night by visiting the neighbor's house. We only did it once, however. It might have been more trouble than it was worth in our case, but I heard that these radio operators serve an important function during times of disaster when normal communications break down.

Besides all these people noted above, I have second cousins. One of them told me I have 64 relatives living in Panama. These were the descendants of Ganny's brother, Ewell Laws. He was the adventurous one who went to Panama and never came back. I think it would be fun to meet them all someday.

"He lived more in his short life than most people live in two."

I'm devoting several sections to my Uncle Josh. Even though I saw him rarely, the stories I heard my mother tell about him have continually influence my life.

I started this section with a quote my mother once said about him. I've recalled her words many times while living my own life—especially at times when I decided to do things I'd never done before. I remember being around him on very few occasions when I was quite young, but I recall those occasions well. And as an artist, Joshua Meador has served as an inspiration for many people other than just me.

Another photo from my grandmother's house now hangs in our home. It shows a family reunion that took place in 1953. In the photo, I was the only baby, sitting on my mother's lap, as the Meador side of the family (with husbands and wives) stood or sat in the back yard at my grandparent's house just as a professional photographer posed everyone other than me. (I'm looking toward the camera while everyone else has his or her head turned slightly toward one direction or the other as the cameraman instructed.) Ganny and Pawpaw are there, along with their three children with their wives and husband (my father), and all their grandchildren, which include my sisters and all my first cousins from the Meador side. It was another well-preserved moment in time. For many years, I only had this photo to look at when people spoke of Uncle Josh, Aunt Libby, and their son, Philip.

Joshua Lawrence Meador was born in March of 1911 in Greenwood, Mississippi. Even at an early age he began to display artistic inclinations. While doing some house painting as a boy, he made a few strokes with a broad paintbrush on the interior wall of the garage at Ganny and Pawpaw's house (mentioned previously). In doing so, he created a mountainous scene that even now looks pretty good despite its simplicity. I recall seeing it whenever I went inside the building. When this garage was torn down a few years ago, this section of the wall was preserved and placed in a small museum dedicated to Josh Meadow's memory in Columbus, Mississippi.

We have an unsigned painting he must have done while still living at home. It originated from Ganny's home when she moved out. It was painted on a piece of thin composite board instead of canvas. We attribute this artwork to Uncle Josh because no one at my grandparent's house painted other than him. It shows a dark forest scene and demonstrates the abilities of someone just beginning. Even so, we think it is good enough to hang in the living room.

I encountered a photo album among the items brought by my mother from Ganny's house after she moved into the rest home. Many of the photos show Josh as a young boy or as a teenager. He seemed to have grown up doing a lot of things, and many of his photos are of outdoor activities. Maybe this left him with a preference for landscape and seascape paintings.

After Uncle Josh graduated from high school, he attended the Art Institute of Chicago. This was during the early 1930s. My mother used to repeat a story he told, which I'll pass along, maybe for the first time in print. Who knows if it is true or not, but it makes a good story; from the information I know, it's probably true.

John M. Moody

Josh lived a number of blocks away from the school, and he often walked to and from classes. His rooms were located not far from the Biograph Theater at the time when John Dillinger was shot and killed there by the FBI (July 22, 1934).

Anyway, as he walked to the institute, he often passed the front of a building where a man sometimes sat on the steps alongside a dog. My uncle sometimes spoke to the man as he passed, and he used to pet the man's dog. Uncle Josh and the man engaged in conversation more and more as the days progressed.

One day the man invited Josh inside to his apartment. Then he opened a trunk containing a lot of weapons to show the young art student. The man then told him (according to my mother's version), "Buddy, you seem to be a nice kid. You're always friendly to me and to my dog. I'll tell ya' what; if ya' ever need anyone bumped off, I'll do it for ya' for free."

My uncle thanked the man very nicely and soon found an excuse to leave. From then on, he changed his route to reach the art institute so he wouldn't have to walk in front of the building where the hitman and his dog lived.

While going through old papers a few years ago, Belkis and I found a letter Josh wrote while living in Chicago. It includes small, pencil drawings to illustrate some of the subjects he spoke about. At one time he worked on a public mural while he was still a student in Chicago.

My mother also described the first time when Josh returned home for vacation. His parents asked to see some of his work in school, but he seemed reluctant to show them much of anything. One late night, Pawpaw somehow got the keys to my uncle's car and opened the trunk to take a look, anyway. He found a lot of paintings of nude women.

At first, Pawpaw felt upset that he had been paying Josh's way to an expensive school just so his son could paint a lot of nude women, but I understand it is a fairly common practice in art schools to use nude models. When my mother asked about it later, Josh explained that when he first stepped into a room with a posing nude, female model, he felt shocked. He said that later, however, he tended to forget about the nude as he started to concentrate on what he was doing. After Josh explained the way the school taught, Ganny and Pawpaw simply had to get used to it. Unremarkably, none of these paints seemed to have survived.

The Artist's Varied Artistic Works

Uncle Josh graduated with honors from the Art Institute of Chicago in 1935. Following art school, he married my Aunt Libby, his childhood sweetheart, and they moved to southern California. He went to work for Walt Disney in 1936 when Disney was beginning to expand his studio. I heard snatches of stories about those times, but I don't know any of them well enough to repeat.

I do recall my mother describing a train trip with Ganny across the southwestern US to California in the late 1930s to visit Josh and Libby. My mother was a teenager at the time. Uncle Josh and Aunt Libby drove them to a drive-in restaurant, which my mother said was a rather new thing in those days. A big car pulled up next to theirs to be waited on, and Josh claimed the person in the other car was Douglas Fairbanks, Jr. My mother said she felt impressed.

Josh Meador later became a well-renowned American artist, known especially for painting marvelous landscapes. My mother told me that the actor Vincent Price owned a number of his paintings. I also read that Fred McMurray, another actor, purchased still more of them. Supposedly, one painting hung in Dwight D. Eisenhower's "Western White House" in Colorado. Walt Disney apparently purchased quite a few of his paintings, which have been passed along to Disney family members. Some of his paintings hang in museums, too. Art galleries, especially in California, still sell his work.

Some of my immediate family members still own early Joshua Meador artworks. When my mother died a few years ago, these were divided. I believe that most of these are his early works because his style progressive became more "impressionistic." I have always been amazed by how an artistic painter can capture an object on canvas using only brush strokes—or in Uncle Josh's case most of the time, palette knife strokes—through differences in color or texture.

When I was young, a Meador snowy mountain scene hung over my bed. When I gazed at this canvas from a distance, I saw the mountainous scene with large rocks and a distant forest. Up close, however, the tiny, individual trees are represented by single strokes with a palette knife or brush. I've read accounts written by other people who describe Josh's work expressing similar amazement.

I've heard he used to arrange family outings to many parts of California, and his paintings seem to reflect his favorite locations. They often show interesting rocky bluffs or snowy mountains. Some show solitary houses or barns. Others show waves crashing against rocks along seashores. Some are described or named by location; they include Carmel and Monterey, Casper and Fort Bragg, Bodega Bay, along the Sierra Nevada, and Paso Robles. Supposedly, in the Alfred Hitchcock movie *The Birds*, one of his Bodega Bay paintings shows up in the background of the café. I have an early painting showing a mountain that isn't identified by location.

When I wrote *Searching for Jennifer*, I had some of my characters travel to Bishop, California, (and beyond) during a critical phase of the novel. I chose Bishop because my mother described it as being one of my uncle's favorite areas. This novel also deals to some extent with art, and I thought of my uncle often while I wrote it. I even use one of his quotes in the story, attributing it to him directly. In another of my novels, *Return to Nowhere*, one of the characters is an artist, and while this person's life and that of Uncle Josh are nothing alike, I modeled the character's personality after my uncle as I remembered him.

Apparently Uncle Josh most often painted using palette knives. At an early age, I received from Ganny an old fishing tackle box that might have belonged to Pawpaw, and inside among the tackle I found a small, flattened knife with dried green oil paint on the ivory-colored, plastic handle. This must have surely belonged to Uncle Josh—also at an early age. I still have it because it once belonged to him.

I earlier described a Joshua Meador painting that hung over the fireplace at Ganny and Pawpaw's home. From a fairly young age I always admired it, and one day Ganny informed me that this painting would go to me after she died. At the time, of course, I never wanted her to die, and I suppose at an early age I never expected to receive the painting. Somewhere along the way she apparently remembered. Ganny sent it to me by way of my mother when she moved out of her house at the age of 100 years old.

This painting shows a small flock of grazing sheep with what looks like early-fall colored trees in the background. Tall poplar trees stand near the center with part of a meadow in the background, and other types of trees stand toward the sides. I have often imagined this painting shows a scene from near Bishop. The story behind this composition is when Uncle Josh set up his canvas, the sheep were grazing randomly. However, when one of them happened to move into a position he liked, he quickly sketched it. As he worked on this sheep or on the background, he kept an eye on the other sheep until he saw another one in a position he liked. In this way he composed the scene in his mind until it ended up looking the way he wanted. This continued until seven sheep are shown, but it is possible the original flock held more or even less animals.

He worked as an animator for Disney Studios during the time when some of Walt Disney Productions most famous animated full-length motion pictures were produced, including films such as *Snow White and the Seven Dwarves* (1937), *Pinocchio* (1940), *Cinderella* (1950), and. *Sleeping Beauty* (1959). His name shows in the credits for many films at this time. His animation specialties were waves, ripples, bubbles, and electricity, and his work shows up in scenes such as when Snow White is speaking into the wishing well or when Cinderella is cleaning the floor and making bubbles. In *Fantasia* (1940), I understand he did a part Disney rejected as being a little too wild for the viewing public at the time, but I've never learned the details. However, I believe he animated the section showing the sound track. I know he did parts of the segments for "The Rite of Spring" and "Night on Bald Mountain." Part of his work animated flowing lava. He also worked on *20,000 Leagues Under the Sea* (Walt Disney Productions, 1954) which won him and a co-worker Oscars for best special effects at the 1954 Academy Awards. Along the street near the family home (previously described), a historical marker now stands. It briefly mentions some of Joshua Meador's accomplishments.

While looking through one of Uncle Josh's photo albums, I came across a group photo showing my uncle posing with fifteen men he apparently worked with. In the corner off to the side, I promptly realized one of the men looked familiar; he was a rather young, dark-haired Walt Disney (wearing suspenders).

The one thing that used to impress me the most—and I used to brag to my grade school friends about—was at the beginning of the television series *Zorro* (1957-1959), Uncle Josh supposedly animated the lightning bolt that comes down to form a big "Z" across the screen. I've never been able to confirm this information, but my mother told me it was true. She might have heard it from him directly. The work appears to be his style and would have fallen into one of his specialties. In any case during later years while living in Venezuela, one television station ran the entire series for a while, and I always remembered Uncle Josh each time I saw the beginning of an episode. I understand that much of his later work on certain Disney projects was "uncredited."

At about the same time in his career, Disney Studios loaned him out to do animation effects for the now-classic science fiction movie *Forbidden Planet* (MGM - 1956). He certainly received credit for this one; his name shows up in big letters at the beginning of the picture. I can see his style in the Monster of the Id, which tries to break through the force field (electricity again). I also thought it was interesting when Lesley Neilson shoots a ray gun at the leaping tiger, and the creature promptly turns into animated stripes that float away. Other animation effects are also apparent.

Around 1960, Uncle Josh and Aunt Libby built a house somewhere between Casper and Fort Bragg, along the northern California coast. The house overlooked the Pacific, and he could descend a cliff to reach the shore where he sometimes gathered abalone. Ganny went to visit them once. She described the place as having a large fireplace in the center, and Uncle Josh had in some way used a "piece of wood with lots of worm holes in it" as part of the structure. Ganny saw it as strange, but I can imagine it as the sort of Bohemian place where an artist would like to live. He then spent more time painting canvases.

Treasure Map

During her visit to his newly-built home, Uncle Josh showed Ganny one of his latest projects. It was a treasure map he purchased from someone. As a young boy, I always wanted to see it. Supposedly, the treasure was located in a remote part of the desert southwest. The map provided location clues, and when he visited certain locations to investigate, he found symbols carved onto rocks. What he did was to set up a canvas and paint a picture of the rock with its symbol to use for future reference. He showed Ganny the map and the paintings of rocks, but it hadn't made any sense when she spoke to him at the time. According to him, however, people sometimes followed him when he went out.

These tales inspired me to write *Brass Puzzle*.

Sunset

Uncle Josh died of a heart attack in August of 1965. I was on a summer trip to visit a friend out of town, and when I returned home, my mother told me he had died a couple of days earlier. He had a heart condition since his youth, and from 1955 until he died, he had arranged to be "on call" for Disney Studios to avoid the stress he felt by working there under tight schedules. Before he started working part-time, he rose to be the head of the animation department.

I understand that on the day he died he had just been awarded a commission to do a painting for the US Air Force, and he felt excited about the news. Aunt Libby left in the afternoon to do some grocery shopping a few miles away, and when she returned home, she found him dead. Uncle Josh had collapsed while standing outside on the back patio. He had been painting a sunset scene, and he still held in his hand a rag he used to wipe the paint from his palette knives. I guess it's appropriate for an artist to die painting a sunset.

Uncle Josh lived to be only 54 years old. When I think of him, I'm reminded of a line from the movie *Blade Runner* again; it is the part when Roy, the "replicant," meets Dr. Tyrell. The doctor tells Roy, "The light that burns twice as bright burns half as long …"

Inspiration

In Venezuela, a number of artists from as far back as 200 years ago have painted the large, forested mountain overlooking Caracas from the north known as El Avila. These men are sometimes referred to as "pintores del Avila" (painters of the Avila) with the mountain providing them inspiration. I once viewed some of these works in a Caracas art museum.

Some years ago between my second and third visits to Venezuela, my thoughts of Joshua Meador urged me to try my hand at painting. After expressing my interest to my parents, they gave me a basic set of paints and a few other items as a Christmas gift. In my free time—and without any training other than my imagination—I set up a canvas and tried to decide what to paint. I got out some photos I had taken while in Venezuela the second time to serve as my models.

I first thought about painting an interesting looking ship I once photographed on Lake Maracaibo, but after making a pencil sketch, I believe I painted only the sky before something else captured my attention at the time. I never painted the ship.

Still later, I decided to paint a scene I photographed one night from an apartment my company rented in the center of Caracas. My photo showed the lights of the city with a dark silhouette in the background. The lower center of the photo shows only a dark pit where a large park was under construction.

I had better luck with this one, finishing it in only a few days. Even so, I still couldn't imagine how Uncle Josh did what he did.

This is the only painting I've made so far as an adult, and I suppose it's not bad. It's possible to recognize nearly everything shown in the painting for what it's supposed to represent. In fact, my parents liked it so much they hung it in the hall leading to their bedroom, but I mostly imagined they liked it because their son painted it.

Following my return to Denison in 2001 after my third extended stay in Venezuela, the painting ended up back in my hands, and I put a nice frame around it. After she saw it, Belkis liked it, too, and it now hangs in our bedroom. And as it turns out, the dark silhouette in the background is actually a mountain—El Avila. Uncle Josh's inspiration inadvertently made me into another "pintor del Avila."

My Father

My father, John M. Moody (the Fifth), was born in Columbus, Mississippi, on April 22, 1918, when World War I was still in progress. Among my parent's things, I found photographs of him as a young boy dressed in a child's soldier uniform, complete with hat and rifle, so I guess he often had the military on his mind while growing up. He lost his father to blood poisoning at about the age of 12, and from then on, he took on the role of "man of the house" for his immediate family, which included his mother and three sisters, previously described.

During the Great Depression years, he became an Eagle Scout, he won a county-wide spelling bee, and he was selected to serve as honorary mayor of Columbus for a day during his high school years. He also worked with a Civilian Conservation Corp crew at some stage. He sent most of the money he earned home to help support his family. He worked occasionally as a surveyor or on construction jobs. Later, he served in the Mississippi National Guard and was once sent to stand guard over Tupelo after a devastating tornado (Fujita Rating F5) damaged that town in April of 1936. He was 17 years old at the time.

War Stories

While I was young, I rarely heard my father speak of his experiences during World War II. As I grew older, however, he began to tell me stories. Besides the stories he told, I sometimes heard other details from my mother. I've also figured out some of what he did through research—along with a little surmising.

While in the Mississippi National Guard, he apparently specialized in field artillery. I once found a copy of an album from this time showing photos of guardsmen posing around obsolete, WWI-vintage artillery pieces such as the M-1916 37mm gun and the 4.7 Inch Gun M-1906, which I understand were often provided to state militias for training purposes.

He was planning to leave the MNG at the end of a normal enlistment term. This was to be early in 1942, but then came Pearl Harbor on December 6, 1941. After this, practically everyone with military experience ended up transferring into the US Army. Because of his gathered knowledge and experience in field artillery, he soon attended officer's training and became a lieutenant. He served for a while as an artillery instructor at Ft. Sill, Oklahoma. Following the Normandy Invasion in June of 1944, he was sent to Europe, specifically to England, Belgium, Germany, and France, as far as I can determine.

During his time in Belgium or Germany, he found (according to him, on a battlefield) a German Army dispatch case containing an

John M. Moody

Agfa camera and extra film. The camera held a partially-exposed roll of film at the time, and he soon began to use the camera, finishing the roll then in progress. When he was able to develop the film, he discovered three photos taken by a German soldier—two of a German hospital ship on a river and one of a group of German soldiers posing for the camera with some civilians. After the war, he kept the negatives and prints from his war years together, and they show some interesting moments of his life and the places he visited.

While overseas, he served as an artillery officer in the 78th Infantry Division, also known as the "Lightning Division," and a few of his photos show artillery-related shots. He apparently used or commanded mostly 105mm howitzers while overseas. Some of his shots show German artillery pieces he must have thought were interesting, and I was especially impressed by a photo of a German Jagdpanzer 38 tank destroyer, which rests askew in a ditch. He described once when a fired burst of 20mm shells blew up on a wall over his head, and he also described how a German 88mm shell blew up right in front of him. The force of the explosion knocked him to the ground, but he came through the experience otherwise unharmed.

During the winter of 1944-1945, he was located just north of the Battle of the Bulge. While this famous engagement was taking place, news reports at home were describing how his division was also surrounded, and my mother said she worried herself sick about it for days until later she learned he was actually unharmed.

One of his photos might have an untold, interesting story behind it. It shows a GI firing a pistol as if doing target practice. I was showing my father's photos to a friend once, and he recognized something unusual about the pistol. He worked at the time with photographic equipment, and to prove his point, he made an enlargement of the hand holding the pistol using the original negative. It shows the pistol is a small Walther, a German-made gun.

My father rarely spoke to me of his time during World War II until the late 1960s, but before that time we enjoyed watching war movies on television together. I can specifically recall the two of us watching *Sargent York*, staring Gary Cooper. He also liked to watch the show *Combat*, staring Vic Marrow and Rick Jason. I recall a time while we watched when an artillery barrage passed overhead in an episode, and he told me it sounded just like the real thing.

I eventually learned that my father served as a "forward artillery observer" while spotting targets from an airplane. Some of his photos show the type of plane he flew in, which is an L-2 "Grasshopper." These small aircraft held only the pilot and an observer.

One day I discovered a book at home which was written directly following the war specifically for his division. It describes some of the actions the soldiers had been involved in during the invasion of Europe. My father found a map in the book and began to describe some of the places he passed through and saw from overhead.

He told about crossing the Rhine River a number of times by air before the opposite territory had been captured. Topography-wise, higher ground bordered the other side of the river, and as they crossed, the German soldiers tried to shoot them down, sometimes using only small arms. He pointed to one place where they fired machine guns at the plane he was in, and at another town on the map, he said a fellow observer returned "with a bullet lodged in his parachute." Along with the service metals most soldiers were awarded for participating in WWII, he also brought home an Air Metal for his service time spent in an airplane.

Some of his photos show German planes on the ground as well. A couple of photos show a German Heinkel HE 162 jet that was captured at an airfield. In one shot, three US soldier are standing next to the plane. Other photos show a "Storch" Fieseler Fi-156 observation plane, which was the German counterpart to the plane he flew in. He also mentioned seeing German V-1 "Buzz Bombs" as they flew overhead. He also saw the smoke trails in the sky of V-2 rockets. Some of his photos show formations of Allied bombers flying high overhead. One of those photos was taken from a street with a French nameplate on a wall, so I imagine it was taken in Belgium late in the war.

Many of his photos are only of places he visited or of army companions. One photo shows him standing on the Autobahn. The German idea was later copied by President Dwight D. Eisenhower to create the US Interstate Highway System beginning soon after the war.

John M. Moody

Noble Bridge

My father and I occasionally watched a television show together entitled *Battleline*. Each episode took the points of view of soldiers from opposite sides of important military engagements, and we watched one about how the Allied Forces crossed the Rhine, specifically the battle for the Remagen bridgehead. The show used an original film taken from the front of a jeep as it crossed the long Ludendorff Bridge, and my father promptly told me he remembered crossing the bridge. I thought it was interesting he had been there, so I later looked into the details of the battle. I found the facts quite fascinating.

The bridge, originally built during World War I, was made for two rail lines and included pedestrian walkways. It was a high-arched frame type with twin stone towers at its entrances on each end. The town of Remagen sat on the west side, and the railroad tracks entered a tunnel through a high bluff on the east side. The German Army had placed artillery and antiaircraft battery positions overlooking the town and the bridge.

Unexpectedly, US soldiers captured the bridge practically intact on March 7, 1945, following a fierce battle. The German Army tried to destroy the bridge, but the explosives failed. The bridge was damaged, but miraculously, it didn't fall. In the meantime, the German Army did everything it could to try to destroy the bridge, including bombing it using aircraft, shooting it with railroad guns, and trying to sneak in demolition frogmen. Other temporary bridges were soon set up, which probably wasn't an easy task in such a short time due to the size of the Rhine River at that point, and the bridge had to be closed to vehicular traffic five days after it was captured while the engineers busied themselves in an attempt to strengthen it. My father must have crossed the bridge within those first five-days when it was open because ten days after it was captured, the bridge collapsed into the river due to the accumulated damage it suffered. During those ten days, the allied high command took advantage of the situation and sent 25,000 troops over to the opposite side using the damaged bridge and other temporary bridges. My father was one of those who crossed the original bridge.

In 1969, United Artists released a highly dramatized film about the battle, and our local movie theater (The Rialto in Denison) announced that anyone who had taken part in the military action could attend the film free. I told my father he would probably be able to see the movie free, but he wasn't interested, and I never knew if he saw the film later on television or not.

Afterward

Between the time he crossed the bridge at Remagen and the end of the war, my father contracted some illness that gave him Yellow Jaundice. I never learned what was wrong with him, but it put him out of action in a field hospital for a number of weeks, and during this time, the war had practically ended. From this time onward, he was never able to donate blood.

He traveled from Germany to France along with other soldiers. One of his photos shows the train they rode in. It looks like all box cars. He then traveled to England, and other photos show the sights throughout London—many of which I also saw on trips there years later.

Following the war, the army sent him home on the British ocean liner *Queen Elizabeth*, which had been converted into a troop transport vessel at the time. One of his photos shows a smokestack of this ship.

He collected military service patches for a while, and his collection of US patches was once pretty sizable. He also brought home a small collection of military insignia, mostly US lapel pens and rank bars, which he kept in a black and ivory colored, plastic box. He let me look through the box as a boy, but I always had to put everything back when I finished.

After many years of living away from where I grew up, Belkis and I, along with Mary Ann, returned to live in my old home place in order to help take care of my mother. One day I was sorting through old boxes in the garage, most of which were about to be discarded. By chance, I came across the same little, black and ivory colored, plastic box, and when I opened it, I felt delighted to find all the US insignia I remembered as a boy. I still have it after believing it lost long ago. I still have the German Army dispatch case, his photos, and even the

Agfa camera, although the bellows of the camera is no longer "light tight." I also found a strange pair of gloves I had never seen before. They are the type an artilleryman would have used during WWII where most fingers are united like a mitten—except for the trigger finger. They must be some he used during the war.

The Katy Railroad

After my father's army discharge following World War II, an uncle of his (whom, I do not know) was able to get him a job with the Missouri Kansas and Texas Railroad, known also as the Katy Railroad. He first worked as a survivor, moving upward through various jobs.

Before I was born (late 1940s to around 1950, I believe), my family, which consisted of my parents and my two sisters, lived in a small house in Grand Prairie, Texas, located between Dallas and Fort Worth—closer to Dallas. I remember my mother driving past the place once when I was little. I think my parents were renting it. Before I was born, they purchased a house on Delaware Street in Oak Cliff (across the Trinity River from Downtown Dallas), which is the home I remember as a small child.

While living at this location, my father took a correspondence course to become a railroad engineer—not the sort who drives trains, but a civil engineer. After he received his certification, he worked in the Katy's Engineering Department, often traveling to locations up and down the line to look at sections of land or to visit companies that wished to use rail services. He helped with the planning of new tracks and knew a lot about the business. He did this sort of job with the Katy until he retired.

When I was in the first grade, the Katy's upper management made a decision to move their Engineering Department and other offices to Denison, Texas. They believed Denison was more centrally located, and maybe they also ended up saving some money by making the change. My parents sold their house in Oak Cliff, and the family relocated halfway through my first school year.

This move changed my future life in what I now consider to be many favorably ways. I grew up in a smaller town. I eventually attended meetings of the Texoma Rockhounds. (This is a club in Denison where people who like minerals, Native American artifacts, fossils, and rocks in general get together and exchange information. I'll discuss this organization in more detail later on.) I met friends and classmates who influenced me. I attended Grayson County College (now called Grayson College). All of these I now look back upon as beneficial to my path in life.

During summers when I was a little older, my father used to take me with him when he went on long business trips. I got a lot out of traveling with him, and at some locations, I often helped him by holding one end of a tape measure or by navigating with a map from one town to the next. I remember visiting Tulsa, Oklahoma City, Houston, and other places. Pryor, Oklahoma, was a town he visited often because the Katy was providing rail service to an industrial park there at the time.

In 1963, the Katy Railroad announced that they would soon eliminate regular passenger service. My mother decided that her children needed to experience rail travel, and my entire family could travel for free because my father was a railroad employee. For my first trip on a train, we traveled down to somewhere south of Dallas on a Saturday morning, returning to Denison the same afternoon. It was fun, but I thought, as a young boy, the trip was rather long. I don't recall my father going with us, but my sisters and my mother were there.

(As a side note, the train track was located along the west side of downtown Dallas. Through the window of the train, I recall seeing a building marked "Texas School Book Depository" as we passed. I asked about the place, thinking I would gladly deposit all my school books there so I wouldn't have to use them. Someone explained it was where Texas public school books were stored and distributed, and apparently the name had been placed on the side of the building earlier that same year. When I heard the name again on the news on November 22, 1963, I recalled the building's exact location. Now the place is famous.)

The train trip I remember most, however, was one to San Antonio, Texas. The entire family boarded the train on a Saturday morning at the Katy Depot, which still stands in downtown Denison, and we rode to the station in downtown San Antonio, arriving shortly after dark. Then we took a really fast taxi a short distance to the Casa Rio restaurant, one the oldest Mexican food establishment of

John M. Moody

downtown San Antonio (1946), which is still located along the River Walk. We ate dinner there, and I remember it tasted delicious.

Then we killed a little time in a novelty store that was open late. It was located in a storefront right next to the stairs that descended to the restaurant. My parents bought me a small key chain with a yellow plastic Mexican sombrero attached, and I might still have it among my things.

Around midnight, we returned to the train station by taxi and boarded another train back to Denison. I slept in a reclining chair all night, and as we approached Dallas, I woke up. We arrived again in Denison later in the day. It was a fun trip full of memories. We basically took the train to San Antonio just to enjoy dinner in a nice restaurant.

While I was in high school, a famous British train, the *Flying Scotsman*, was making a tour of the US. It was steam powered. This train came to Denison and stopped at the depot late in the afternoon. My father saw it from his office window, which looked down on the tracks just north of the main depot building. He viewed the train's visit as an important event, so as soon as he got home from work right after 5:00 PM, he drove me back to see it. I thought it looked pretty neat at the time; the sides were olive green. The train stayed overnight in Denison, and the next morning, its shrill steam whistle could be heard all the way to our house as it continued its journey.

At about the time of a railroad downsizing or a merger during the late 1970s or early 1980s, my father was offered a deal to take early retirement from the Katy, and he took it after working there for about 32 years. When the train depot and adjoining plaza in downtown Denison were being restored, he contributed to the project in some way, and his name appears on a pink granite monument that stands just north of the central fountain. (I describe this plaza, the fountain, and the monument in one of my novels, *Shards of Time*. In my story, one of the main characters visits the location twice because her grandfather's name [supposedly] is on the monument.)

The Denison Public Library set up a project called *Railroad in My Blood* so the memories of some Katy employees and others related to the railroads of Denison would be preserved. (At around this time the Katy's name was about to go out of existence as an active railroad, being absorbed by the Missouri Pacific Railroad, a part of the

Union Pacific). My father participated in the project. He went down to the library and recorded on tape a story about one of his early experiences as a railroad worker. Not long ago, the library's catalogue showed they still have the recording.

Smoker

When my family lived in Oak Cliff, my father smoked cigarettes and sometimes a pipe. I even remembering the brand of cigarettes he smoked because at a young age, I saw a pack on a table in the living room; they were Winstons. He probably picked up the habit when he was young or possibly while serving in Europe because one of his army photos shows him smoking.

Before we left Oak Cliff, however, he gave up the habit because he didn't want my sisters or me to smoke. He said later he gave up cigarettes "cold turkey." From one day to the next, he simply stopped smoking, depending mostly on willpower to stop. He claimed that one thing helped; each time he felt a craving for a cigarette, he simply chewed a stick of gum. He stopped smoking his pipe as well.

I guess it worked. I never smoked a cigarette in my life.

Rocks, Fossils, and Artifacts

In the early 1960s, I became interested in the Texoma Rockhounds after vising one of their annual shows in a building on Main Street in downtown Denison. My father learned about a meeting, and he accompanied me; I was too young to attend without an adult. I recall the night quite well; the club's guest was an inventor of a commercial metal detector. The speaker showed coins and items from early ship wrecks. Although he spoke of finding treasure along Padre Island instead of true rock hound subjects, it was really interesting for a boy like me. I learned a lot by being there.

Unexpectedly, my father discovered that people he knew from his job at the railroad were also members. In particular, I remember John Taylor from that first meeting. He collected fossil echinoids (sea urchins, for those less biologically inclined). My father also enjoyed the meeting.

We learned about field trips, and once again, an adult needed to be with any children, so my father went with me. On the first trip, he seemed to have as much fun as I did. He began to arrange non-club-related trips with people he met, and when he went on a trip, I usually went with him. It started something the entire family enjoyed for years. We often traveled as a family to collect whatever sorts of rocks, minerals, fossils, or artifacts the field trip location had to offer. My mother—who I have to describe as outgoing and friendly—began to take as much of an interest in collecting as my father did.

He especially became interested in echinoids, the same as John Taylor, and over the years, my father amassed a pretty good collection of local specimens. He also traded duplicate examples over the years, ending up with many out-of-area and even international varieties. He didn't collect only echinoids, either. He ended up collecting a little of everything dealing with rocks, fossils, and early Native American artifacts.

Many times he and I took trips with no one else along. Although he had collected some "arrowheads" as a boy or while he worked as a surveyor for the Katy Railroad, my father wasn't as interested in the artifacts starting out. Later, however, he went out on weekends with friends specifically to search for artifacts, especially in cultivated fields throughout north Texas and southern Oklahoma. One area that drew his attention was the North Sulphur River in the area of Ladonia, Texas, where at one time artifacts could be found frequently in the river gravel. His collection grew to be quite sizeable.

He also liked the vertebrate fossils that the river gravels held from some of the same locations. The most common items in his collection were the bones and teeth of Cretaceous mosasaurs, plesiosaurs, and fish. Some of the individual bones and teeth he collected were remarkably well preserved. I also took an interest in everything he found (as I will describe in more detail further on), and later, as a university student, I was able to help him identify some of the specimens. A few of his fossils were eventually photographed and published in guidebooks, specifically *A Field Guide to Fossils of Texas* by Charles Finsley (various publishers, three editions, 1989, 1996, & 1999) as well as *Fossil Collector's Guidebook to the North Sulphur River* by the Dallas Paleontological Society (2001).

When I was busy with high school, college, or university activities and couldn't go with him, he sometimes went alone to the North Sulphur River when he couldn't find anyone else to go with him. On occasion, he looked for access points to reach the river bed that weren't near bridge crossings. Farmers usually didn't mind if he crossed their land to reach the river once he told them what he was doing. One time when the soil was still wet from recent rains, he drove the car along a road and got it stuck in the mud. A local farmer had to pull him out with a tractor.

My father's interests expanded, and during later annual rock shows presented by the Texoma Rockhounds, he began to display prized fossils from his collection. Through a friend at my work, I was able to supply him with simple computer software that allowed him to catalogue his collection.

In his later years after his retirement, his passion for collecting never ceased. He used to go out with a retired rockhound friend, Henry Doshier, to collect fossils along the shores of Lake Texoma. Once, however, Henry made a misstep and fell, breaking his leg. My father had to get him back to the car and drive him to receive medical attention. Following this incident, my mother wouldn't let my father go out alone to collect fossils anymore.

Other Hobbies

My father enjoyed a number other hobbies besides collecting rocks, fossils, and artifacts. He first collected postage stamps, beginning to some extent as a boy, but he expanded his collection once he became more financially stable. Because of his service in the army in Germany during World War II, he specializing in German issues, but he collected a little of everything.

He was always interested in old coins, and he saved them whenever he found them, but I guess he didn't actively collect them. He gathered an interesting collection of international coins and paper money while overseas, but most of them remained for years in an old wallet. When I began to take an interest in international paper money following a trip to London in 1979, he gave me what he had accumulated to add to my collection.

John M. Moody

My father enjoyed watching sports events in his free time, especially during winter months. He started out with baseball, but his favorite later was American football. When neither of those was in season, he watched basketball.

He watched birds as a hobby, and as many birders do, he kept a "life list." It was another hobby we shared, although he went about it more formally than me, eventually volunteering at Hagerman Wildlife Refuge on Lake Texoma just west of Denison. He participated each year in the refuge's "Christmas count," where they statistically look for any trends in bird populations from year to year. He received a plaque in recognition for his service one year. I was able to help him expand his life list considerably over ten days when my mother and father came to visit me in Venezuela in the fall of 1983.

As a writer, I once created a character who is an avid birdwatcher for my book *Woman in White, Cage of Black*. In another of my novels, *Many Shades of Green*, I use a character who pretends to be a birdwatcher as he watches his "target." I drew upon the experiences I shared with my father for these personalities.

In a letter I received while I lived in Venezuela, my mother described my father "going gleefully from one hobby to another."

A Tumble on the Ice

In October of 1999, Belkis and I traveled from Venezuela to visit my parents, and at the same time, I made arrangements to attend a paleontology convention in Denver. My parents decided to travel with us. In fact, they suggested we travel in their van. We made plans to visit several locations in Colorado prior to the convention, and my father and I hoped to watch birds at some locations.

We encountered snow in several areas during the trip. By the time we reached Estes Park, where we planned to stay for a couple of days before returning to Denver, the roads into the upper reaches of Rocky Mountain National Park were closed, but some of the lower locations were still open. It was a cloudy afternoon in the park, and I worried we might get caught in the snow on the way back to the motel if we drove too far away. Even so, my father wanted to see if he could spot an eagle he had once seen near one of the lakes a short distance up the road.

I was driving. I stopped at a stop sign on the way out of a parking area. Toward the left, the road led to the lake; toward the right, it led back to the motel. I now wish I turned right, but I decided to turn left to give my father the chance to see the eagle.

We reached the lake and searched the skies, but we didn't see the eagle. Belkis snapped a photo of my father and me at the spot. Then we headed back toward the van with my father moving rapidly ahead. The walkway had some packed snow on it. Just as the thought entered my mind that my father should slow down, his feet slipped out from under him. I heard a sharp crack when he hit the ground. I thought he broke his hip.

As a result of his fall, he broke his upper arm bone (his humerus). A man a few feet away at the time was a registered nurse on vacation. He quickly went over to check my father before anyone would let him move. When he learned it was his arm and not his hip, the man helped my father to stand while I carefully hurried to get the van. We got him into the vehicle and headed toward the park entrance further down the hill.

We told the people at the park entrance what happened, but since they didn't have advanced medical facilities there, I decided to drive on to the hospital in Estes Park. Even so, a park ranger showed up about an hour later to inquire and investigate because the incident occurred in a national park.

For some reason, the doctor didn't put a cast on my father's arm. The staff put him in a special kind of sling to use until we returned to Denison, where his regular doctor would take a look at his arm first.

For the next several days, he had to deal with the broken arm everywhere we went. Even so, I was able to introduce my father to some of the paleontology researchers I knew, and I could tell he was pleased.

Once we returned to Denison, my mother and father began to take care of the problem through his regular doctor. Belkis and I returned to Venezuela, but we later heard that the break wasn't healing properly.

Finally, he had to have an operation to install a rod to hold his arm while the bone tried to heal. He was still going through the healing process when he died.

My Father's Death

My father died at the age of 81 on March 26, 2000, after suffering an aneurism in a lung. After first realizing something was wrong, he passed out rapidly and died within a couple of minutes before anyone could do anything to help him.

I was in Venezuela at the time, and I couldn't travel to the US immediately. Belkis and I had already made plans to relocate to the US the following year, and I was looking forward to visiting regularly with both my parents. I lost this opportunity.

His body was cremated. I came back for several weeks in April to drive my mother to Columbus for the burial of his remains in the same cemetery where his ancestors are buried. My mother and I had the man at the cemetery bury a fossil echinoid with his ashes. It was his favorite type of fossil.

At about the same time, I helped to arrange a grave marker through the Veteran's Administration, which we learned would pay for a stone marker for anyone who had served in the military. It gives his name, his birthdate, his date of death, and his military rank.

Also because of his military service, my sisters and I paid to install an engraved brick with his name on it for the Eisenhower Memorial at Loy Lake Park, southwest of Denison. The memorial can be seen along US Highway 75 in Denison on the way to Sherman.

In general, I think my father had a full and varied life, but it ended too suddenly. His life—and his death in such a quick and unexpected way—have also influenced my novels.

My Mother – A Most Remarkable Woman

My mother, Mary Esther Meador Moody was Ganny and Pawpaw's only daughter. She was born in the small community of Electric Mills, Mississippi, in 1919. It was named that way because an all-electric sawmill was built there in 1913, but after milling operations ceased around 1941, the town mostly evaporated. I remember seeing it once, probably in the mid-1960s, but I don't think anyone in particular lived there at the time. As I've already described, my mother had two brothers. Throughout most of her childhood, Mary Meador Moody lived in Columbus, Mississippi, in the house on the hill previously described. She had cats around the house as a child, but later in life, she developed a cat allergy. I know little else of her childhood except for the following story.

"Zeppelin" Visit

My mother told me a story once about a visit over Columbus by a "zeppelin," most likely a large airship. I was pretty young when I first heard her story, and later in life when I asked her about it again, I didn't learn anything new. She said she was around ten or twelve years old at the time. Her father learned (possible through the local newspaper) that an airship would pass over Columbus on a certain day. When she told me the story, she thought it might have been the Graf Zeppelin on its round-the-world journey in 1929, but when I searched the various routes of this craft, I never found a time when it passed over Mississippi. In any case, between 1929 and around 1933, several other large airships might have been flying the Mississippi skies. (Through a little research, I discovered that between October 12 and 15, the airship *Macon* flew from Lakehurst, New Jersey, to Sunnyvale, California, by way of Macon, Georgia, which would have probably taken it over Columbus. My mother would have been just under 13 years old at the time.)

According to her story, the airship approached, and Pawpaw called everyone at home at the time to come out to see it. She said it looked huge, and it flew rather low to the ground as it drew nearer. In fact, she said it looked so massive, she feared it would crash down on everyone in town. She ran back into the house, jumped onto her bed, and pulled a pillow over her head.

A Reading Teacher with a Touch of Science

My mother attended Mississippi State College for Women (now Mississippi University for Women) in Columbus where she trained to be a school teacher. She already knew my father by then, but long ago I recall my mother bragging to my sisters that she had several boys interested in her during high school. From what I understand, my father had been somewhat shy.

After she graduated, she took a job teaching in Meridian, Mississippi. She had family there to help her get started, but she didn't stay too long, maybe only a year. About that time World War II broke out. My father had become a soldier because he had been in the Mississippi National Guard, and he asked her to marry him some time about then. She was a June bride, marrying in 1942. They weren't married at a church. Instead, I believe they were married while standing in the dining room at Ganny and Pawpaw's house. Then they returned to Mama Moody's house for a while before they left town the same day. I've seen some photos, and this is what I gather after looking at them.

They really didn't go on a honeymoon. My father was then in active service, and he had to travel somewhere as soon as they were married. He had already obtained the rank of lieutenant by then. My mother spoke of going to the train station to travel with him while still wearing her wedding corsage. The station was pretty busy and full of military personnel going one place or another. In the restroom before they left, she removed the corsage and threw it into the trash so no one would know she was a newlywed.

The train was so full of passengers, they had standing-room only for a while. However, a couple of soldiers with seats spotted them. One of the soldiers stepped over and gave my father a salute, asking them if they would both like to take their places. My mother said she felt pretty impressed.

My sister Esther was born while my father was still performing military duties in the US, but he learned he would soon be transferred overseas to Europe. While my grandparents took care of Esther, my mother and father took a few days to be together, and they traveled to New York City. They saw some of the sights there, although my mother mentioned that every time they wanted to go to the observation deck of the Empire State Building, the top always seemed to be hidden by clouds. They never went to the top. They also saw the Rockettes at Radio City Music Hall. At one exhibit—maybe at the same location—she saw a television for the first time.

One afternoon they left a museum (maybe the American Museum of Natural History), but they couldn't find a cab to take them to the hotel. It was raining hard with a tremendous wind blowing, and they had to walk several blocks. They were completely drenched and cold, but when the hotel staff saw them, they rushed in to help, bringing them extra towels. (I thought of this when I wrote one part of my novel *Many Shades of Green*.)

Soon afterward, the army sent my father to England, but the Normandy invasion had already taken place. Then he traveled to Belgium. My sister, Frances, was born while my father was overseas. At the time, my mother was back in Columbus living with her parents until my father returned. My mother spoke several times of not knowing anything of his whereabouts during the war until weeks after he was no longer there. During the Battle of the Bulge in December of 1944 (as I mentioned earlier), the news reports claimed that his unit was surrounded. Actually, his group was holding an area toward the north, and they were never surrounded. Even so, she worried about him all the time. He didn't know that my sister Frances had been born until the news caught up with him a couple of weeks later.

After the war, they moved to Texas because an uncle worked on the railroad. They lived in a small place in Grand Prairie, as I mentioned previously. One detail I remember my mother describing was how much she disliked having to use an ice box in the place of a real refrigerator. The return to production of peace-time goods was apparently slow, and for a while, my parents simply couldn't buy a refrigerator because none were available. Their names were on a list.

My mother said she disliked having to buy ice regularly from the ice man who passed the house daily. She hated having to empty the melted water from the tray on a regular basis so it wouldn't overflow onto the floor.

Finally, they were able to buy a refrigerator. People who served in the military were given priority when it came to purchasing certain items.

They moved to Oak Cliff before I was born. I'll describe some of this time elsewhere. Then we moved to Denison.

My mother usually drove us everywhere we went. Even during family outings and vacations she drove because she felt too nervous in the car with my father driving. My mother was an excellent driver, and I don't believe she ever had an accident.

She also took care of banking matters for the family. Once when my father complained about having trouble balancing the checkbook, she took over. She worked out some sort of system to make it easier. She was a good money manager, too.

When I was still in elementary school, my mother began to teach again. She started out as a substitute teacher, but in order to be hired as a regular, full-time teacher, the State of Texas required a few courses she didn't have. One of those was Texas History.

However, it wasn't long before she was hired to teach second grade at Lane Elementary School in Denison. Not long ago I drove to this location, and now it's only a vacant lot. All that remains are a few sidewalks.

During summer months, she had a lot of extra time. My family usually spent my father's entire vacation in Columbus, Mississippi, to visit with family, but later, she wanted to travel to other places in Texas and to neighboring states, mostly toward the west. We also took trips into northern Mexico a few times. It used to be a running joke in my family that "gipsy blood" flowed through our veins. We all ended up traveling quite a bit.

When I was 14, we took our first trip to Colorado because Esther got a job teaching in Arvada, near Denver. (It seems we were all teachers at one time or another, even my father while in the army.) We enjoyed our trip to Colorado so much that we went back about once a year over a few years. (I'll describe later how we bought some land in the San Luis Valley of southern Colorado.) We eventually traveled to many places while on summer vacations. During my first summer after high school, we started traveling to the Big Bend area fairly regularly, and my parents eventually bought some land there.

My mother liked wildflowers, and after she took a photography course at Grayson County College, she used her camera often to take pictures of those as well as of everything else she saw along her path. She became interested in county court houses in Texas, and over the years, I believe she took photos of all of them except for one, along with some old jails she encountered in the process. She took photos of mountains, especially those in the Big Bend area of Texas. I believe I like photography because of growing up in this sort of environment, and I've learned to take photos for my book covers.

She taught at Lane Elementary for several years, but then she decided to earn her master's degree at Austin College in Sherman. All the while, she continued to teach. With her master's, she moved into a

US Government funded program to improve reading skills in children entering middle school. She worked at McDaniel Junior High (the old high school building) not far from home, and I was either attending high school or college by this time.

The program was called "remedial reading," and her job was to try to find out why particular children couldn't read by the time they reached middle school. (It was a new program at the time, and I understand that students are now tested at a much younger age.) She discovered that some of them only needed glasses. They couldn't read because they couldn't see properly, and up to then, the problem simply hadn't been caught. She identified others with different types of vision problems, and she routinely tested children entering the program. From what I understand, she was good at her job, and a lot of people became successful after passing through her class.

My sisters are both older than me, and my mother said she returned to work to help pay for our higher educations. In this she succeeded, too. While we often had summer jobs, we never had to work while we took college or university classes except to earn some extra spending money.

Along with collecting rocks, fossils, and Native American artifacts the same as the rest of the family, my mother also collected picture post cards. Whenever she went on a trip, she mailed a card back to herself for her collection. I got to where I also mailed postcards from places I visited (although from some locations, they never arrived).

My mother also enjoyed traveling to Mexico. On one trip in the 1960s, she traveled with a group of school teacher friends to Chihuahua and took a tour of Pancho Villa's home. The famous revolutionary's widow still lived in the house at the time, and the woman came out during the tour to greet visitors. A photographer took a group photo, and a few moments later, someone caught up with the tour selling copies as mementos. My mother bought one, and she is shown standing directly behind Señora Villa.

My mother also enjoyed the train trip with some friends through Copper Canyon in northern Mexico on the Chihuahua al Pacifico Railroad. On the trip, she met an author named Jonathon F. Cassel who wrote a book titled *Tarahumara Indians*. These tribes live in the same area. They possess extraordinary stamina when it comes to running long distances. I used my mother's autographed copy of this book while doing research for my novel *Intersecting Destinies*.

After 22 years, my mother retired from teaching. My father also retired about this time. We children were grown and mostly lived away from home. My parents then built onto the back of house and placed large windows in the back so they could watch birds in the yard. They also traveled regularly, taking trips with family and friends. Sometimes they visited relatives who lived far away. This was when my mother also got interested in genealogy and did a lot of her research, which I have drawn upon while writing portions of this book.

After my father died in 2000, she wasn't nearly as active. Belkis, Mary Ann, and I returned to Denison soon afterward to watch after her. She had suffered from several health problems over the years, but it was congestive heart failure that finally caught up with her. She died on February 22, 2006, after about two months of being in either a hospital or a rest home while trying to recover from shortness of breath.

X-Ray

My mother died late at night. My sisters and I were taking turns sitting with her in the hospital, and in the early morning hours, I received a call saying she had passed. We congregated in her hospital room for a few moments and talked about what had to be done next.

As it turned out, Mary Ann suffered a medical problem about two days later, so Belkis and I took her to my daughter's pediatrician to see about it. The doctor's office was located in a building directly next to the hospital. The doctor decided to take an X-ray, so he wrote up an order and sent us next door.

When the X-ray technician saw the name on the request, he asked, "Are you any relation to Mary Moody?"

I answered, "Yes, she was my mother, our daughter's grandmother."

The technician then told us he had just read the obituary in the newspaper. He went on to say how sorry he felt because she taught him in school. I don't know if it had been during his time in second grade or later in middle school when she ran the reading program, but the man offered his sincere condolences, claiming she had been one of his nicest teachers—someone who made a difference in his life.

The x-ray technician wasn't the only one. I now see how my mother subtly guided me to appreciate things in special ways by presenting me with unique opportunities. (For example, when I was an early teen, I began to ask questions about classical music. She bought me a couple of classical albums to try, and I found I truly enjoyed them.) I've learned to enjoy life much more because of her. While the knowledge I gained in school was important for my future, my mother taught me much more, which I later found to be essential. She influenced me more than anyone else.

Wildflowers

The family also took my mother's remains back to Columbus, Mississippi, to be laid to rest beside my father's. The funeral homes in Denison and Columbus took care of all the arrangements, and a number of family members from several parts of the country showed up to pay their respects. At my mother's request, we only arranged to have a single basket of flowers at the gravesite, but when we arrived that morning, we found the entire cemetery full of spring wildflowers. It was perfect for her funeral.

My Sisters

My sisters, Esther Alford and Frances Tucker, have played an important part in my life. Although several years separates us in age—with me being the baby of the family—they've remained close to my heart despite long distances. I refer to them in some of my stories, but at this point, let it suffice that I love them. I also thank them for all their help and advice over the years. With regard to my writing, they have become some of my biggest fans.

John M. Moody

My Early Life in Dallas

A Small Boy in a Big City

An Operation

I was born in Methodist Hospital in Dallas, Texas. I don't recall much about my early life in the Dallas area. I spent my first seven years in a suburb of Dallas across the Trinity River from downtown known as Oak Cliff.

I used to believe that my earliest memory was of looking out a window of the hospital toward downtown Dallas next to my mother shortly after I was born. It was nighttime. My mother later informed me this simply wasn't possible.

Even so, one of my earliest memories *was* of looking from the window of a hospital room and seeing the lights of the Downtown Dallas skyline at night while next to my mother. It was probably at the same hospital where I was born. At the time, the tallest building in Dallas with lights on it was the Mercantile National Bank Building, but quite prominent was also the "flying, red horse"—or "the fryin' red rorse," as I then pronounced it—on top of the Magnolia Building. At least that's what I used to call the Pegasus figure on the Magnolia Petroleum/Mobil Oil logo each time I spotted it as a young boy on the top of the building.

This memory of looking through the hospital room window revolves around a time when I was two and a half years old; I was admitted to the hospital for a hernia operation. In relation to this, my *actual* first memory was of riding in the car on the way to the hospital. I had my stuffed, sleeping, yellow rabbit with me. I called it Bunny

Rabbit. I remember crossing a long bridge over the Trinity River with a view toward downtown, and I held Bunny Rabbit close to the car window for him to see out. (I later used part of this memory in one of my novels, *Woman in White, Cage of Black*, when a young girl is in a clinic with her favorite stuffed-cloth animal toy, a sleeping yellow rabbit.)

Besides the view from that window, I recall some other details about being in the hospital, both good and bad. I recall when the hospital staff gave me anesthesia with a mask in a gaseous form. At one moment, I saw a bright light from the operating room overhead and felt terrified. Then I remember nothing until I woke up feeling thirsty. However, when I asked for water, the nurse brought me a shot in a hypodermic needle. I think this is where I lost my full confidence in the medical profession, which continues today.

Two good things happened, though. Some of the medical staff made an airplane for me out of wooden tongue depressors and rubber bands. Also, when I watched the doctor examining me with a flashlight, I apparently expressed so much interest in it that he bought me a small flashlight. I think I've liked flashlights ever since, but he failed in overcoming my distrust of doctors. I express some of this distrust in my novel, *Return to Nowhere*, where one of the doctors at a clinic is a truly despicable character.

My later recovery at home following the operation was another time I remember well. A number of people—most likely friends of my parents, including people from their church—visited our home, and they brought me all sorts of gifts. Someone gave me a set of plastic, toy, farm animals. I recall in particular a rooster and a light brown calf. Another friend of my parents brought me a set of second-hand puzzles. They were for a much older child (although still for children), but even at two and a half years old, I began to work them. One of the puzzles was of Hansel and Gretel, showing the wicked witch. A boxed set of other puzzles included maps of North and South America. I still recall playing with the map puzzles as an older child, perhaps at about nine years old. I think I like geography because of these puzzles, and I suppose this is also why I've been fascinated with South America from an early age.

John M. Moody

The Witches of Delaware Street

I remember much about the house where my family lived in Oak Cliff. The front door in the living room faced the street, and in an age before everyone had air conditioning, my mother used to lock me as a toddler inside the screen door and leave the wooden door open for air circulation. This kept me safely inside and somewhat entertained while she did things around the house.

I recall random images of the following events—but just barely, so most of the details are based on my mother's perspective as she told it when I was much older. At the time of the story, I was around three years old.

St. Joseph Home for Girls, run by the Catholic Church, stood a couple of blocks away near the ended of the street toward the east. Frequently during the summer months, the nuns took the girls swimming in a pool on South Adams Avenue. The pool was located in a tree-shaded corner of the same plot of land holding John F. Peeler Elementary, and today only the trees remain. The girls—in their swimsuits, complete with bathing caps if I remember correctly—walked single file from the orphanage west along Delaware to turn onto Adams, and several nuns always escorted them.

My mother found me inside the screen door one day calling out to one of the nuns as she passed, "Hello, old witch!" It was most likely a time, mentioned earlier, after I received my Hansel and Gretel puzzle showing a witch on the picture. I naturally identified women in long, black dresses wearing heavy, black shoes as witches. I wasn't afraid of her; I was just trying to be friendly.

My mother quickly pulled me away and shut the wooden door. She didn't know if any of the nuns heard me or not, but she tried to keep the door closed after that when they strolled past.

Lost in a Downtown Dallas Department Store

My mother used to cross the Trinity River in our old, deep-purple Plymouth to go shopping in downtown, and she pushed me around in a metal stroller. She said she had to keep it constantly in motion while she examined store displays because if she ever stopped, I was out in a flash. I might have been around three years old one day when I made an escape to go exploring. She said I was there one minute and gone the next.

She didn't know where I was, but I wasn't worried. I knew exactly where I was and how to get back to her—only she wouldn't have been in the same spot if I ever decided to go back because she had gone looking for me. As a child, that part of the logic still hadn't dawned on me.

Eventually, someone found me standing in front of a moving escalator, half mesmerized as the steps disappeared in front of me. I recall that part of the incident quite clearly. Whoever found me returned me to my mother safe and sound.

On the way home in the car, I recall her scolding me for running off. She told me how much she worried about me. I recall her saying she had been afraid that a "bad man" might have gotten me.

Random Memories of Oak Cliff

A Red Bryans Barbeque restaurant used to be located in Oak Cliff near the southwest corner of Jefferson Boulevard with Llewellyn Avenue. I remember as a young child how delicious the barbeque tasted as I sat with my mother and sisters in a booth there. My family didn't eat out often unless we were traveling, and it was always a treat to stop there to eat so close to home. According to Google Street View, the building still stands, but that particular restaurant has long since closed down. Years later, I rode with someone at lunchtime to pick up barbeque sandwiches at Sonny Bryans in another Dallas location, and I fondly recalled the sandwiches in Oak Cliff.

If I remember correctly, a large Sears, Roebuck & Co. store sat on the north side of the street across from the restaurant. (I used to believe my mother said "Sears robot" when she spoke of the place.) It was surrounded by a parking lot that took up the rest of the block. I think the old building is gone, and a small shopping center replaced it.

Raven Pharmacy sat on the corner a block or so east along Jefferson from Red Bryans, and it had a metal sign showing a large, black raven that revolved. I always looked for the raven as a young child when my mother drove to that part of town. The drug store is apparently something else now, but the sign with the bird was still there the last time I checked.

The Texas Theater still stands a couple of blocks further east on the north side of the street. I saw my first indoor movie there, and I couldn't have been more than six years old. I even remember the movie; it was *The Vikings* with Kirk Douglas and Tony Curtis. For years afterward I recalled certain scenes, such as when the Viking ship traveled up the fjord after a raid. Another scene was the part when the Viking chief sentenced Tony Curtis to death by drowning, and the crabs were going to eat him, but he was saved by a change of wind. Not long ago I saw the movie again. It was much as I remembered, as vivid a memory as it must have been. I grew up enjoying movies.

Years later when President Kennedy was assassinated, I watched all the reports on the news. I lived in Denison at the time, but I knew exactly where Lee Harvey Oswald had been caught because I still recalled the theater's name.

At Home in Oak Cliff

My family's home in Oak Cliff was a small, frame house. I think it had only two real bedrooms with a single bathroom in between on the east side. My parents used the bedroom toward the front while my sisters used the one toward the back. The west side had a living room/dining room as a single room in front, with a separate kitchen toward the back. The living room had a gas heater in a hearth that looked a little like a fireplace. The house also had a fully-enclosed porch behind the kitchen, which became my room after I stopped using a crib. I used a metal-framed single bed along the back wall of the house, and the cement floor, which had once been the back porch, sloped slightly downhill.

The cement floor of my "room" had expansion joints—those grooves placed in cement, hoping that if the slab ever breaks, it will separate along lines of weakness. I recall that some of my toys were colorful glass marbles. I have no idea where they came from, but I surely got them second-hand. I kept them (or maybe I received them) in an old, metal, pipe tobacco can with no lid. I used to play for hours with the marbles on the grooves extending across the floor. I lined the marbles up on a groove parallel to my bed, and as I rolled them toward an intersecting groove, they made a 90 degree turn and rolled downslope to the other side of the room. Then I gathered them up and did it again, over and over. I could only roll the marbles from right to left along the groove, however, because at the down-slope corner, the expansion joint didn't quite work, leaving a broken corner shaped like a jagged triangle. I'm amazed I can recall so much detail about a cement floor, but after all, it also served as one of my favorite playthings when I was young.

I especially recall one marble in particular. It was made of transparent, red glass, and it had a few nicks or defects in it. I used to hold it up to my eye and look through it toward the light. As I turned it in different orientations, I imagined seeing an entire world inside as the nicks or other spots floated by on the opposite surface.

In the back yard, my parents planted a pecan tree. They did it hoping someday for the shade it would provide, as well as for the pecans it would produce. They took good care of it, and it was just beginning to bear its desired fruit when we moved away. Whenever we returned to Oak Cliff to visit one-time neighbors, my mother occasionally wondered if the people living there were enjoying the pecans. Based on Google's Street View, the tree still seems to be thriving.

A girl named Linda Jo of my same age lived directly behind our house when I was only a toddler. I think her parents were living with her grandmother at the time. (The grandmother was a piano teacher. Years later, my mother claimed that Van Cliburn—at an early age—was once her student, but I never heard first-hand confirmation.)

My friend's yard and mine joined in the back. Our parents were friends, and they arranged it so our sand boxes were nearly together, separated only by a chain-link fence. (As another side note, Ganny and Pawpaw bought the chain-link fence for my parents after I was born to keep me safely in the yard. I tried to climb it once and failed miserably.) Linda Jo and I could play together while not actually being together. About the worst we could do was throw sand at each other. As I grew older, I thought of her as my girlfriend.

Linda Jo's grandmother owned a large, old, dark gray hound. At some later time when our parents let us play together, I went inside the dog's doghouse, where I contracted ringworm on my stomach.

My friend's father sold golf equipment, and in the mid-to-late 1950s, it was apparently a good business. Her family prospered, and when I was about five or so, they moved into a brick home in a nice neighborhood in a far-away Dallas suburb. My mother drove me to her house a couple of times to play, but things were never quite the same.

Even after my family also moved out of Oak Cliff, our parents stayed in contact for a while. Linda Jo's family once paid my family a visit in Denison. My mother told me they were on the way, and I waited in the front yard under a tree for about an hour in anticipation.

When they finally arrived, her father was driving a second-hand, full-size passenger bus he had converted into a combination living trailer and golf equipment showroom. During summer months he drove the family to all the famous golf tournaments and events around the country to sell equipment to attendees and spectators, and he stopped by our house just to say hello on the way to somewhere else. Their stay lasted only a few moments at the most—or it seemed that way to me. It was the last time I saw Linda Jo. My thoughts of rekindling our friendship (romance?) came to an abrupt end. I was about nine years old at the time.

I had another friend who lived two doors down. His name was Paul. He was a little younger than me, but other than Linda Jo, he was my best friend. His mother sometimes made popcorn for us in one of those popcorn poppers where a person had to crank a handle. I guess those were the only times I ever saw a device of this type used. Popcorn might now be one of my favorite foods because of her.

One day Paul and I were playing in his parent's garage. I was about five at the time; maybe he was four. He opened the door of his family's car (surely a 1950s something, built like a tank). Then he told me that if he held his hand in the gap of the car door and I closed the door, it wouldn't hurt. He convinced me to try it. Sure enough, he held his hand in the gap, and I closed the door on his hand. Remarkably, he didn't get hurt. Then it was my turn to hold my hand inside the gap, but when he closed the door, it hurt like hell. My fingers were hurt pretty badly. I never did it again, and to this day, I still can't figure out why it didn't hurt him in the first place.

I was playing with a young friend in the back yard once. I don't think he was Paul. We pretended to be mountain climbers, and the house was the mountain (although we weren't really climbing anything, only pretending to climb). At one moment, I gazed toward the lofty peak above, and I spied a lot of smoke rising into the air over the roof of our house. I shouted, "There's a fire on top of the mountain!"

Luckily, my family's home wasn't on fire. My friend and I excitedly hurried around to the front yard, and a wood-frame house across the street was burning. Within moments, the fire department arrived and quickly extinguished the flames, but not before the house was a total loss. No one was hurt. The fire had been caused by an electric iron someone forgot to turn off before leaving that morning. The owners eventually tore down the building. A brick home now stands on the spot.

In the late 1950s, I came home one afternoon to find a neighbor (one of my mother's good friends) and another woman sitting on our living room sofa. A small, light-colored poodle also sat on the sofa next to the woman. The other woman turned out to be Debbie Reynolds' mother, who had stopped by to visit the neighbor (an old friend). In turn, the neighbor brought Debbie Reynolds' mother to meet my mother. The dog, I was told, was Debbie Reynolds' poodle. The mother took care of the dog while the actress was working. I recall the dog being especially well-mannered.

Over the years afterward whenever I heard about Debbie Reynolds and her career, I always remembered that her dog (as well as her mother) once sat on my family's sofa.

The Case of the Crawling Bag

When I was about three or four years old, my family took a summer trip to Mississippi. We probably spent time with family in Columbus, but on the way home, we made a detour to Biloxi and Gulfport. (As a young girl, my mother used to spend weeks during summers in a house that had a view of the gulf, so she enjoyed returning to the area. The house was destroyed by Hurricane Katrina in 2005.)

During our trip, we rode an excursion boat from Gulfport to West Ship Island to see the sights. It may have been my first experience in a boat, and I know it was my first over such a large body of water. I recall sitting on a wooden bench near my parents with my back toward the water. The boat pitched up and down so much I felt afraid I might lose a child's sand bucket I brought along. We saw porpoises along the way, and I know this was another first for me. At one point, my parents let me use a brown-paper sack to walk along the beach and collect seashells. I remember finding a lot of them.

As soon as we returned to the mainland, one of my parents drove us all the way back to Oak Cliff, where we arrived the same evening. My father unpacked the car—an old, dark-purple Plymouth—and mother soon sent me off to take a bath after the long trip. While I was bathing, however, I heard a commotion somewhere else in the house. When I finished my bath, I learned that my paper bag full of seashells "started to crawl across the kitchen floor." When it first began to move, it startled my mother and my sisters tremendously.

My father had to set the bag outside, and by the next day, many of my sea shells had crawled away. Thinking back now, I suppose the shells must have contained hermit crabs.

Teddy Bear

My sister Frances had a small, brown teddy bear, and when she became older, I used to play with it, too. By that time, it was several years old, and the poor, stuffed animal had lost both its eyes.

One day our mother announced that she would perform "an operation" to restore its eyesight. She selected two, baby-blue buttons and carefully sewed them on in the correct spots. However, she wouldn't let me play with it right away. She reclined the bear face-up on a table with a rag covering its eyes, and I couldn't touch it for half an hour until it "healed" properly. I recall the anticipation I felt as I asked her frequently during that half hour if enough time had passed. Afterward, I was careful not to pull on the buttons. I believe that Frances still has this bear at her home, and it still has the same, blue-button eyes.

No Nursery Today

Our family attended Christ Episcopal Church in Oak Cliff, and I guess I was baptized there. During certain times, maybe when my mother attended women's service group meetings organized by the church, she used to take me to a children's nursery (these days called a day care center), which was also run by the church. This nursery was located in a dark red-brick house across South Llewellyn Avenue from the church sanctuary. The room facing the church was probably a large, open living room where the children could play, and I remember lots of children to play with.

One thing that impressed me once was when a toddler much younger than me brought a sack lunch, and when the attendants at the nursery pulled out a banana from the brown paper bag he brought, it was completely black. As I thought about it over the years, especially after becoming an adult, I couldn't imagine how any parent would have sent a banana that was so overly ripe in his or her child's lunch.

When I last looked on a Google Street View, the house still stood in the location, and it still appeared to be in good condition, much like I remembered it. The cement steps facing the church and leading up to a porch are flanked by short, brick walls capped by cement slabs. The reason I describe the stairs in so much detail is because of an adventure I experienced there.

When I was a little older child, my mother had to go to a meeting at the church. She dropped me off at the sidewalk and told me to go inside the nursery. However, she mentioned that she wasn't sure if the nursery was open or not that day. Even so, she was in a great hurry for some reason. She said if it wasn't open, I could just wait on the steps. She then drove off somewhere to park.

Sure enough, the nursery wasn't open. I knocked on the door several times, but no one answered. I sat alone on a side wall of the porch steps—the one on the right side as a person faces the house. I remember feeling a little frightened as I sat there, just waiting for what felt like a long time—until my mother came back to find me there. These days Child Protective Services might have been called, but I was fine. My mother praised me for simply sitting there and waiting (without getting into any trouble).

I attended elementary school in Oak Cliff for half a year, but I'll describe it in more detail further on.

The Dallas Tornado

No, I'm not talking about a sports team. A few years ago I stumbled across a webpage dedicated to the tornado that struck Dallas in 1957. I felt so impressed by the information, I decided to write its creator and editor, Robert Butsch, and I now include my slightly-edited and updated correspondence below. I think this information is important. As it turned out, Mr. Butsch didn't often check for messages, but several months later he contacted me to thank me for my input.

Dear Mr. Butsch,

I discovered your very interesting and detailed account on the 1957 Dallas tornado today, and I wanted to tell you how informative I found it to be. I was living in Oak Cliff in 1957, and I watched the tornado from my front yard. I decided to write to add my "two cents."

My family lived, if my memory for numbers still serves me, at *** Delaware *(Note - Information deleted for this publication)*. I confirmed from a Google Map of Dallas and a Street View photo of the property that this location is only six blocks east of "Minute 13" of your timeline. At the time, I was a few months less than five years old, but seeing this tornado impressed me so much, it remains one of my most vivid memories from my years living in Dallas. Even though I was very young, I can still picture many of the details of that afternoon in my mind.

At the time, my father worked in an office [in the Katy Building] on the western side of downtown, not far from the present day Kennedy Memorial. He heard about the tornado and called my mother, probably concerned for our safety. She stepped out the front door to take a look, and I tagged along. I believe my sisters were still at school. (I also believe the house is still standing.) An elementary school with a large, open playground stood in the block just to our west. (A different school building seems to be there now.) This open playground gave us an excellent field of view. It wasn't raining, but my mother years later described the morning before the tornado struck as feeling "sticky" with humidity.

As we left the house, the tornado was passing directly to our west. The tornado appeared to be on the ground just the other side of a line of houses in the block beyond the school. I remember how tremendous and truly awesome it appeared. The funnel was a very dark, rotating mass that looked almost solid, and it was very well defined from the ground high into the clouds. My mother didn't think to get the camera. (Most of the photos I have seen do not look like I remember it, but it is possible I saw it from a closer distance or at a different time than the photos I've seen.)

Some neighbors stood outside with us. No one seemed to be afraid. My mother had never seen a tornado before, and she misjudged its size. I remember her saying to neighbors something like, "Oh, it's just a small one. Look at all the trash it's kicking up." As I mentioned earlier, instead of the tornado being three blocks away, the true distance was six blocks at the time. The "trash" she pointed out was probably walls and roofs of houses.

We stood outside in the front yard and watched until the tornado was quite far away toward the northwest. You mentioned the possibility of there being two funnels when the tornado neared the Trinity River. When the tornado was so far away that it looked like a narrow "finger" connecting the dark cloud to the ground, I watched as a second funnel formed next to the first. Very soon there were two, one not far from the other. I'm sure of this because it impressed me to see two "fingers" that both looked about the same size and shape. I'm sorry to say we were too far away to tell if both funnels were on the ground at the same time or not. Not long afterward, we couldn't see it anymore.

My parents never took me to see any of the destruction, but I believe I saw the half-hour documentary on television. It was either that or I saw a lot of news coverage. In any case, a couple of thing I can remember about the film reports impressed me. One segment showed a house that had been completely destroyed, but a small, delicate table still stood, and on the table there was a vase with a check for $20 dollars under it. I understood the report to say the tornado had taken away the house but left the table, vase, and check as shown for the report. Thinking back, it could have been an easy thing to stage for the camera, but I guess I'll never know for sure. I think I can also recall hearing that the tornado took a man's "wooden" leg off of his body, but he wasn't killed. I'm not sure it really happened, but it is one of my memories from the aftermath.

For many years, I used to dream about tornados. In the dreams, I usually wanted to take a photo of a tornado, but I would not have a camera, or the camera would not have film, or just as I was preparing to take the photo, something else would happen to prevent me from taking the shot. However, the dreams were never nightmares, and I guess one of the reasons was because everyone around me watched the 1957 Dallas tornado very calmly as it passed. I'm sure the dreams were a product of my experience.

As I read the website, it struck me that I also saw something significant and historical so long ago, and if I never shared my experience with someone who appreciates it, the memory will be lost forever. Anyway, I hope you will find the account of a boy less than five years old to be useful. If you have any questions, please feel free to contact me.

Sincerely,
John M. Moody

I describe a woman and her young daughter experiencing a tornado strike in my book *Woman in White, Cage of Black*, and I feel certain my experience in 1957 created my fascination for these meteorological phenomena. As for the dreams, a shrink would probably have a wonderful time with this sort of information, but I've now left these dreams behind with age. (And as for the photos, these were pre-digital days—no cameras on cell phones. I might have an easier time of it now.)

The closest I've come to seeing another tornado was as an older teenager. I was on a trip with family near the Texas Gulf Coast, riding in the back of a station wagon. The weather was stormy with plenty of low, dark clouds. Back along the highway and off to the left, I spotted a funnel cloud in the distance. The dark, slim finger extended halfway to the ground. I had my mother's camera with me, and it contained film. I aimed through the viewfinder to take a picture, but I delayed, hoping for a better shot. Seconds later, the car's forward motion brought a rain shower between me and the potential tornado. Once the rain shower was out of the way, the funnel had disappeared into the clouds—just like in a dream.

The Dallas to Denison Transition

When describing my father, I have already written about how my family came to live in Denison, Texas. Denison was a nice place in which to grow up. I had good friends. I learned from good teachers (for the most part). The surrounding area allowed me to learn about nature, fossils, and Native American artifacts, which later influenced one of my branches in life immeasurable. I can probably list dozens of reasons why living in Denison eventually shaped me to be who I am, but I prefer to simply describe some of my memories from growing up.

John M. Moody

My Life in Denison

Growing Up in a Nice Place ... At Least Most of the Time

When my family first moved to Denison, I guess I was around seven years old. For half a year, we lived in a rent house on Morgan Street until my parents began to buy a house further north. The rent house was near Houston School, and both are still standing. The school continues to be active, too. On the playground, I recall horned toads running around, but I guess too many students trying to catch them made them become locally extinct.

My main memory of living in the rent house was listening to a crystal radio at night. The device was made of red plastic and looked like a rocket ship. By twisting a small knob on the rocket's nose I could change the radio station.

The house sat on the steep slope of a hill, and one block further west down the hill the pavement ended to become a dirt road, which extended for only another block, ending in a dead end. I tried to walk down that way once, but an older boy blocked my way telling me it might be dangerous. He never said why, and I never tried to go that way afterward. The pavement extends for at least three blocks now. It no longer appears dangerous, but the street still terminates at a dead end.

After we moved, I was able to attend Central Ward Elementary School, which once stood between Sears and Morton Streets next to Armstrong Avenue. I have a lot of memories of Central Ward School, but I'll group most of them with my school life later on. The rest of this section deals especially with growing up in and around Denison.

The Day I Saw Eisenhower

President Dwight D. Eisenhower was born in Denison. As I understand it, even he didn't know this fact until he was much older. His family moved to Abilene, Kansas, when the leader was only a small child. As a result, he thought he was born in Kansas when he filled out his application for West Point. It wasn't until he began to move into the top command position during World War II when someone in Denison remembered his parents and the general as a young boy.

General Eisenhower returned to Denison twice before my time because I've seen photos of these occasions. After he served as president, he returned again, and I saw him that time.

When the new high school auditorium was built in 1965, the school decided to name it after the former president and military commander. He accepted an invitation to speak at the dedication. Everyone apparently knew he was coming, and in some way my mother knew about the time he would arrive. She drove my sisters and me to a street corner along US Highways 75 and 69 just after they joined and entered Denison from the direction of Sherman. I can almost remember the exact corner, but I'm not positive because so much has changed since then. US Highway 69 is still there, but US 75 now bypasses downtown completely toward the west.

My sisters and I stood on the corner and waited for only a few moments. Then someone spotted a large, black car with an escort. "Here he comes!" someone said.

I gazed hard toward the car. The windows weren't tinted, and I saw him sitting in the back. My sisters and I waved at him, and he waved back. We were the only people on the corner, and I suppose we were the first people in Denison that day to welcome him back to his birthplace.

Later, we went to the auditorium. We found seats early, but later the place had standing-room only. The news stations from Dallas were all there. The former president came out and gave a speech, but I don't remember what he said; I was too young at the time. The news services brought mounted cameras, which were equipped with bright lights, but sometimes the lights pointed in our direction, making it difficult to see the speaker at the podium. I recall one man somewhere behind us who wasn't pleased with the lights, either, and he shouted out to have them turned off. I felt embarrassed by the demonstration because a former president was trying to speak on stage. Even so, they turned off the lights, and we got to see the speaker much better afterward.

When President Eisenhower died in 1969, I saved a copy of the Denison newspaper at the time, *The Denison Herald*. I wrapped it in plastic as a way of preserving it. I simply thought it might be valuable someday, being a report of his death from the town where he was born.

In my novel, *Searching for Jennifer*, the principal female protagonist mentions being from a Texas town on the Red River where a president was born, and this information later brings the principal male character to Denison in search of her.

Lake Texoma

A large part of my life growing up in Denison revolved around Lake Texoma. This lake, created during the early 1940 by the construction of Denison Dam, is still one the largest man-made lakes in the United States.

Over the years, I guess I've seen most of it at one time or another. I collected some amazing fossils and Native American artifacts from its shores in several locations. I even found an arrowhead on one of its islands. I used to swim at beaches east and west of Burns Run near the Oklahoma side of Denison Dam and further west. I've also camped along its shores in Texas and Oklahoma. I went boating with friends whose parents owned boats, and I even waterskied once—for about 10 seconds.

Near the lake, I've watched birds, alone and with my father many times. He worked as a volunteer at Hagerman Wildlife Refuge throughout his retirement years, and whenever I returned home after being away for long periods of time, we went birdwatching there.

Later on I'll describe how I came up with my idea to write *Shards of Time*, my "Denison" murder mystery, during a trip with Mary Ann to hunt for fossils at the lake. I'll also describe some of the fossils from Lake Texoma.

Scouts

I was in Cub Scouts and Boy Scouts. During those years, I learned a number of skills that served me later.

In Cub Scouts, our group met at a friend's parent's home. The Den Mother, the mother of my friend, organized all sorts of great activities for us to do. We went downtown once to watch how ice cream was made at Ashburn's Ice Cream. The building still stands on Main Street. We went to a local company that made paper products. We visited the Safeway Plant that once operated just north of Denison, and at the conclusion of the tour, they gave us samples of freshly packaged margarine and newly bottled pickles. We also took a tour of the power plant at Denison Dam, which I found especially interesting.

One year my father and I attended a father-son camp for a weekend on Lake Texoma. I recall that someone brought one of those hand exercise devices that helped to build muscles by squeezing it closed. Our group of boys tried to squeeze it closed, even using both hands, and none of us could do it. My father took the device in his hand and squeezed it closed several times rapidly. I heard one of my fellow Cub Scouts say, "Wow!" I felt pretty proud of my father that day.

We took several hikes during the day, and on one of these outings, I picked up a long walking stick. We returned to screened-in cabins at night to sleep on cots, and before I went inside, I placed my walking stick up next to the cabin under a roof so it would be out of the way. I planned to use it the following day.

During the night, it rained extremely hard. By the following morning, all the firewood was wet. The older men couldn't start a fire for fixing breakfast.

Then I remembered my walking stick. It was still dry, so I took it to my father. He used his pocket knife to carve enough shavings to get a small fire started, and from that, the men were able to dry out enough wood to get a larger blaze going. We had a late breakfast, but we ate. I used this experience when writing a small portion of *Journey from Mezet*.

On my first camp-out in Boy Scouts on Lake Texoma, I went through a "branding ceremony," a form of initiation. I had heard about it even before I became a scout, and the thought of it was almost enough to make me not want to become one. It involved the branding of first-time campers with a hot stick—or so I thought.

On the first night, the older scouts built a campfire by the beach. Then they took the first-timers like me into semi-seclusion. They kept several of us grouped apart some distance from the beach.

They led us shirtless, one at a time, to the campfire. I felt worried. I couldn't understand why the adults didn't step in to stop the practice, but I saw them grouped together on one side, merely watching. The older boys said they would only touch my stomach quickly with the hot stick, and it wouldn't hurt much. Even so, I had heard the screams of the boys who were led away ahead of me, so I didn't have much confidence in what they told me.

Regardless, I felt determined to face up to it in front of the other boys. After all, a scout was supposed to be brave, wasn't he?

They removed a hot stick from the fire and showed it to me. I still have the image in my mind. It was large and had a glowing, fiery-red tip. Then they blindfolded me. I asked them to let me brace myself in a stance, and I waited for the burn. Then I felt it. I felt it burning—only it wasn't burning wood. They had stuck my stomach with a piece of ice.

After that, they sent me to sit with the other initiates. They had me pretend to be recovering from a burn on my stomach until the rest of the group went through the ordeal.

I suppose it wouldn't be allowed now days, but that's what they did. However, I believe they had already discontinued the practice a year or so later. Still, I found out I was braver than I thought.

As a Boy Scout, I learned many skills. Most importantly, I learned about maps and how to navigate through a forest. I learned to make a fire in the wild with no problem when needed, but I never needed to do it until I reached Venezuela, where I cooked roasted meat over a bed of coals fairly often. Even now when I start a fire for cooking outside, I never use fire starter fluids. To stay in practice, I always build fires the old-fashion way with wood shavings and sticks—and usually a single match. I even learned to start a fire with flint and steel with little problem. I gathered knowledge about nature, survival skills, and camping over the years. These skills show up in all three books of my "Mezet Trilogy" (*Journey from Mezet, Second*

Book of Marc, and *Marc's Final Journey*) and in *Return to Nowhere*. More recently, I also refer to them in *Snake Bluff Lodge*.

Our scout group once took a trip to an area along the Glover River in the Kiamichi Mountains of eastern Oklahoma. On one day, we crossed the river a few at a time in a rowboat and visited a spot where we collected quartz crystals. I found several nice ones, and I used this memory in *Return to Nowhere*. Paul, the principal male protagonist, always carries around a quartz crystal he found during summer camp. It represents a keepsake from a perfect day of his childhood.

Early one summer when I was still in middle school, a call went out to all the Boy Scouts that an elderly woman with mild dementia never returned home after she went for a walk. It was Saturday morning, and she had been missing since the previous afternoon.

The woman told a person she happened to pass the day before that she planned to walk to Dallas (about 75 miles away), and she was known to walk long distances around town. Earlier, it had never been a problem because she always returned home in the evening. Many of the Boy Scout troops of Denison gathered at McDaniel Junior High to form search parties organized by the Denison Fire Department.

Boys fanned out all over town as they searched for her. We went in pairs in most cases. In that way if we found her, one boy could stay with her while the other reported to the fire department.

Initially, I started out to search with another boy in the eastern part of town near where the woman was last seen. We were riding in a car with George Cravens, the Fire Chief at the time, as he drove us toward a search area. However, he all at once received a call on his radio that someone located a woman.

Chief Cravens immediately turned and headed to a sand and gravel quarry not far south of the US Highway 75/69 bridge across the Red River. (This was in the opposite direction from Dallas.) The woman turned out to be the one who had gone missing.

When we arrived, she was still sitting in a spot where one of the searchers spotted her, and she ended up alive that day because of the boy's sharp eyes—and a little pure luck. The boy was just about to leave the area when he happened to glance back toward a pile of sand. He saw something fluttering in the breeze. It happened to be a white scarf the woman wore on her head. She had wandered into the quarry during the night and had fallen into a depression in the soft sand where she couldn't stand up. As she sat there, the top of the scarf was the only thing still visible behind the sand pile.

The chief gave her small sips of water from a canteen one of us carried while he talked to her. She had been in the spot much of the night up to late in the morning, so she was pretty thirsty, but the chief wouldn't let her drink too much at one time. An ambulance soon arrived to check her before they attempted to move her. In the end, she was okay except for dehydration.

Later in the summer, my family went on our annual trip to Mississippi to see relatives. When I returned home two weeks later, a friend told me the same woman had left her house and gone for another walk. My friend and others searched for her again, but they never found her. I don't know if anyone ever did.

During several summers, I attended a Boy Scout camp called Camp Texoma on the Texas side of the lake. The camp occupied a large plot of wooded land and had a lot of facilities. I especially enjoyed when they fired a brass cannon in the morning to wake everyone up. I often tried to get up early enough to watch them load it and fire it. I guess I first fired a gun, a .22 single-shot rifle, on my first visit to the camp, and the camp staff seemed surprised by my marksmanship. During a camping trip there one year, I learned how to handle both a rowboat and a canoe, earning merit badges for both of those. I later drew upon my experience with a canoe in *Return to Nowhere*.

Our troop camped once in seriously freezing weather. It was in late November of 1963, and President John F. Kennedy had just been assassinated. It dropped to 17 degrees Fahrenheit overnight. In the morning after I cooked breakfast, I used a hot washcloth to wash the skillet, and I set the cloth down for a few seconds to toss the water from the pan. When I turned around and picked up the washcloth again, it had frozen solid. I know this is no big deal for people living in cold climates, but I was unaccustomed to working outside in this sort of weather; I felt amazed at how the water froze so rapidly. (Years later, I got used to the cold while in Colorado. I went out one night with some friends to buy ice cream. The temperature was 6 below, and I wasn't wearing socks.)

Different Lives in One

On another occasion at summer camp, I was out walking around the camp one night when I heard a group from one troop raiding another troop. Some big kids started bullying a group of younger ones, and I stepped right in to stand up for the younger ones. When I told the bullies to stop, one of them taunted, "Who's gonna make us?"

I told them, "I am!"

Up until then, I guess it was the bravest thing I had ever done. At the time, I was tall, but not especially large, and I knew I was no match for several of them at once.

However, my boldness caused the bigger kids to back down and go away. I made some young friends that night.

I was chosen to be in the Order of the Arrow, which was modeled after Native American traditions. It was a special honor, and I had to be selected. Afterward, other boys and I were instructed to attend a weekend camp and go through a special ordeal. For one thing, we weren't allowed to talk to anyone as we worked various manual labor projects at the camp during the entire weekend.

In our free moments, we were expected to carve an arrow out of wood, and if we didn't do this, we wouldn't be admitted to the final recognition ceremony. If any of the councilors caught someone breaking the rules, they carved a large notch in the arrow, and three notches resulted in the arrow being broken. A person had to start over and carve another arrow if that happened to be the case. As it turned out, my arrow didn't have any notches.

On top of that, we were fed very little food. I think we got a piece of bread and some water for breakfast, and a package of cheese crackers and water for lunch.

At the end of the ordeal, they presented us with our symbols of recognition—a white sash with an embroidered red arrow across it—showing we had successfully completed the requirements. Then they let us talk again, and they fed us a steak dinner. During the following year, I participated in a second camp where I earned the next higher level of the order.

I never made it to Eagle Scout, and as I look back, I remember why. I had a fear of diving head-first into water, regardless of if I was at a pool or at a lake. I knew how to swim quite well. I even earned a Mile Swim badge at summer camp. I worked on the swimming merit badge and did everything else, but when it came to the final part—diving head-first into the water—I simply couldn't do it correctly. I usually hit my stomach whenever I tried. Therefore, I didn't earn the award, and without this one, which was required to become an Eagle Scout, I simply gave up trying.

Eventually I got older and had too many activities in and out of high school to keep up with them all. I dropped out of nearly everything other than school activities to concentrate on the ones I had to do to pass my courses. And while I never became an Eagle Scout, I learned everything I could while I was in the organization.

Texoma Rockhounds

I suppose no other group influenced me more in my later life than the Texoma Rockhounds. I learned a lot from its members, several of whom were geologists—or at least serious amateur rock and fossil collectors possessing a world of knowledge. As I've already described, I started going to meetings as a child with my father, and eventually the entire family became involved.

During the early 1960s when I first went to meetings and on field trips, attendance in the club was high. I guess between 50 and 60 people came to meetings fairly regularly during good weather. Half of that number usually showed up on field trips. The club's field trip chairman tried to organize an outing each month for the club—again depending on the weather. About once or twice a year, the trips to more distant locations lasted overnight. With a group of this size, it wasn't easy to find accommodations.

We took trips to all sorts of places. My first visit to the North Sulphur River was with the Texoma Rockhounds, and it became one of my favorite areas to collect artifacts and fossils over the years.

My family's first visit to the Stillwell area of Oklahoma was with the club. Areas north of Stillwell were once great places to collect artifacts from plowed fields during the 1960s. Native American tribes had evidently camped in the area between about 9,000 BCE to 200 ACE based on some of the artifacts other family members collected. (My mother once collected a "paleo" type of dart point from the older end of the scale, and my father once found part of a trade pipe that probably dates from the early 1800s).

On a few overnight trips, we also collected rocks and minerals, or we went to "rock swaps," where people traded, bought, and sold anything rockhound related. We visited all sorts of locations across northern Texas and southern Oklahoma. Regardless of what we collected or did, I enjoyed it all.

A typical club meeting went through the usual motions such as treasurers report, minutes from the past meeting, old business, new business, etc. Then they presented a speaker. Sometimes it was a person from the club, but they often invited someone from out of town. Someone always served refreshments such as coffee, Kool-Aid, and cookies. For December meetings, they had a pot-luck supper where everyone brought different dishes for everyone else to share. I describe a part of *Journey from Mezet* where a group of people does something similar as a form of celebration, and my idea came directly from my memories of these delightful events.

My mother served as the president of the club one year. (My father was too busy with his job when they asked him, so they asked her.) Later, she served as the club's historian, keeping yearly scrapbooks of club activities until she was no longer able to keep up with it.

During the fall of each year for many years, the club organized a public show over a weekend. The general public came to see displays of rocks, fossils, minerals, and artifacts shown by club members. My family used to participate. The club usually invited a rock dealer who sold items during the events, and in later years, they allowed several dealers to compete with each other. In most cases, however, every dealer sold enough to make a profit as long as the crowds were large.

I went off to the university and later to work in Dallas. Still later, I began to work overseas. Even so, the club continued to function, and my parents still attended regularly. On one of my return trips from Venezuela to visit my parents, I gave a presentation on fossils I worked with at the museum, and the crowd was still fairly sizable.

Today the group continues to meet, but I usually find I'm too busy to go anymore. Even so, I suppose I became a geologist and a curator of paleontology in a museum because of my background gained through of this group.

Woodcarving

While living in Denison, I began to make wood carvings at a young age, and I continued to make things out of wood for many years up to recently.

The first thing I remember making was a wooden cannon. I had just seen a movie on television showing a big cannon on wheels, so I made one to play with. I later carved boats, and as a Boy Scout, I carved neckerchief slides. I thought some of them were pretty creative, and I won second place with one of them in a competition.

I carved guns, too. I'll later describe how I made realistic models of Thompson sub-machine guns, but some of the other guns I carved include an Astra Model 400 pistol, a World War II Japanese Nambu pistol, a revolver with a revolving cylinder, and a Smith & Wesson sub-machine gun. I gave the Nambu (still showing the wood with only a light-stained finish of linseed oil) to a Denison man who owned the actual pistol I modeled it after, and he seemed quite impressed.

Later on, I carved fossil animal skeletons while at the university. I did most of them as decorative plaques to hang on a wall, but in one case I carved a three-dimensional model of a mosasaur skeleton. I had to design the base in a special way so the ribs—all carved individually—were supported.

Sometimes during my university years I made items to give away to impress girls. One of these was a small horse, and another was an airplane. People sometimes made requests for specific items, and I tried to comply, but when people wanted me to carve items and offered to pay, I never made money—and at the same time, I usually ended up spending time carving something I wasn't especially interested in making.

In the late 1970s, Core Lab, the company I worked for, wrote an article about my woodcarving for the company's magazine. While searching through my mother's file cabinets that hold her genealogy research, I discovered she had saved a copy.

When I worked for a while in Houston for this same company, they made some improvements to the lab there, and part of what they did was to place long, oak boards along the tops of some of the lab counters. In the process, they trimmed off a foot-long piece of hard

Different Lives in One

oak and discarded it. I carried it to my apartment to see if I could find a use for it. I soon realized the wood was too hard and too thin for me to use to create a free-standing figure of any form I could imagine. When I examined the surface, however, I found a tiny knot on one side. I spent a while wondering if I might use this knot to my advantage because it looked like a tiny eye. I eventually made a relief carving of a sperm whale with the knot as its left eye. Then I gave it an antique finish. While writing my novel *Brass Puzzle*, I describe a similar figure, which plays an important part early in the story.

The disadvantage of woodcarving is getting cut. My right hand has slipped more times than I care to remember, usually cutting my left one in the process. While working on a large, wooden gun when I was 16 or 17 years old, the knife slipped, and I cut my left thumb rather badly on the top. I had to go to the doctor's office to get four stiches. I mention a similar episode in *Shards of Time*.

As I said above, I occasionally carved items to impress girls. When I started to date Belkis, I discovered she likes turtles. I ended up carving four of them for her. One is a sea turtle. Another is a terrestrial tortoise standing on four legs. The other two, from a single piece of wood, are tiny box turtles who face each other, kissing. She still has them.

Safe Cracking

When I was fairly young, I could look at diagrams and figure out how things worked. I became interested in locks and keys. Collecting old keys became one of my hobbies, and I learned a lot about how locks work. After studying a diagram of the mechanical dial lock on a safe, I understood the basic principles of how those work, too.

In about the tenth grade, a friend named Wayne called me one Saturday morning to say he knew of a large, combination-lock safe in an old building. It had been locked with the door open, and the building's new owner (a friend of Wayne's father) didn't know the combination. Wayne recalled my interest in locks and keys. I packed up some tools and walked to the building located north of downtown. The owner sat talking to someone in front while Wayne, another mutual friend, and I went to work on the safe. Using my acquired knowledge, we opened the back of the safe's door and figure out the combination a short time later. When we demonstrated by locking the safe and opening it again, the owner was noticeably surprised and pleased. He said he planned to use the safe for its intended purpose at a later date.

Years later, I was able to do the same thing on a much smaller safe in a house where I lived for a while.

Since then, I used these experiences in my novel, *Land on the Verge of Darkness*, where the principal female protagonist does the same thing with the safe in her mother's home—and makes a surprising discovery in the process.

For the Birds

As I mentioned, my father was an avid birdwatcher. He used to go on outings specifically to watch birds, and some of his fascination for these creatures rubbed off on me. He kept a life list, and I do, too. After I finished a natural history course at the University of Texas at Arlington (described in more detail later), my parents gave me several important reference books as Christmas presents, and I still use them on occasion. My US bird book was one of the most useful over the years, but each time I moved to a different country—or even when I only planned to visit a region for a few days, I purchased a bird identification book to keep track of what I saw.

I could probably say a lot more about some of the birds I've seen in different parts of the world, but I don't think I will. However, when I worked with fossils in Venezuela, bird species made up an important part of the fauna at one location in particular, as I'll describe later. I sent the first box of bones to the US to be identified from that location because I realized their importance.

Cats

There doesn't seem to be any better place to write about this, but I'm a cat person in a family of cat people. For years before I traveled to Venezuela the third time, I've had cats around the house doing mostly what they wanted to do while manipulating me through their cuteness. Normally the cats were in twos and threes, but at one

Different Lives in One

point, Belkis and I were trying to keep 23 cats alive. Most of those were abandoned kittens. Not all of them survived, but we did our best. When we could, we found homes for them.

Certain cats over the years were quite special, and I want to describe one in particular. Ronaldo was a Venezuelan, black and white, male cat who I took care of ever since he came into my life as a dirty, somewhat older kitten. He had been abandoned near where I lived at the time. At a young age, I once caught him seated in front of the television, staring up at the screen, and I took a photo. When I developed the film, he was watching the cartoon show *Tom and Jerry*.

This cat loved to be petted. He often jumped onto my lap for me to pet his head, but after I started, he also started to get comfortable. Little by little, he positioned himself sideways and then up-side down to the point where I could more easily rub his stomach. When visitors were at the house, they were amazed to see Ronaldo stretched out on my lap, spread-eagle, with me rubbing his chest and stomach while he had a look of perfect contentment on his up-turned face. Of all the cats I've seen, I've never had one that was so trusting. I could carry him in my arms like a baby, and he never tried to get away from me when he was tired of someone carrying him, the way most cats do.

Once, Belkis and I came home to find Ronaldo injured in a strange way. He was on the roof of the house making an unusual sound—a sort of muffled meow—and he didn't want to come down. We had to bring him down with a ladder. I don't know how he did it, but he had a deep cut across the *back* of his tongue. His mouth was bloody. I took him to the veterinarian and had to leave him for a couple of days. The vet warned me that if he couldn't use his tongue to eat and drink, he wouldn't survive.

The next day I stopped in to check on him. Ronaldo had already started using his tongue to drink water. When I heard the news, I felt pretty pleased. He had to eat only soft foods for a while, but he lasted for seven more years.

The vet told me later (and I paraphrase), "Cats are pretty resistant animals. I've found you can cut them in half and place the two parts pretty close to each other in a cage, and the parts tend to join back together before long." I thought it was a rather strange way of putting it, especially for a vet.

Once when Belkis and I were on a three-week trip to the US, we left Ronaldo with other cats at home, and a friend took care of them daily. As soon as we returned home and opened the gate to the driveway, Ronaldo came running up to us crying the strangest and most desperate sounding cry. It was his way of showing us how much he missed us. The other cats didn't much seem to care. Some people say cats forget their owners after two weeks, but I know it's not true. Ronaldo lived about fourteen years, which isn't bad for an outdoors cat in Venezuela.

We still have two cats around the house. I once posted on Facebook how one of our latest black and white cats sometimes curls up in the crook of my arm while I sit at the computer to write, but none of them have ever been as pleasant as Ronaldo.

My Life as a Student

School, College, and University Days

Elementary

In March of 2018, the City of Denison began to demolish the old Central Ward School building. It had stood on the spot for a hundred years, but it hadn't been used as an elementary school for quite some time. For a while, some sort of industry occupied the building, but I guess the company had been gone for about twenty years before some official group decided the structure was too far gone to save. Driving by and seeing the building always brought back memories, and seeing the ruins made me sad. From the second through sixth grades, I attended there.

Central Ward wasn't my first school. I first attended John F. Peeler Elementary School in Oak Cliff south of downtown Dallas. I attended part of the first grade there, and the school stood within sight of my family's home. (Kindergarten wasn't mandatory, and hardly anyone other than the wealthy educated children before first grade back then, as far as I know.) I remember having a nice, sweet teacher in Oak Cliff named Mrs. Doocy (although I'm not sure how it was actually spelled). I was a good student, and I seemed to be learning to read pretty well. I recall the teacher praising me once when I read out loud for the class. The book we used starting out was titled *Tip*, by Paul McKee, and it was about a dog that often got into trouble. If I remember correctly, Tip's owners were a young boy and girl. That's all I recall about the book, but it was a long time ago.

The next book in the series was titled *Tip and Mitten (Reading for Meaning)*, also by Paul McKee, and halfway through the first grade when my family moved to Denison because of my father's job, my teacher gave me a copy of this book to take with me. I still have the copy stored away, and the value of a used example has increased considerably.

One other thing I remember about Peeler Elementary was walking down the hall in the company of another teacher on the way to the classroom. I saw a piece of paper in the hall, and I reached down to pick it up to throw it away once we reached the room. (I suppose I was spotting things and picking them up even back then, which later helped me with geology and paleontology.) Anyway, I stepped over to my desk in the classroom, but the teacher, in front of the entire class, called Mrs. Doocy's attention to the fact that I had picked up a piece of trash in the hallway without being told to do it. I felt both proud and embarrassed at the same time.

As I described earlier, my family first rented a house on Morgan Street near Houston School when we first moved to Denison. My first grade teacher for the second half of the school year was old and grouchy (in the opinion of a first grader), and she probably should have retired before the school system allowed her to "burn out." She complained constantly to my parents through notes she wrote home that I couldn't read.

This teacher divided the class into groups based on student's reading speeds. The fastest were the "Rockets," the next fastest were the "Jets," and the slowest were the "Bombers." When I learned that one group was named Bombers, I thought it was neat until my classmates warned me I didn't want to be included among their number. The teacher sometimes made the Bombers stay inside during recess to practice their reading skills, which I suspect is a practice that present-day schools would frown upon. For this reason, I tended to alternate between a slow jet and a bomber, pushed into the higher category by sheer force of will in order to enjoy recess. I don't know what happened between one school and the other, but I believe this teacher's heavy-handed methods set me back for years when it came to reading, giving me a mental block against wanting to do it. It was so bad for a while, it's a small wonder I ever became a writer.

Within a few months my parents found a home to buy, and thankfully, I was no longer in the Houston School district. For the second grade, I attended Central Ward, which was a short walk from our new home. My second grade teacher was Mrs. Guilloud, and I remember telling my mother after the first day that she was as nice as Mrs. Doocy. Mrs. Guilloud started me on the road to recovery when it came to my education.

I have a lot of memories of going to Central Ward. In the third grade, I attended Mrs. Cooper's class. We had a large jar full of water with small, black tadpoles someone collected, and on the top of the water, a large water bug swam or floated around. Overnight each night, a tadpole always disappeared. This happened for several days, and no one could figure out what was happening to them. As a young naturalist in the making, it was my suggestion that the bug was eating the tadpoles. When the teacher removed the bug to another jar, the tadpoles stopped disappearing. However, the bug eventually died without his food supply.

In the fifth grade, I was walking on the back playground while talking to a friend one day, when all at once another student ran into me so hard it broke my front tooth. Without realizing it, I had wandered onto a track where students were running races, and the student who hit me had been so anxious to win, he didn't try to avoid me in his path.

In Miss Carter's sixth grade, I recall when a student who listened to a portable radio during lunchtime heard that President John F. Kennedy had been shot. One teacher had a black and white television on our floor (the third floor), and the teachers rolled it into our room where students from other classes joined us to watch the events during the remainder of the school day. I vividly recall some of the other student's reactions—mostly tears, disbelief, and shock.

The school building had a tall, iron fire escape in the back, and I remember climbing it to the top on weekends when no one was around. On one occasion, one of my sister's boyfriends brought me an air-force-blue, silk, cargo parachute to play with. I attached a heavy, wooden box to it and carried it to the top of the fire escape. Then I threw it off. The parachute worked perfectly. It looked great from above as the box floated gently to the ground. Thinking back, I'm glad it didn't hit any windows along the way.

On the north side of the back playground, a twisted bois d'arc tree grew near a gap in the fence toward Morton Street. A little further south toward the school, a group of large, red ants had established a colony. Some of my friends and I used to enjoy watching the creatures as they carried items to their nest entrance. Over the years, they had cleared away all the vegetation for about 18 inches surrounding the hole. One of the school's custodians tried to poison the ants once, but my friends and I felt delighted when after a few days the ants reemerged and continued with their work. Years later, I returned and found them still there.

The largest tree on the playground was a pecan, which still stands near the northeast corner of the block. In the fall, it produced pecans we could crack and eat. A line of chinaberry trees still grows toward the southwest corner of the lot, and one year a type of painfully stinging moth larva infested this area. Some of the students organized a group that sought out these larvae to destroy them on the school grounds, and the next season they weren't nearly as common.

One morning before school, a group of students were throwing the cut-off tops of large, steel, food cans into the air like Frisbees. They had salvaged these from the cafeteria trash. One of these came down and hit a boy across the top of the head, edge first, cutting him badly enough to require stiches.

Something similar happened one afternoon because of me. I took a baseball to the school. The problem was we weren't supposed to play with real baseballs, only softballs. The principal had made an announcement only a few days earlier on a day when I wasn't there. However, all the other boys knew we weren't supposed to play with them, but they didn't tell me.

At lunch recess, the group used my ball to play baseball, and one boy hit a high home run right into a crowd of other students halfway across the playground. The ball hit a boy in the head really hard, immediately creating a swollen bump the size of a chicken egg.

The entire group (including me) was called into the principal's office. The principal asked everyone questions. When my turn came, I had to admit it was my baseball, but I explained my ignorance of his recently-imposed rule. I have often heard, "Ignorance of the law is no excuse," but because the others never told me, they all got in trouble, and I merely walked away with my baseball after promising never to bring it back. Luckily, the boy who was hit in the head made a full recovery.

Hamburgers Across from the School

While I attended school at Central Ward Elementary, a tiny hamburger place operated near the northwest corner of Sears Street and Armstrong Avenue. It sat roughly behind a white house and faced Armstrong. The shop had a counter, behind which someone cooked and fixed the burgers. The rest of the building consisted of small tables or booths. My favorite spot to sit was a booth next to a window looking back toward the school.

It was possible in the shop to buy a hamburger for 15 cents, a bag of Fritos for a nickel, and a bottled Coke for another nickel. A child could have an entire meal for a quarter. I ate there occasionally, but most of the time my parents preferred for me to eat in the school cafeteria.

Much later, I read in a newspaper story about how the family that ran the business used to make sure no child ever went hungry. Even if the child didn't have any money, the family still provided a hamburger and a drink. I also recall a "birthday list." They wrote it in chalk and posted it on the wall. If you told them your birthday (just the day of the month when your birthday occurred), they drew a number from 1 through 31 each day. If your number came up, they placed your name on the list as eligible to receive a free hamburger. I remember eating lunch in the cafeteria one day, and when I went outside, a friend told me he saw my name on the list. I ran across the street and also ate a free hamburger.

Upon moving back to Texas after living many years away, I discovered that the building once housing the burger shop still stood, but it appeared as if it might collapse at any moment. I took pictures of it. Not long afterward someone demolished it, as well as the house where the family once lived, after both places could no longer be saved from abandonment. Isn't it curious how the memory works? Even though it was impossible and truly impractical to save the place, I felt sad to see it go.

John M. Moody

A Dangerous Act

While attending McDaniel Junior High, which had once been the old high school downtown, I have plenty of memories, but not many of them stand out enough to share. I do recall a time when I might have been in the eighth grade. After lunch, I went early to my health class, which was on the third floor near the center of the building. As I waited for class to begin, a couple of other boys from my class also entered the classroom. I don't remember now who they were. A window was open, and one of the boys walked over and started looking outside. A window into a restroom stood open at a nearby corner of the building.

Then the first boy told the other one, "I'll bet I can get to that open window by climbing along the ledge." I don't recall what the second boy said, but the first one evidently viewed it as a challenge.

He climbed out the window and started working his way along the narrow, cement ledge by holding onto the spaces between the bricks. I recall feeling really frightened that he was going to slip. Even though I was only an observer, I couldn't imagine what I would have told the teacher if it happened. The hard cement three stories down would have been the only thing to stop his fall.

Luckily, he made it to the other window and climbed inside. I don't guess I ever felt more relieved. After a moment, the boy stepped around the corner from the restroom as if entering the room for the first time. When the teacher arrived, no one said a word.

A Bug in a Box

For a junior high English class, I once acted in a play, *Cheaper by the Dozen*, which we performed for an assembly in the McDaniel Junior High auditorium. During the preparations, I was changing clothes in a room under the stage when I spotted a dead cockroach. I also saw a small, discarded, cylindrical, plastic container of the type once used to sell ribbon and lace. I decided to place the cockroach into the container, and I sealed it. Then I placed it on a high ledge where it was difficult to see.

About four years later I returned to the auditorium for a program, and I found my way under the stage. To my delight, I found

Different Lives in One

the container right where I left it with the roach still preserved inside. After I looked at it for a moment, I returned it to the same spot on the ledge.

When workers were in the process of demolishing the building a few years ago, I walked around it with my camera various times to take pictures. When an outer wing of the building was gone, I could plainly see the two windows and the ledge where the boy walked. I still couldn't believe he had actually been stupid enough to do what he did with so much at stake.

I also wanted to go under the auditorium stage to take another look, but I never had the chance.

DHS Band

I played in the band during junior high and high school. My best friends in high school were also in the band. During my senior year, we had a great, precision marching band that attended all the football games. I thought our organization rivaled those of many schools much larger than ours. Unfortunately, our football team didn't win a single game of the regular season. Following one of the games, I overheard a couple of people as they left the stadium. They were talking about losing the game—again. But then one of them remarked, "Yeah, but the band was good." It made me feel better about having to attend every game when my team wasn't winning.

Lights! Camera! Action!

As a high school senior, I enjoyed my English class. For one thing, three of my best friends (Wayne, John, and Dwight) were in the same class. I also felt that the teacher, Mrs. Sickles, inspired us. I've had a lot of teachers over the years, but I'll always remember her as one of the best.

For our final book report of the year, Mrs. Sickles told us we could make a movie of a book to show the rest of the class, and we could do it as a group project. My friends and I thought it would be a fun project. Wayne had access to his father's Super-8 movie camera, and his parents paid for the film and the later processing, which would

John M. Moody

have otherwise been beyond our budget. However, the camera we used didn't have sound capabilities in those days, so it ended up being a silent movie. This also meant we had to do more with the action to tell the story. I was reading some spy novels at the time, so I suggested we film Ian Fleming's *Moonraker*. (This was pre-Roger Moore, and our film actually followed the plot of the novel with a good degree of accuracy.) Wayne did most of the filming because he had experience with the camera. Dwight played the role of James Bond. John and I played additional characters, and we got several other students to help. We worked on it for several weeks.

For one early scene, James Bond had to travel to a secret, government rocket base in England. We selected a stretch of Texas FM 131 west of Denison, just south of its intersection with Texas FM 120. It is near a large hill with a wide curve in the road. I still drive this road frequently, and I often recall the filming of this scene.

Dwight rode his motorcycle. He didn't use a helmet, which was illegal at the time. Instead, he used a pair of wrap-around dark glasses. Since the story is set in England, we needed to film him riding on the wrong side of the road. To accomplish this, Wayne climbed onto the luggage rack of my family's Chevrolet station wagon, which I drove slowly in the right lane as Dwight sped past on the left around a blind curve. Luckily, the road didn't carry much traffic back then, and the scene turned out well.

For the next scene, "Bond" had to travel through a security checkpoint. We used Wayne's grandfather's land where a gate entered the property. We set up a fake machinegun with an armed guard, and Dwayne was supposed to ride up to the guard and show his identification in order to pass through the gate. As we began to film the scene, we all noticed that Dwayne approached the gate a little too rapidly. At the last moment, however, he slid his motorcycle sideways on the gravel and nonchalantly reached into his back pocket to show the guard his wallet. It looked great on film.

One scene required a submarine, but of course, we didn't have one. We did the next best thing. The group attached a rod resembling a periscope to the end of a wooden float. The lower end of the float was connected by a rope to a pulley underwater at Lake Texoma. Then while Wayne filmed, John rowed a rowboat as fast as he could to pull on the opposite end of the rope. His efforts, in turn, pulled the rod underwater. When John stopped rowing, the rod returned to the surface. It took several tries before they got it just right. During editing, the film section was cut in the middle to reverse the order. We ended up with a periscope emerge from the water and then going back down again. Between these two segments, we filmed "James Bond" seeing it all through a pair of binoculars.

Dwayne's parents owned a house on Lake Texoma. It had a trapdoor opening onto a flat roof. We made it look like the trapdoor opened automatically so several of our actors could walk up to look at the rocket on the launch pad. I played the part of one of the evil scientists. Dressed in a white lab coat, my big scene was to point out the rocket to Bond. Then the scene in the movie switches to a view of a foot-long model rockets on a launch pad—some of my handiwork.

For the rocket in flight, we attached a black thread to the model's nose and set off a small smoke bomb in the tail to simulate a fiery engine as the rocket was slowly pulled skyward. A moment later with the model mounted on a stick, the smoke bomb in front of a house fan gave an illusion of the rocket streaming through clouds. As the rocket appeared to fly, Wayne slowly turned the camera up-side down to make the rocket look like it went up and then straight down. The explosion at the end was accomplished using a little flash powder. The special effects looked remarkably good, all things considered.

We all received an "A" as a grade for this project. Wayne became the film's caretaker at the time. I wonder if it still exists.

Grayson

I first attended Grayson County College (now Grayson College) not too many years after it was first built on a high hill southwest of Denison. When I first graduated from high school, I didn't really know what sort of career I wanted, but I knew I was better at science and engineering than with the humanities. (This was still a likely carry-over from my problems with reading in the second half of the first grade.)

It was great to have an institution of higher learning only a few miles from where I lived. A friend of the family taught some of the basic engineering courses, and I car-pooled with him for a while during my first two semesters of college. I also met a good friend named Keith while in class there, and I'll discuss Keith in greater detail in other sections. (Years later, I returned to work at Grayson as a part-time professor and lab instructor, but that's another story.)

Part of the way through my first year at Grayson, I decided to become a mining engineer because I liked geology, but at the time, I really knew little about what these studies or this career would involve. I had two reasonable choices of where to study mining engineering, Missouri School of Mines in Rolla and Colorado School of Mines in Golden. I chose to go to Colorado.

Mines

It was a somewhat frightening experience to leave home for the first extended period of time and travel by myself by car all the way to Golden, Colorado. Sometimes I still think of it as a small wonder I survived. I had all my stuff packed into my green, rust-spotted, 1955 Chevy four-door as I set out rather blindly. I arrived in Golden and found a motel room. I didn't even know I was supposed to reserve a dorm room, and the next day when I went to the campus to register, I discovered that all the rooms at the dorm were full.

However, someone provided me with a tip; I might be able to find a temporary room in an old building close to downtown. Sure enough, the nice, elderly couple who managed the property said they had one room still available, but the woman warned me; "I'm afraid you'll have to find another place within a month or so because the city plans to tear down this building to expand a city parking lot."

Golden experienced an early snow that year. I think it was my second week there, and it snowed 13 inches, taking everyone by surprise. It was a "wet snow," sticking to and burying everything. I saw a set of 55 gallon barrels in an alley that were being used as garbage cans, and snow had built up around the rims, making them appear quite pretty. I later used my recollection of these cans when writing my novel *Intersecting Destinies* as Chris Mitchell, the principal male protagonist, describes a similar scene to a woman he wishes to impress.

That snow melted, but being Colorado, it snowed again and again until it began to snow again before the previous one melted completely. Some of my geology student friends joked that the process would eventually lead to the creation of glacial ice flowing down the streets.

The Astor House

My second-floor room in the old building appeared rather austere, with a single bed and a writing desk. A window overlooked the street in front of the building. A bare light bulb hung from a wire in the center of the room. I soon found a metal shade for the bulb, which helped a little. Several rooms on the second floor shared a bathroom. Even so, I felt pretty comfortable living there for a while. Almost immediately, however, I started searching for another room out of fear I would soon need another place to live.

Over the next several weeks while attending classes, I visited with the old couple downstairs and eventually learned more about the old building where I resided. They described it as "the oldest stone hotel in Colorado," known as the Astor House. It had been built during the mining boom days in 1867 when Colorado was still a territory. The elderly woman, who knew some of the building's history, claimed that a lot of famous characters had stayed there over the years.

I once asked them, "Why isn't anyone trying to save the building? Isn't it an historical landmark?"

The elderly woman explained that not many local people, especially city officials, seemed to care about the history. The building was going to be torn down by the city to add about six extra parking places to accommodate downtown commerce.

During some moments when not in class, I recall paying visits to the public library. I spoke to a woman I met there and talked about how it would be better to save the building and preserve it rather than add a few more parking spaces. I remember telling her how the town back in Texas where I lived tended to preserve old houses or other buildings that were historically significant, and once the old hotel was gone, the town would never get it back.

In the meantime after a few weeks, I found another room in a house on the same street a couple of blocks away. By mid-October, I was in the new place. It was a nice, second-floor room a little closer to the campus, both larger and more comfortable.

John M. Moody

Even so, my talk with the woman at the library might have done some good. It wasn't long before the newspapers started to print stories describing growing support for the preservation of the hotel. One article even described how "young people" (me and maybe others) were voicing favorable opinions toward saving the structure.

I used to go back to visit with the old couple at the former hotel. A few weeks later, they said that public opinion was growing in favor of saving the place to make it into a museum, but by the time I left Colorado to return to Denison, nothing had been decided.

A couple of years later, however, I returned to Golden along with my parents to see what happened. The old hotel still stood. It had been painted white, and on the side in large letters, I saw a painted sign reading "The Astor House 1867." I think it's still standing.

Two Life-Changing Experiences

As a new student of mining engineering at Colorado School of Mines, I was required to take my first geology course. Remarkably as a sophomore mining student, I still wasn't taking any classes that dealt directly with mining. However, one of the other mining majors talked a professor into taking a group of us to the experimental mine near Idaho Springs so we could find out what mining was all about.

It was an interesting trip. They showed us all the equipment in use and even took us deep into a shaft to show us where explosives had been set to do some blasting at a later time. However, by the end of the day, I looked into some of the dirty, bearded faces of the more advanced students who worked in the mine, and I had a thought; do I really want to spend much of the rest of my life working in a deep hole in the ground where I'll rarely see the sun? I soon decided I no longer wanted to be a mining engineer, but I wasn't really sure what else I wanted to be. (And by the way, when I informed my parents, I soon learned that my mother never much liked the idea of me being a miner, anyway.)

I don't know why I never thought about it before then, but I had been dealing with geology from an early age by being associated with the Texoma Rockhounds. One of the men in the club was a geology professor named "Doc" Walters, who taught at Grayson

County College. Doc had formerly been associated with the petroleum industry.

One of my classes at Colorado School of Mines was physical geology. A lot of students were taking the class, so they held it in a large auditorium. I guess there were about three hundred of us, and at the time, it was the largest class I had ever attended.

The geology professor was a man named Dr. Moore, and the rumors reported he only received a dollar of salary from the college because his main job was to be on call for the government whenever they needed a geological consultant in a hurry. (I don't know if it was true or not, but that's what other students said.)

By far, it was the best and most enjoyable class I took at Colorado School of Mines. Dr. Moore really knew what he was talking about, and in my case, I was literally on the edge of my seat by the end of each class, as interesting as I found his lectures. Dr. Moore also illustrated great examples on the board and told many stories, often accompanied by colored slides he personally photographed at locations where the government had called upon him to examine serious geological problems throughout the western US. He is the reason I returned to Texas (where it was far less expensive to go to school). After only one semester at Colorado School of Mines, I returned to Grayson and began to work on a geology degree.

Trips to Places

On weekends while at Colorado School of Mines, I often took trips to places as long as the weather allowed—which was up to about the end of October. As a teen, my mother and I bought a few acres of land in the San Luis Valley in south central Colorado (As part of my education, I did the searching, research, and correspondence to select the site while she paid for it on an instalment plan until we owned it.) On a couple of my weekend road trips, I paid a visit to this land again. I explored much of the San Luis Valley during these trips, and I visited some really interesting locations that are off the paved roads. During all this time, my 16 year old Chevy performed marvelously.

I kept a map of Colorado where I marked every road I traveled. The part showing central and southern Colorado had most of its major roads marked by the time I left.

One day I happened to be studying the map and noticed a spot in the northeastern corner of the state called Pawnee Buttes. As I understood it, the spot was a couple of flat-topped hills that had served as landmarks for earlier travelers through the region. One nice Friday afternoon after class I decided to visit them, so I filled the car's tank with gasoline and set off on an adventure. I drove my car as close to the base of the buttes as I could get without going onto private land.

Then when I looked at where I ended up, I noticed that Nebraska wasn't far away. I thought, *I've never been to Nebraska.* I drove north until I entered the state and reached a major highway. Then I turned west and drove to Cheyenne, Wyoming, turning south toward Denver and back to Golden, arriving at about 8:00 at night.

On some days I visited museums or sights around Denver. One friend I met at the school went with me to a nice botanical garden, and the memory of so many tropical plants growing in a cold place like central Colorado eventually provided ideas to add to my novel *Into the Center of the Shadow.*

I sometimes traveled for the day into the Rocky Mountains, alone or occasionally with friends. Most of them didn't own cars, and they were often anxious to get out of Golden on weekends. I once traveled with a group of cave explorers down to the Colorado Springs area. I climbed much of the way to the top of Mount Elbert. I went into the woods as often as I could, and some of my experiences eventually helped to add details to my novel *Snake Bluff Lodge.*

I guess it's possible I don't care much for cold weather after living for a while in Colorado as a student. By the time I traveled home by jet for the long Thanksgiving break, I hadn't been able to travel much of anywhere outside the Denver area for a couple of weeks due to all the snow. When I arrived in Denison, everything still appeared green. I guess it was then when I felt certain I no longer wanted to continue attending Colorado School of Mines.

The Trip Home

I feel this is the proper place to describe an incredible experience that occurred on my trip home from Golden, Colorado. It was mid-December. I attended my last class in the morning to take a final exam. On the night before, I had packed my belongings, ready to leave Golden by around noon. I carried some cold soft drinks in a cooler, and to keep them cold, I used a rock hammer to break off a large icicle hanging from the roof of the school gym. I also took along a few other snacks, too, planning not to stop until evening. I made plans to find a motel at that time because I knew I wouldn't make it all the way home safely after leaving town so late in the day.

The car I drove was still my faithful, green, four-door, 1955 Chevrolet. (This car was my companion during many adventures. When I had a vehicle, I tended to drive it for long periods of time.) On this trip, for a change, I decided to drive the "plains route," US 287, which crosses the Colorado flatlands at a southeastern angle to later turn south to reach the Oklahoma panhandle. Later, it turns southeast again to enter the Texas panhandle. I thought I might reach Amarillo before dark.

One of the features that impressed me along the way was looking back across the plains and seeing only the top of Pike's Peak—just as Zebulon Pike must have seen it for the first time.

I made it to Oklahoma, and the car had been running all afternoon without stopping except once for gasoline. I reached Boise City and turned southeast as planned along US 287. It was already late in the day by then, and much of the land at the time was pretty much devoid of anything other than reddish dirt, scrub brush, and rocks.

My car started to climb a slope when all at once I felt a jolt. I had no idea what the problem might be, but I started to lose velocity, even though the engine continued to run. I had the impression that something was plugging my exhaust manifold. In any case, the car ran slower and slower until I decided to pull off the highway. Just as I did, the engine died. From the time I first noted the problem to the time the car went dead, it had traveled about half a mile while heading uphill.

I gazed around and saw nothing nearby. In the distance further up the road, I spotted a cluster of buildings; one of them looked taller than the rest, like it might have been a grain storage silo. It was a pretty desolate location to be having car trouble.

To make matters worse, just as I stepped from the car to take a look, a strong cold front hit my location. I must have been traveling just ahead of it the entire afternoon. The temperature started to drop rapidly.

John M. Moody

I still had the notion of something blocking my exhaust, so I got some tools and went under the car to see if I could loosen the exhaust pipe enough to start the car again.

While I was half under the car, all of a sudden I noticed that another car had pulled off the road just ahead of mine. A man got out. He said something about being on his way to San Antonio, and he had part of his family with him. He offered to check out my problem. I don't guess I had been stopped along the road for more than ten minutes when they arrived.

He quickly removed the fuel line and told me to try to start it. He found it wasn't my fuel pump. He removed the coil wire on top of the distributor and said I had spark from the coil. He couldn't figure out why it wouldn't start, but he said he had a chain and would tow my car further up the hill to the buildings in the distance where I might find help.

The trip took a few minutes, as slowly as we traveled and as far as we had to go to reach the buildings, which were actually several miles away. As soon as he reached the first building, he unhooked the chain, wished me luck, and went on his way, heading southward.

The building nearest my car just happened to be a hardware store. As I stepped inside, it felt pretty weird, like crossing a time warp or stepped into an episode of *The Twilight Zone*. Rattlesnake skins and frames containing mounted arrowheads hung from the walls. Off to the side, a wire cage held a couple of prairie dogs, which ran around on an exercise wheel. Several men stood talking near the front counter. One of them wore blue jeans, a jean jacket with a fur-lined collar, and, of course, cowboy boots. He had a handlebar mustache and looked like he had just gotten off a horse—and walked off an old west movie set.

I stepped to the counter, and right away the man behind it asked what I needed.

"I'm having some car trouble. It won't start. Someone just towed it to the front of the building." (I paraphrase because I can't recall my exact words.)

"What kind of car is it?"

"It's '55 Chevy."

"Is it a V-8 or a 6 cylinder?"

"It's a 6."

"That's good. Then maybe it won't be too complicated for me.

"Where are ya' headed, son?"

"I'm on my way home to Denison, Texas, after attending school in Colorado."

A moment later, he opened the hood, and I explained what the other man had already discovered while searching for the problem. Half a moment later, the man disconnected the distributor cap and immediately exclaimed, "There's your problem! The bug's broke!"

He had discovered that the rotor in the center of the distributor, or the "bug," as he called it—the part that spins around providing an intermittent electrical spark from the coil to each of the six spark plugs—had broken off completely at BOTH contacts, on the top and at the tip of the rotor. My faithful, old car had traveled half a mile uphill without receiving any spark to the spark plugs.

Later, a friend who knew something about vehicles speculated that the engine had been so hot from running it all afternoon that it "dieseled." It might have worked much like a diesel engine where the fuel ignited in a hot cylinder without the need of a spark. Then again, it might have continued to run due to magic. Much else that occurred the same afternoon and evening impressed me as being rather magical.

The man from the hardware store said he would go to check in the back to see if he just happened to have a replacement part. Remarkably, he actually had similar parts for other cars—some of them rather old—but he didn't have one for a '55 Chevy, 6 cylinder.

By then I figured I might be sleeping in my car that night. The sky was already about to turn dark. I had to dig out a warm coat.

However, another man had been standing silently off to the side the entire time, listening to my conversation with the store owner. He promptly stepped up and said he might be able to help. Then I watched as he walked over to a pay phone hanging from the wall and made a call.

I heard him say, "Honey, we've got a young college boy here whose car has broken down. Do you think I can bring him home to get something to eat?" I couldn't believe it.

The hardware store was about to close, but this other man drove me to his home in his pickup truck. The distance wasn't far. It was down the highway and across a railroad track, but the exact route was rather confusing in the dark. The taller building was indeed a grain silo. It served as the nucleus of a small community, which wasn't apparent from the highway. When we reached the man's home, a Christmas party was in progress.

The man's wife introduced me to several people, the names of whom I immediately forgot due to the confusion I felt. Then she served me plenty to eat.

After I tasted some salad she served me, I told her I loved the taste of the dressing and asked her about it. She said it was a mix from an envelope, and she showed me the package. I read "Hidden Valley" and "Ranch." It was the first time I ever heard of it. Apparently, it was a rather new product in Texas at the time. I later found it in a store, and when I read the instructions, the mixture required real buttermilk and mayonnaise in order to do it right. Since then I believe a lot of people have agreed with me about the taste of "ranch" dressing. I understand it is now the most requested flavor in the world, and it took a crisis for me to first find out about it.

But back to the story, while I sat there, tasting new delicacies and discussed Christmas party cuisine, the woman's husband had figured out a way to call an auto parts store in Stratford, Texas, located about 22 miles away. He apparently knew a man who worked there. The store was already closed, but he arranged to meet the man later that night just so I could purchase the part I needed.

After the meal, I rode in the man's pickup to Stratford, where we waited for only a few minutes downtown before the auto parts dealer showed up. He reopened the store at about 8:00 PM. Then he went to the back and brought me a small box. It cost a total of 58 cents, including tax. The man wrote out a receipt for it, which I still conserve somewhere—all that trouble for a 58-cent part!

I thanked him and told him I was sorry he had to come and open the store for such a small sale.

He responded, "Don't worry. I know an engine won't run without it."

As the man with the pickup drove me back to my car across the dark countryside (another 22 miles), I mentioned that after they had gone to so much trouble, I hoped the part was the only problem. I still recalled the jolt I felt like something might be restricting the exhaust pipe.

The man with the pickup responded, "Well, if you can't get it started tonight, we can put you up at our place." It made me wonder what planet I had landed on that was populated by so many nice people.

When we arrived in front of the hardware store again, the man held a flashlight as I snapped on the new rotor and reconnected the distributor cap. I pumped the gas for a moment, and sure enough, my car started right away. As the engine warmed up, I thanked the man profusely, and as heroes often do, he told me it was "nothin'." He said he was just happy to see me on my way.

I wasn't even sure if I had been in Oklahoma or in Texas when I broke down. When I asked him the name of the place, I thought he said it was called Derrick, Texas, but the wind was still blowing pretty hard. He explained that the man from San Antonio who towed me to the hardware store had stopped right after crossing into Texas. The man and I exchanged names, and I told him to look me up if he was ever in Denison, but I never heard from him again, and I have never passed that way again, either.

That night after we said our goodbyes, I drove back to Stafford (22 miles again) and found a room in a motel—still feeling somewhat in awe and disoriented after the amazing experience. I slept in a warm bed that night instead of in my car—but I guess I would have slept in a warm bed either way.

The next morning outside the motel I tightened the exhaust pipe I loosened slightly the day before. There had been nothing wrong with it. I was soon back on the road, arriving in Denison that same afternoon.

When I looked at the first map of Texas I could find after I returned to Denison, it didn't show a town on US 287 just south of the border between Oklahoma and Texas. This disturbed me a little. I later tried to look for Derrick, Texas, by name on a better map, but it didn't seem to exist. This disturbed me even more. However, I have since learned that I didn't hear the man correctly. The name is actually Kerrick, Texas. Now days it even shows up on Wikipedia. It just doesn't show up on a lot of large-scale maps because it is an unincorporated community and still quite small.

When I wrote *Intersecting Destinies*, I refer to a similar incident as part of my story. One of the characters describes how someone helped him after being stranded out in the middle of nowhere while crossing the Texas Panhandle. As he helps a couple of the novel's main characters who have also become stranded, he says he's only paying back a favor. I've often thought about all the people who helped me that day to eventually send me on my way. Whenever I could over the years since then I've also tried to help people, especially when I saw them having car trouble. And I've sent a good number of them on to their destinations without further incident.

UTA

After another semester in Grayson County College following my decision in Colorado to become a geologist, I registered at the University of Texas at Arlington, about a two-hour drive from Denison. One of the reasons I went to UTA was because a professor at Grayson spoke highly of the university. I later learned that the school had an excellent geology department. The seasoned professors possessed a wide variety of practical experience among them.

For my first year, I lived in Brazos Hall (also known as Brazos House). This was one of the oldest buildings remaining on campus at the time. Built in 1936, it had been a dorm when the school was a military college, and the room I shared with only one roommate once held six students in three-tiered bunk beds. Two rooms connected to a single bathroom between them, so originally 12 student soldiers once tried to shave, shower, and use the restroom in the shared space each day. In the summer of 2018, the university demolished this building, and pieces were being offered for sale. I couldn't afford anything.

I noticed something comical while living in Brazos Hall. A sign outside the dorm office announced the availability of an engraving tool so dorm residents could mark personal property in case of theft or loss. A couple of days later another small sign appeared under the first one requesting the person who borrowed the engraving tool to please return it. I just saw it as rather ironic. Was the engraving tool marked with an ID number? If so, how was it done—except with another engraving tool? I ended up using this story in *Brass Puzzle*.

I recall one evening soon after a semester started when I returning to the dorm. I found everyone watching something on television in a lobby on the lowest floor. The Munich Massacre had just begun at the Olympic Games. Most of the young men were practically in shock.

For my geology classes, I earned mostly high grades. Dr. Charles Dodge was the head of the Geology Department at the time. He had worked on one of the formations in the Arlington area as a student. He also had experience in petroleum geology and field geology, which later served me well when the time came to get a job, not to mention during oilfield geological studies or while solving stratigraphic problems with respect to paleontology.

One of our professors was Dr. Fritz Fischer. He was the university's resident "hard-rock" petrologist. His father was Dr. Al Fischer, who with two other men wrote a widely-used paleontology text book. The older Dr. Fischer also did important research in the Guadeloupe Mountains of southwest Texas and southeastern New Mexico. On one Christmas break between semesters, I joined a group led by both Drs. Fischer into these mountains, and I probably learned more in ten days than I would have at the university in a semester. (I also took along my copy of Al Fischer's paleontology book, and he graciously autographed it.)

We visited all sorts of geological "environments" in the area, and we went to a lot of really special places. One of them was an extremely deep potash mine. On another day, we climbed the north side of Guadeloupe Peak. (These later provided insight for my novel *Into the Center of the Shadow*.) For me, the most impressive place we visited was the lower cave at Carlsbad Caverns.

We visited the cave during the day to make the arrangements, but that night we returned after all the tourists were gone and took the elevators straight to the bottom. Then a guide led us to a point of deviation from the regular trail to descend even lower into the parts of the cave where tourists never go. It was "unimproved." We had to carry kerosene lanterns. I saw a lot of impressive sights, but one incident turned momentarily frightening.

We walked in a line along a dirt trail, but at times it was necessary to climb over large rocks. At one spot, I was the last person in line, and I carried one of the lanterns. Everyone ahead of me climbed over a large rock, but when my turn came, I realized I couldn't climb and hold onto the lantern at the same time. In addition, I couldn't set the lantern down and climb over because then I wouldn't be able to reach the lantern. About then the lantern began to flicker like it wanted to go out. I believed I was about to be left behind in the lower part of Carlsbad Caverns with no light.

As I pondered my predicament, all at once the younger Dr. Fischer stuck his head over the rock and asked, "John, are you coming?"

"Yes, but I need some help. Can you please hold my lantern?" Problem instantly solved.

Just before my last full semester at UTA, most of the geology students of my graduating class attended the Geology Summer Field Course in west Texas. Dr. Dodge was the professor. We all traveled to Alpine, Texas, where we stayed in the community college dorm when we weren't camping in areas too far away to return to Alpine at night. Our group spent six weeks working on all sorts of projects throughout Brewster County. Some exercises took only a day or two, while the final project took more than a week to complete. (I'll describe more about this project shortly.)

As something of a tradition for the field classes, Dr. Dodge selected a piece of weathered, light gray rock about the size of the palm of a hand and about an inch and a half thick. He called it "The Stupid Stone." The professor or the professor's field assistant could assign a student to carry this rock, but it was only passed on to a student who made some sort of grand blunder during field work or who asked a question he or she should have known how to answer. This student carried the stone until the next student did something the professor thought of as deserving, and so forth. A couple of fellow students seemed to constantly pass the stone from one to the other.

The course was a great learning experience, and I got to see some amazing geology. We even did work in Big Bend National Park. Later on, I will describe some of the things I found during this trip.

One of our vehicles was an old, unidentified, rustic, people carrier of some sort. Dr. Dodge called it "The Goose." Occasionally, he got us to "fly The Goose." As he drove down the road, he positioned students next to the windows on both sides. We then extended our arms outside the window. On his command, we moved our arms up and down in unison to make it appear as if the vehicle "flapped its wings."

I collected a lot of fine, colorful, rock samples in one local rock formations known as the Santiago Chert, and some of these are still around the house after more than 40 years. I used one sample in particular to illustrate a series of complex geological processes to students at a private school during some summers.

One day, early during our course, the professor took the class to see an igneous formation in the distance along the road between Alpine and Fort Davis. My roommate in Alpine was a slightly older student who happened to be a licensed pilot. Later, he decided he wanted a better view of the formation. He rented a single-engine airplane from the Alpine airport, and we split the costs among three of us, with the pilot taking me and another student one at a time to see the formation from a bird's perspective.

After we saw the formation and took photos, he demonstrated a "stall," how to recover from a tailspin, and how to "feather" and glide the plane (which was an operation I didn't much care for). Then as we headed back, he asked me, "Would you like to see how it feels to fly for a while?" He let me take over the controls, and with minimum instruction, I was able to align the plane with the runway. It wasn't my first time to be in a plane, but it was my first (and only) time to *fly* a plane without being aware when I took off that I would.

While we worked in the northern part of Big Bend National Park, I explored alone one afternoon on a mapping project when I happened to look down. I spotted a large, dinosaur, limb bone. It lay on the ground in a number of pieces, with some of them already displaced from the point of origin. Our class didn't have permission to collect fossils in the park during our studies, so I gathered all the pieces together and stacked them into a pile for the next person to find. Who knows? They might still be there, as desolate as the country appeared.

We had 21 students in our class. For our last project, we were expected to gather surface data and then draw a geological map based on what we observed. Our study area was a geologically-complex region on private land north of the national park. Dr. Dodge and his assistant divided us into teams of two students each, but after everyone else had been chosen, I was the twenty-first person. I didn't have a partner. I immediately pointed this out, and they told me, "Yes, we know. What we're going to do is let you work alone, but don't worry; we'll take into consideration that you don't have a partner when we assign grades."

I shrugged my shoulders and said, "Okay ... if you say so."

We went into the area the following day, and I began to collect data. On about the second day I noticed that working alone was more efficient. When pairs of students visited spots to take measurements and make observations, they sometimes argued with each other as to what the data revealed. When working by myself, I simply went to the spot, examined it, took measurements, drew a conclusion, and moved on to the next spot.

In the end, I had gathered as much data as any two of them put together—enough to do a full map all by myself. I was always pretty good when it came to drawing maps, so I sat down and drew, transferring the data as I worked. At the end of the project, my map looked better than any of the others. When I presented my final results, the professor and the graduate student assistant appeared pretty impressed. They said they planned to use my map as a standard of comparison for future courses.

On the final day of our class, Dr. Dodge took back the "Stupid Stone" from the person who carried it at the time. Then he formally presented it to me in front of the other students in honor of being the top student for the course. His actions came as a complete surprise. I still have the stone guarded away in a box.

Natural History

As part of my university education, I took a Natural History class as an elective. I can't think of any other class besides some of my geology classes that impressed me more. We went on several overnight field trips. The professor led us to some great locations, and I learned about a lot of interesting animals.

During this class, I also learned how to write journal notes describing my field trip activities. From this point on, I wrote down information while on trips, and I continued to do it for more than 25 years until I was no longer actively going on field trips. At first I carried the journal with me into the field, but later I started to write down notes in a regular field notebook, which I faithfully transcribed and expanded into my journals to make them readable as soon as I returned home following a trip.

To the Bat Cave

During one of my field trips, our class visited Marble Falls State Park in central Texas. The professor had obtained permission to capture bats from a cave nearby for his studies. I worked with the bat cave group part of the time.

On our first afternoon there, which happened to be on a Friday, the instructors told us to stretch a black net across the cave mouth to see what we could catch. A couple of hours after dark we returned to see if we caught anything. What we found was a net full of holes with no bats in it. It seemed that bats flew out of the cave and became trapped just as planned, but they quickly chewed through the net and escaped before we got there.

By late Saturday afternoon, the instructors decided to try something different. Instead of stretching the net across the cave mouth, they made preparations to run a section of net straight down the center of the cave near the entrance.

However, we arrived a little late. Some of the bats were already becoming active with the arrival of night. One of the graduate students handed me a big, powerful flashlight and told me to head further into the cave to shine the light toward where the bats would be coming from. The idea was to try to fool the bats into thinking it was still daytime until the others could get the net set up properly using poles on each end.

As I stood there, I heard the bats chirping at me. Their biological clocks were telling them it was time to eat, but the light I held told them otherwise. Occasionally, I saw one or two as they flew in my direction, but they always flew back into the darkness beyond the light I held.

Within just a couple of minutes, my companions told me they were ready, adding, "Okay, turn off the light." I did. Right away I heard bats fluttering by my ears for several moments, but none of them so much as brushed me as they passed.

Half a minute later, they told me to turn on the light again and to come to the net. We counted 80 bats in the net—far more than they needed. And who knows how many went past without getting trapped? All those bats flew past me while I stood in the dark in the middle of the cave—and not one of them touched me.

For my writing, I used this experience twice. In *Second Book of Marc*, I describe how the hero of the story, Marc of Mezet, has just discovered a passageway full of bats, and when he drops a burning stick he carries, all the bats fly past him to escape. None of the bats touch him. In *Woman in White, Cage of Black*, I describe the story much like it happened as the hero of the book is required to stand and tell a scary story at a party in front of a group of strangers, including the party's weird host.

The Barred Owl

Another of our biology field trips was to east Texas, and I got to see all sorts of creatures I had never seen before. The professor was a herpetologist, and he could identify the various species of frogs at night by their calls. (I have an idea for an adventure novel, and perhaps I'll model one of the characters after him.) Snakes were common there, too.

One night we left our camp in search of barred owls. We took along our flashlights, and as I recall, it was raining lightly at the time. At one location, we heard a call from the trees far away, and the professor identified it as that of a barred owl. The forest was thick, which made traveling at night a little slow, but we soon heard the calls from more than one direction.

We divided up. As I traveled alone through the forest toward one of the calls, I had an idea. I decided to imitate the call to see if I could lure the bird to me. I remained in one spot and turned off my flashlight. Then I listened carefully to the call and tried to imitate it as precisely as I could. After about three tries, I believed my call sounded as good as the owl itself—although I never heard the owl's opinion. Satisfied, I continued to make owl calls as I scanned the dark tree branches overhead for movement.

After a few minutes of repeating my calls, I promptly noticed a small collection of flashlights converging on my location. The professor and several students believed I was the owl. I didn't see a barred owl that night, but my trick had been good enough to lure a trained biologists.

Collecting Dead Animals

I was always interested in bones while growing up, especially skulls. While working in my natural history class, I learned something about biology museums—which at the time, I didn't realize how much benefit the information would eventually provide.

Even after I was no longer in the class, I continued to help the biology museum by bringing in specimens. During the geology field class, I encountered a couple of skulls and collected them to bring back to Arlington. I later donated a pronghorn cranium and a spotted skunk skull to the biology museum at UTA, and afterward, the graduate student in charge of the museum was always glad to see me because those specimens were the first of either animal to be included in the university's collection. The skunk skull in particular ended up as a welcomed prize for one of the professors who was doing research on Texas skunks. The example I collected had five lower incisors in the jaw in the place of four.

I later brought in anything I found as road-kill. I once spotted a freshly-killed, female, great-tailed grackle on an Arlington street and took it in. The graduate student congratulated me because I had just doubled the number of female boat-tailed grackles in the collection. On another occasion, I encountered a dead mole in one of the green spaces on the UTA campus and took it in. It wasn't in good condition, and the student in charge joked with me about it not being as good as my other discoveries—but he accepted it all the same. I felt happy to bring in parts of already-dead animals because I could supply the museum with specimens to study without doing harm. It was one of the things about paleontology I liked; I didn't have to kill anything because the animal remains I collected were of creatures long dead.

Baker Street Irregulars

For years, I read and enjoyed Sherlock Holmes stories. In fact, I read them all—some of them several times. Perhaps by reading these stories, I became more curious.

The first Sherlock Holmes book I ever looked at was one in the school library at Central Ward Elementary School. It was only a children's book with colorful illustrations and easy text.

John M. Moody

The reason I became more interested in Sherlock Holmes stories was because an older friend down the street from where I lived had started reading the original stories by Sir Arthur Conan Doyle and told me about them. I soon became a fanatic for anything related to the subject, and my interest has stayed with me up to the present in varying degrees. I once had a Victorian Period coat made with a short cape similar to those in illustrations from some of the stories. Someone I knew at UTA gave me a deer-stalker cap. Even now, I occasionally wear a similar cap during local, public events. I once bought a dark lantern, the sort of illumination device used in some of the original stories, and I found a plastic pipe to use whenever I decide to dress up in full regalia for Halloween.

A few years after my interest in the subject increased, I recalled the first Sherlock Holmes book I read. Being the small world where we live, the librarian at the Central Ward School library happened to be a friend of the family. She was married to a professor I had later at Grayson County College. When I asked about it, she told me the book still sat on the shelf. I arranged a visit to the school one afternoon to see it. She had the book waiting for me when I arrived. It appeared a little tattered after years of use. When I examined the check-out card in the back, I found my name still there near the top. She then allowed me to borrow the book from the library for a while and take it home, adding my name to the card again. And by the way, only about ten or twelve students had checked out the book during the years since I last saw it. I returned it a few days later. However, when the school system eventually closed the school, she discontinued the book due to its condition and presented it to me as a gift. I still have it.

While I attended UTA, I learned that one of the administrators in the university library was a Sherlock Holmes fan, and she ran a local chapter of the Baker Street Irregulars. This is a group dedicated to anything Sherlockian. I met with them whenever I could. We attended movies and plays as a group at times. For some events, I wore my deer-stalker cap and Victorian coat. I had fun meeting with them, but some of what they did was too rich for me. Many of them were working professionals with steady incomes, while I was only a poor university student. Dinner parties at fancy restaurants accompanied by drinks weren't in my budget. Still, I enjoyed the time I spend with them.

Years later when I first traveled to London, I took along notes listing specific locations mentioned in some of the stories. During my free time, I visited all of them I could find. I walked along Baker Street. I visited the Sherlock Holmes Pub where they have a reproduction of Holmes' and Watson's sitting room for visitors to view. I rode the underground to reach Aldgate Station. I walked along Whitechapel. I walked past the old Scotland Yard building (which I much later saw used in period British mystery productions imported into the US). My interest in these places added fresh and exciting elements to my trip.

The Sherlock Holmes stories also helped in other ways. For my own writing, I often add an element of mystery, which relates back directly to my enjoyment of these tales.

I graduated from UTA with a Bachelor of Science in Geology, and I went to work at a full-time job in a service company for the petroleum industry, as I will soon describe. And I took what I learned with me.

John M. Moody

My Working Life

Various Jobs with Company-Paid Adventures

I've held a number of interesting jobs in different companies. Even in the same organizations, I've held different positions and worked on a variety of projects.

I've also been fortunate to have worked for companies that sent me places. Not only did they send me to company offices to complete tasks in their names, I also took advantage of being at these locations to see plenty of extra places and sights during my free time. No matter where I went, I tried to see as much as possible in the time available. I had it in mind that it might be my only chance (or last chance) to visit certain places, and in many cases, I was right ... so far.

"The smell of grass ..."

There's something about the way fresh St. Augustine grass smells when it's freshly cut. The aroma stimulates memories of summer. From the time I was about eleven years old, my father gave me a job—to mow our lawn whenever it was needed.

The lawn mower I used when I first started probably came from Sears. My father often bought his equipment at Sears, and he had been using it for several years by the time he taught me how to use it. The mower was beige and brown with a gasoline motor for the blade, but I had to push it. It was necessary to remove the back handle to transport it in the trunk of a car.

Different Lives in One

My father went outside with me the first time and showed me some safety tips. One was to always wear shoes. I was also supposed to place my foot on top of the carriage when starting the mower with a pull cord, which would assure that my food wouldn't be under the blade when it started. I knew it was serious business, so I took his training seriously.

He paid me for each job I did well. If I remember correctly, I received $2.25 for mowing the front, the back, and the alley behind the house, but I sometimes had to trim the front and prepare the lawn to be cut in spring, which was part of the overall task. As I grew older, my father raised my pay.

One time not long after I started, I missed some spots in the front. I was probably mentally distracted while I pushed the mower along. When he returned home that day, he pointed out the spots where the grass was too long, and I had to go back and cut them before he paid me. It was a good lesson. I heard later in life during a company-sponsored training course, "Do it right the first time."

When my parent's friends discovered I was able to mow lawns, a lot of them started asking me to mow their lawns, too. Mostly the locations were within a few blocks of my house, so I was able to push the mover to each location. I could earn up to $4.50 for a single lawn depending on its size, and in the mid-1960s, this was pretty good money for a young teenager when I had a constant flow of jobs. By the age of about fourteen, I was making pretty good summer money by mowing lawns, and I did a good job. I can only recall one time when someone who was merely a friend of a friend of a friend didn't pay what I considered to be enough money for a really difficult job, and I simply declined to go back. I occasionally received compliments about how particular lawns appeared after I finished with them.

After I had been using the mower for several years, a front wheel tended of falling off. I had a way of fixing it, but my fix got worse and worse to the point where I had to start hammering part of it to try to keep the wheel on. Later, I had to fix it using bailing wire, which seemed to work well until the wire started slipping off. In time, the motor's kill switch stopped working, but I figured out a way to carry a claw hammer as I mowed, which I used to electrically short the spark plug whenever I needed the mower blade to stop.

Eventually, the wheel on the old mower fell off one too many times, and I couldn't fix it. My father bought a new mower for me to use (at Sears again). The new model had a light-weight, magnesium frame, and the handle folded down onto itself for easy transport. I was able to do an even better job with it than before.

We were getting rid of the old mower about then, and despite the problems I use to have with it, I actually felt sad because I had been using the same piece of equipment for years. I don't remember if Sears was coming to get it or if my parents gave it to a junk dealer. In any case, I knew it was about to be picked up, so I pushed it onto the front lawn, I set the wheel in place one last time, and I took a photo using my mother's camera. As it happened, a friend from high school was riding by in front of my house as I was taking the photo, and the next day he asked me why I was taking a picture of my lawn mower. I just told him we were getting rid of it after I had been using it for years, and he thought it was a silly thing to do. I found the photo a few weeks ago, and it brought back plenty of memories of when I captured the photo and of mowing lawns in general, so I'm glad I took the photo despite how silly it seemed to my friend.

Fore!

The MK&T Railroad had a lot of benefits for its employees when it was a profitable business. For one, it had its own nine-hole golf course right in Denison. The Katy Golf Course was located on both sides of Crawford Street at around the 1900 block close to where a railroad crossing still stands. The track divided the south side of the golf course into two parts, and the railroad even built a short tunnel of corrugated metal under the track to allow golf carts to pass easily.

When I drive down Crawford Street now, I see no signs that the golf course ever existed. Only the track is still there in the same location. An area on the north side of the street around the 2000 block is now a set of sports fields, and many more houses have been built toward the west of where the northern part once stood.

I used to go there with friends to "hang out." I even went exploring there at night, but my friends and I were good kids; we never did anything to damage property or to get ourselves into trouble (although if anyone of authority ever found us there and decided to do something, we might have found ourselves in trouble).

Every so often my friends and I discovered golf balls as we crossed through the area. On one occasion, I found two golf balls in pretty good condition, and I showed them to a golfer. He offered to buy them from me, and he paid twenty-five cents each for them, which at the time was pretty good money.

I sometimes built Estes brand model rocket kits, and my friends and I went to the golf course to shoot them once. It provided a nice, open area, allowing us to recover the rocket bodies after we fired them.

One day during the early summer when I was about thirteen years old, a friend called to say that the golf course manager was hiring a team of guys to do maintenance work on the golf course. I went right over, and sure enough, he hired me. The pay was $1.25 per hour, and we worked for eight hours per day. At the end of a week, the manager approached me and a select group of others to see if we'd like to work for another week, and I did, alongside a few of my friends. At the end of two weeks, I had earned $100, which for me was a small fortune. I held onto this money for a long time, spending only a little at a time when I found something I really liked.

The job at the golf course allowed me to work a variety of jobs using a number of pieces of specialized equipment. One of our jobs was to punch can-sized holes in some of the greens in order to plant a special variety of grass there. This grass was to later spread and take the place of the grass already growing there. I recall digging a hole in one location and finding a .380 brass cartridge case that might have been buried there for years.

They called one machine a "verti-cutter." It had a series of blades that rotated vertically. I don't know why, but I think they used it on the special grass covering the greens. I also used a really heavy device that punched small-diameter holes into the green so fertilizer would enter deeper into the soil.

One day someone was driving an old pickup truck from one location to another, and I needed to go to the new area, too. The new location was only a couple of hundred yards away, but everyone was relocating at the same time. The truck cab was full, and the back contained equipment and maybe people, too, but there wasn't any more room left for me. The truck was old enough to have "running boards," those flat, narrow platforms along the side of a vehicle that mostly serve as steps for entering the cab. I had seen gangster movies where men holding sub-machine guns rode on the running boards of old cars, so I figured I could travel that way, too. I ran over and jumped on. The truck began to roll along a fairway that wasn't especially smooth. Within a few yards, the old vehicle began to bounce. It might have been traveling at a speed of 15 or 20 miles per hour. I lost my footing due to the bouncing, and I let go of my handhold, pushing myself away from the truck at the same time so as not to get run over by the back wheels. When I hit the ground, I rolled along the fairway for a moment. Some of the others saw me fall, and the truck stopped to check on me. Luckily, I wasn't hurt. I walked the rest of the way, and I don't think I ever tried to ride on a running board again.

"I've been workin' on the railroad ..." ♪

In the summer of 1971 after I completed two semesters at Grayson County College, I knew I was going to Colorado School of Mines for my next fall semester. I needed to earn some extra money. As I understood it at the time, railroads were pretty close-knit organizations, and the MK&T Railroad was no exception. Because my father worked at the Katy, however, I was able to get a job there for a full summer. I passed the physical, and soon I reported to a mechanical shop run by the Signal Department. At our shop, we rebuilt and repaired train traffic signals that were utilized up and down the entire line. (These were broken most often by people using them for target practice. I once found a .22 bullet inside one.) This shop was located just west of the old US Highway 69/75 overpass, a few blocks south of downtown Denison. The building where I worked is no longer standing, although the building next door is still there.

An older guy was in charge of the shop. He was about to retire, having almost reached 65 years old. He made me feel welcome at the shop.

The main full-time assistant wasn't quite as old, but he was also very nice. They taught me a lot of things when it came to restoring light fixtures, sanding, painting, making gaskets, and other jobs. I learned pretty rapidly, and I ended up doing this for about a month until they decided I could join one of the road gangs working on the actual repairs in the field. They selected me to join the northern crew, with a territory covering Oklahoma, Kansas, and Missouri.

Before I left to go off to work in the field, the older shop manager retired. We had a small, going-away party for him on his last day. After years of working with the Katy—surely many of them spent running the shop—he looked forward to going fishing.

At the end of the summer, I learned that the former shop manager had died of a heart attack. I've always remembered how happy he seemed to finally be able to relax for the rest of his life, but unfortunately, the rest of his life didn't last very long. My memories of this man have pointed out to me how death might step in at most any time, and they have also taught me to try to finish things if I think they are important.

During the summer, my crew started in Tulsa. Then we traveled to Bartlesville. From there, we went to Parsons for a few weeks. After a few days back in Tulsa, we spent the rest of the summer at Muskogee. One day while working out of Parsons, I noticed we were north of Baxter Springs, Kansas, which sits only two miles from the Missouri state line and only about five miles from Joplin. We never went to Missouri while I worked for the Katy, and I have never had the chance to visit that state since then. (Even so, one of my novels, *Intersecting Destinies*, is set, in part, in Kansas City.)

We lived in a trailer we parked on railroad property in locations near where we happened to be working. In Tulsa where I started out, someone had parked the trailer across the street and just up the track from the main depot downtown. In Bartlesville, we parked it on a big plot of land south of town near a set of tracks. In Parsons, Kansas, the trailer sat west across the tracks from the large downtown depot building.

In Muskogee, Oklahoma, we stayed in the strangest location of all. The trailer sat between two railroad tracks directly below a concrete street overpass in downtown. At nine or ten o'clock at night, a north-bound train passed about six feet in front of the trailer, blowing its whistle right next to us. The noise reverberated from the overpass, making it sound pretty loud. Then a south-bound train passed and blew its whistle about three feet behind the trailer at about three in the

John M. Moody

morning, sounding even louder. The 3:00 AM train always woke me up, but after a few days, I was able to go back to sleep with the train still rolling by after the engineer stopped blowing the whistle.

The crews were generally small. Most of the time our crew consisted of only three people, except when we worked in larger towns or cities where local supervisors joined us. Some of what we did was to change light bulbs and replace broken light fixtures. I once thought it was interesting when I opened a wrapped package containing a light fixture to use for repairing a train signal and discovered I had been the person who rebuilt it and packed it at the shop just a few weeks earlier.

I usually drove home for weekends at first, although sometimes it seemed like a long trip. It took about three hours on a Friday evening to drive from Tulsa, and on Sunday afternoon, I had to drive back to be there by early Monday morning. One Sunday afternoon I remember going to see *Lawrence of Arabia* at the Rialto in Denison on its second time in theaters, and after the movie ended, I got in my car and drove to Parsons, Kansas.

On that particular trip, I had a problem along the way. At the time, my car was the same green, 1955, four-door Chevy I described previously. The car was 16 years old, and it had a few minor quirks. One of them was with the fuel gage.

I remember just crossing from Oklahoma into Kansas, and my gas gage was reading pretty low, but I figured I could make it to Parsons before I needed to fill the tank. I was mistaken.

Northeastern Oklahoma and southeastern Kansas have a lot of wide-open land with little on it other than farms or ranches. Remarkably, I had just driven into one of the few small towns in the area when my car died along the side of a street. I had run out of gas. Thinking back, it could have happened most anywhere before or after, but it happened as I passed through the center of town.

I looked up the street and spotted a gas station that was open, so I walked over and explained to the station attendant what happened. The man loaned me a gas can. I filled it with a couple of gallons and paid him. Then I poured most of the gas from the can into the tank, hoping it was my only problem. The engine still wouldn't start.

I walked back to the gas station and explained what happened. The man suggested I should "prime my engine." I removed the air filter and poured the little gas left in the can directly into my carburetor. I tried it, and the car started. I drove back to the gas station, gave the guy the gas can back, filled up my tank from the pump, and thanked the attendant for all his help. I was back on the road within about 20 minutes.

I felt pretty lucky. It could have been much more serious. I could have been stranded out in the middle of nowhere overnight. Ever since then I've never run out of gas. I decided then and there to establish a system; when on long trips, I always filling my vehicle's fuel tank when it marks half a tank low.

On the job, the guys I worked with were friendly. One of them lived in Muskogee, so he stayed the night at home when we worked there. Another new-hire employee also lived somewhere in Texas, but he tended to go home each weekend.

I sometimes stayed over a weekend if the trailer was located in a place where I might have something interesting to do on a Saturday. Sometimes I visited local museums. I went to the Gilcrease Museum once while in Tulsa. I visited the Woolaroc Wildlife Preserve and Museum while at Bartlesville. I went to a movie once while in Muskogee, and one Saturday, in the same town, I went on a date with a waitress from a restaurant where our crew used to eat lunch. Muskogee, however, was close enough to go home most weekends.

Our crew truck was large, and it had a lifting crane on the back. I operated the crane at times, and occasionally the supervisor had me drive the truck from one location to another, even though I didn't have the proper license. No one seemed to care.

Once when we relocated our trailer from Oklahoma to Kansas, we were one man short. One of the crew had to drive the truck to pull the trailer, but he also needed his car. I had to drive his car, and it had a manual transmission (stick shift). Before that day, I had never driven anything other than an automatic transmission. After a crash course lasting about half a minute, I drove his car for fifty miles until we reached Parsons. We returned to get my car after a day or two.

I performed a wide variety of manual labor jobs while working with this field crew. Rarely, I had to use lineman's climbing gear to climb telegraph poles alongside the railroad, but usually the supervisor climbed the wooden poles. At the time, we were running a set of copper wires from a signal to a control house. We spliced the wires together using a Nicopress crimping tool. (It's a name that has stayed with me all these years.) Then we raised the wires to the tops of the poles.

Once, however, the supervisor had climbed pretty high up a very old pole when it broke in the middle. He fell and ended up with part of the pole and the cross arm on top of his leg. I recall rushing over and pulling it off of him. His leg was bleeding. We had to take him into town to have it bandaged. In the end, he only suffered a puncture wound with no broken bones, and he was back at work performing limited duties the next day.

In Parsons, Kansas, a local maintenance supervisor had adapted a small, motorized scooter so it would fit on a railroad track. He did this by welding a pair of special, concave wheels to the frame near the rubber tires. Then he attached a crossbar holding a tool tray to the frame, and the end of the crossbar had a wide, steel roller. While the rubber tires and the concave wheels rested on one rail of the train track, the roller rested on the other. The traction of the rubber tires moved the scooter, and the concave wheels kept it on the track. It could zip along at about 15 or twenty miles per hour. If a train was coming, the device was light-weight enough for one man to easily remove it from the track. The pieces could be disassembled to fit into the back of his pickup truck when not in use. This arrangement allowed him to reach train signals in remote locations more rapidly in order to change lamp bulbs. He set up a regular schedule for replacing bulbs, so he didn't often have to leave home at night. He let us use the scooter when we worked in his area.

Another job I performed was to connect bonding cables to sections of track to assure that electrical current would flow between a signal light and a power source when the train wheels closed a circuit. This was one of the neatest jobs. We first took a battery-powered grinding wheel, which we pulled along on a cart, and we ground the outsides of two adjacent rail sections until patches of shiny metal were exposed. Then we placed two stone or ceramic molds up against the track sections. These molds also held in place a specially-made piece of braded copper cable so it rested against each rail section. Using small, plastic containers holding pre-measured amounts of thermite powder, we filled the molds, making sure to dump all the powder from the plastic container into a mold because the powder in the bottom of the container served as an igniter. Then we shot at the powder using a small sparker pistol. The powder ignited, and within seconds, the thermite melted and re-solidified, flowing around the copper cable until it bonded to the steel of the rail on both sides. Then all we had to do was to hit it a few times with a hammer to test the strength of the bond.

In areas where bonding cables already existed, we had to remove the old cables that had become loose on one end or the other. To do this, we used a hammer and a chisel. Then we started the process of attaching a fresh cable. In areas where new track sections had been laid, we had to place cables for the first time.

We often walked along lengths of track to inspect the cables. Some lengths requiring cables were quite long or in unusual locations. We took turns walking track in some remote areas. For these, the truck dropped us off at a road crossing and picked us up at the next one along the line. Whenever I knew of an unusual section of track to be examined ahead, I always volunteered to cover it. My co-workers probably thought I was a little odd for wanting to inspect these sections, but they never protested. My main reason for wanting to do this was to gather the experiences of being in these places. Part of it might have had something to do with my Uncle Josh, who liked to visit unusual places. Maybe I already possessed a subconscious desire to be a writer, and I was gathering experiences to describe later.

I once walked across a long railway bridge while checking bonding cables, and I reached the opposite end from where I start just before a train came rapidly over the bridge from behind me. I suppose I could have found a place along the bridge to wait for a passing train, but it would have been more dangerous.

On several occasions, I walked through tunnels. I had to carry a flashlight in order to inspect the track. Sometimes I turned off the light for a moment just to see how dark it was. One in particular was located near Eufaula, Oklahoma, and it was especially long, resulting in total darkness without the light I carried. As I walked along deep inside one of these tunnels, I promptly encountered a large, dead dog that had been killed by a train months earlier. I felt just a little bit startled by this discovery. I remember noting it wore a collar with a dog tag.

Walking through tunnels, in particular, provided experiences I later shared to some extent in my stories. In my novel, *Second Book of Marc*, I describe traveling through a tunnel, a trip that lasts several

John M. Moody

days in my tale, much of which must be undertaken in complete darkness.

I remember a time when our crew went out to inspect bonding cables at a particular location, and we finished in the evening to return to the trailer. That night at about ten, the same section of track experienced a major derailment involving about fifteen train cars. Our supervisor received word that we needed to check the same section of track to see if the accident had damaged any cables. We arrived on location by about 8:15 AM. Sure enough, we found a lot of cables that were sheared off and had to be replaced, but the most amazing thing to me was the fact that all the derailed train cars had been removed before we arrived. We observed plenty of damage to some wooden ties, and the emergency road crew had already replaced some of the worst ones. To keep the track in operation, they did an amazing amount of repair work starting after 10:00 PM and finishing before 8:15 the next day.

One day while working in Tulsa, an extremely long, metal tank that had been fabricated for some sort of liquid came into town, and we saw it roll by from the side of the track. It was round on both ends and was painted with a dull red, rust-preventive coating, so it looked like a giant hotdog. It measured long enough to span three railroad flatcars. That evening while I visited with a man who ran the depot's night shift, the tank came through, and it was his job to weigh it. I had previously watched when they brought a train car over a scale and recorded the weight of the freight, car by car, but in this case the metal tank was only being supported by the cars on either end. They allowed the flatcar in the middle to simply roll across the scale. They only had to weigh the two end cars and add the weights together to determine the total mass. We later saw a similar tank, but it was even longer.

In Tulsa one Sunday night, the city experienced a violent thunderstorm just as I arrived at the trailer. The local weather service measured winds of around 70 miles per hour with heavy rain and plenty of lightning. About a block away from the depot a large power line fell, leaving the trailer in darkness. The cable, as it jumped and sparked on the ground, looked like lightening, itself, until an electric company crew came to turn off the power. By dawn the next morning, all the tall buildings in downtown that I observed a couple of blocks away—especially those with large, mirror-glass windows—displayed multiple points of damage, and I felt glad our trailer didn't sit directly under a glass-covered skyscraper.

In several places where we stayed, I met "hoboes," men who tended to travel from one place to another by hopping rides in train box cars. It wasn't legal. It certainly wasn't safe, either, and if switchmen happened to catch them, they ordered the riders off. Box cars in those days often traveled from one place to another with the doors open, making it pretty easy for a person to jump in if the train wasn't traveling too fast. I understand that now the railroads tend to keep box car doors closed to discourage people from jumping trains.

In particular, I remember one old guy I met in Tulsa outside the trailer one evening. He stopped to talk for a while when he saw me sitting on the steps. He mostly wanted to sell me a fountain pen he found, but I didn't buy it. He didn't have a regular place to live. Instead, he said he spent most of the month traveling from one place to another by train. However, at a certain time each month he always returned to one town where he regularly received a social security check at a post office box. Once he cashed it, however, he was on the road again.

As our crew worked, we stopped to watch trains as they rolled by. They taught us to look for problems and signal to a conductor in the caboose if we spotted potential trouble. As a result, we sometimes saw men riding in box cars as the trains passed. Once we spotted a family group consisting of a man, a woman, and two children as they rolled by.

It was an interesting summer, and I earned a good bit of money, most of which I saved to use for college in Colorado that year. After I had already left the job just before I was scheduled to travel to Colorado, one of the men I worked with at the shop in town dropped by my house to bring me my union card. It normally wasn't issued until a person had been working non-stop for three months. He explained that by being a part of the union and with my experience, I could go back to work for them whenever I wished. It had been my first "adult" job, which left me with the assurance that if college didn't work out for me, I could find a job doing something else. However, my life continued along a different path.

Stone Cylinders from Out of the Ground

After I left Colorado School of Mines, I returned to Grayson County College for the spring semester where I took my second geology class, Historical Geology. Professor Walter, whom I knew from Texoma Rockhounds, had become ill, but another petroleum geologist from the club, Paul Steele, stepped in to take his place. I found I liked geology even more, so I arranged to attend the University of Texas at Arlington in the fall.

After I attended there for two semesters, one of my UTA professors, Dr. Charles Dodge, approached a select group of students (me included) and asked us if we would like summer jobs at Core Laboratories in Dallas. I decided to take some night classes and work during the day. I was even able to live in one of the dorms, so I had a rather inexpensive place to sleep at night, although the trip from Arlington to Dallas took about 45 minutes each direction.

Even so, it was better than commuting from my family home in Denison, which was about an hour and a half each direction with heavy traffic. I actually did this commute for a week until my place in the dorm was sorted out, and I ended up doing little more than working, driving, and sleeping that week.

The work at Core Lab was interesting. They placed me in the Special Core Analysis Lab, which everyone referred to as "SCAL." The "Core" part referred to oil well core samples. When companies drill wells, they sometimes cut long cylinders of rock (commonly from two to four inches in diameter) when they drill with special bits. They bring these cylinders to the surface for geological description and analysis. The information a company can get from the actually rock samples can be valuable for a lot of reasons, and it was our job in the lab to extract some of this information.

We sometimes sliced the longer cores into short cylinders and ran tests we called whole-core analyses. More commonly, however, we drilled plugs from the sides of the core and ran tests on smaller, easier-to-handle samples. To perform the tests, we had to mount the rocks into special holders—which sometimes wasn't an easy process.

I must stop here to explain something. The concept of extracting oil from the ground from an oil well is rather misunderstood. When artists depict a cross-section of an oil reservoir in a magazine, it looks like the well on the surface is tapping into a vast, underground lake of liquid petroleum. This idea is totally wrong. The oil of a reservoir is normally present in the tiny spaces between sand grains in a reservoir consisting of sandstone, or in the cracks or natural cavities in a limestone reservoir. When I first began to work in the company, core samples from underground could typically have between 15 to 25 percent "void space" (known as pore space) where the oil or other natural fluids resided. Years later when I visited well drilling sites and observed the core samples as they were first brought to the surface, it was possible to see the rocks "bleed" oil from their pores.

But back in the lab, we took these core samples and filled them with water, gas, or oil (depending on the test) to see how well the fluids flowed through them. Other tests measured the electrical resistance of a particular type of rock when saturated with salt water—like might be found underground. This data was compared to oil well logs, which are measured from electrical devices sent into a well to measure the resistance of the complete reservoir. Companies used our data to calibrate the data from these tools. We also injected one type of fluid into a rock to see how efficiently it displaced another type of fluid—such as in the case of taking a rock saturated with oil to see how much we could remove by pumping water through it. (Remember, oil does not normally mix with water.) Usually a large percent of the oil never comes out no matter how much water is pumped in to replace it.

For simplicity's sake, I'm describing these tests in the most uncomplicated way I can, but an entire science has evolved to study the best ways to extract oil from wells. No test performed is exactly like another, not even from inch to inch along a core sample.

As I mentioned, it was an interesting job, and it lasted all summer until I started school full-time in the fall.

I wasn't able to work at the same lab during the following summer because I had to take my geology summer field course, but before I graduated in the spring of the following year, I had already approached Core Lab about working for them permanently and full-time again as soon as I left the university. They also expressed an interest in having me back and arranged an interview.

I recall the day I went back to Core Lab in Dallas to talk to them. I first went into a reception area where a female secretary sat at her desk. Another man also came in to be interviewed, but first the secretary gave us an aptitude test. It had only 25 questions. I sat on one end of the room at a desk while the other guy sat some distance away at a table. We had a time limit. With regard to the subjects it covered, I only recall the test having some math problems, and I felt I was pretty good at math. In my opinion, the exam didn't seem difficult, but I rechecked my answers as best I could before I handed it back to the secretary. Shortly, the other guy turned in his exam, too

Out of the corner of my eye, I watched the secretary from a distance. The other guy's exam rested on top of mine, so when the woman went to grade them, I knew she graded his first. She took out a red pen and started to run it down his answers while referring to some sort of answer key. I saw her make six or eight marks as she read certain answers, and I assumed she marked only the wrong ones.

Then she set the other guy's exam aside and ran her eyes down mine with the same pen in hand. I saw her make only two marks. I felt elated. I continued on to the interview, and I never saw the other guy again.

Still later, two of the bosses of the lab invited me to a sandwich shop for lunch while they continued to ask me questions about my education, and afterward, we just talked. After a while, one of them asked about my math skills again. I remarked, "When it comes to higher mathematics, I'm not especially good. I only made a 'C' in second semester calculus."

He laughed and said, "No, I don't mean that. Can you add and subtract?"

I smiled at him and said, "No problem."

Once I started back at Core Lab, they placed me in a specialized section of SCAL called the "Reservoir Conditions Lab." I ended up performing some of the tests described previously, only now I had to do the tests in an oven to simulate the temperature underground in the reservoir while also using actual crude oil and water from the well. On one occasion, I ran a series of tests using crude oil containing poisonous hydrogen sulfide gas, and I had to wear a gas mask. I also learned to inject live steam into samples at temperatures up to 500 degrees Fahrenheit, which wasn't a simple process.

I worked with some really nice guys. The head of the department was an older man named Mark, and he taught me how to run the tests. He was a veteran who served in the Pacific during World War II. Another co-worker of about my age was named Jim, and he was super intelligent. Another older man who started in our department later was named George. He was extremely smart as well, but George possessed a lot of practical experience. He had worked in lab environments for a petroleum company much of his life, but he was also a good machinist. When it came to equipment, he knew just about everything, and he taught me a lot. We soon discovered we all enjoyed classical music. While we worked, we listened constantly to the Dallas FM station WRR that broadcasted only classical music from a station in Fair Park. People in other labs usually listened to pop music, and our group famously distinguished itself for being different. We also gave a "serious" impression when company tours stopped in to see our department. I learned a lot about classical music during the years I worked there.

For a while, I rode to work in a carpool to save money. It was during a period of national gasoline shortages when energy conservation was being encouraged on numerous fronts. Three or four other people from the lab gathered at a church parking lot, or we pick up each other from our various homes, depending on circumstances and traffic conditions. We took turns driving our vehicles. I recall one morning when we traveled toward downtown Dallas from the west. It was especially foggy. All at once our vehicle reached a high point where we usually had a view of downtown, but on that particular day only the tops of the skyscrapers were in view above the fog. The sun had just come up showing pinkish colors, but most of the glass-faced buildings appeared blue. It reminded me of a city floating in space like in a sci-fi movie.

After working in the reservoir conditions lab for a couple of years, the bosses selected me for promotion. I started scheduling tests and writing reports on test results for the clients. I'll speak something more about this job later, but from that point on, I was considered "an executive," even though I didn't often have to wear a suit. Still later, I became a supervisor over three lab sections, including the reservoir conditions department where I once work as a technician.

From October of 1980 to July of 1981, I worked as a supervisor in the company's Houston office. Even so, I already knew I would soon be heading to South America. This job served as good practice for my future duties.

Still later, the Dallas offices moved into a new building in the Las Colinas area of Irving (next to Dallas), and I continued to work on special lab projects where we often pushed the limits of our equipment. Certain tests I worked on actually explode on occasion, but I felt happy that the failures weren't my fault. They were usually due to faulty equipment designs, which our failed tests helped to correct.

Over the years, my jobs as an executive with a technical background have provided a lot of insight into the inner workings of an office environment. This gave me an excellent opportunity to write my novel *Intersecting Destinies*, which begins as something of a simple, one-sided, office romance and later evolves into a dangerous adventure.

A Defining Moment

For my first years working at Core Lab, I wasn't especially assertive. I knew my job technically, but I didn't think of myself as a salesman or having managerial material. I felt too unsure of myself—insecure. The company most likely selected me for promotion because I did a good job in the lab, not because they saw me as a "born leader."

I had been this way throughout most of my high school and university years. I don't know how or when it started. Even during my time as a successful lab supervisor, I give the credit for getting things done to the staff under my supervision. They were all professionals with good knowledge of their jobs. All I had to do was give them assignments, and they did them. My insecurity continued throughout most of the time I worked in Houston. Naturally, I kept it to myself. It wasn't the sort of thing I wanted to share, especially with bosses.

For several days in the spring, the Houston office sponsored an intra-company workshop. Up-and-coming lab supervisors and sales people from all over the US came to the Houston office to discuss work matters and to learn about technical advancements in our industry. We usually worked during the day, but in the evening, our local lab manager arranged entertainment activities for the entire group.

The guys from out of town were all staying in a hotel near the office. I lived in an apartment complex practically within view of this same hotel. The plan for the final evening was to have dinner at Houston's Petroleum Club in downtown. We arranged to meet in the parking lot behind the hotel at a certain hour to travel there together in several cars.

It was a cloudy, dark evening. I left my apartment to walk over to meet them, but when I was within sight of the parking lot, it started to sprinkle. I gazed toward the parking lot and spied some of them waiting near the cars. For me to reach the parking lot, I had a pretty long walk because I had to navigate around a long, cement drainage ditch. I was still early for the arranged meeting time, so I hurried back to my apartment to get an umbrella. I don't believe it took me more than four or five minutes. I was still on time.

However, when I rushed back and finally reached the parking lot, everyone was gone. I gazed around me for a moment, unsure of what to do. Everyone had already left—and before the agreed time. I almost decided to return to my place and forget the whole thing. I figured they wouldn't miss me. After all, they hadn't missed me when they drove away and left me behind.

It was raining steadily by then. As I began to head back toward my apartment, something inside urged me to try to catch up with the group. I didn't even know the location of the club, but I knew of a telephone book inside the hotel. It sat in a public phone booth in the lobby. (This was before the common use of cell phones and navigation software.) I changed directions and hurried inside to look up the address. When I returned to my apartment where I parked my car, I studied a map I kept in the glove compartment. I located the street on the map, and I figured out the best highways and exits to take in order to reach my destination. I drove there. It rained the entire distance. The trip took about 40 minutes.

I located the building and parked as close as I could. It was still raining, but at least I then carried my umbrella. A doorman in the lobby confirmed I was in the right place. The club sat on the top floor of the building. I took the elevator. At the entrance to the club, I identified myself as a member of the Core Lab party. He directed me to the correct reserved room.

As soon as I turned the corner and stepped into the room, the entire group applauded when they saw me. They had left the parking lot early because it started to rain, leaving me behind by mistake. In the confusion, each group simply assumed I was in one of the other cars. When they arrived at the club, the lab manager immediately realized I wasn't there, and he started making phone calls to the people working at night in the lab to go see if they could find me. Of course, by then I was already on my way to the club, so no one could locate me. I learned that everyone had been worried about me. Some of them later said they felt embarrassed or guilty for not checking for sure if I traveled among the group. I never imagined how concerned they would be to discover I wasn't there.

All at once, I felt glad I made the effort to find them. While some readers may view this story as trivial, I consider my decision to try to solve the problem and to catch up with the group as another pivotal moment in my life. From then on I tried a little harder to do the things I needed to do despite how difficult they appeared.

Frozen Core

A few months after Core Lab sent me to Maracaibo for the second time to become the manager of Venezuela's only Special Core Analysis Lab, we learned of a future project that would involve "Pressure Retained Core Analysis." A certain company had devised a way to extract oil well cores and quick-freeze them while still under pressure as soon as they reached the surface. Although the process was still experimental at the time, INTEVEP, the research branch of the Venezuelan national oil company (PDVSA), saw advantages to using this service. However, not only was the process extremely difficult to perform correctly, it was *very* expensive. At the time, projects to remove a set of cores of this type from a well and freeze them could cost hundreds of thousands of dollars—and this amount did not include the lab analysis. In any case, it was to be a first for Venezuela.

Our company was hired to collect the frozen core from the oil company, cut open the steel barrels to release the rock samples while still keeping them frozen, and perform a controlled thaw to measure the fluids trapped inside. The responsibility for the project fell under the umbrella of a department other than mine, but nearly everyone in our office was involved to some extent.

In Venezuela, I viewed the project as a logistical nightmare involving several outside contractors. For one thing, keeping anything at sub-zero temperatures for an extended period of time in the heat of western Venezuela wasn't easy. Everything had to be planned weeks in advance. Special equipment had to be brought in from the US or constructed locally. We also needed the services of a machine shop, and it had to be located close to the lab. To take care of the actual core handling process and analysis, the company sent a man named Chuck down from the Dallas lab to serve as our resident expert. I knew him from when I worked in Dallas. Chuck was serious about doing a good job, and we got along well.

The coring operation took place at one of the reservoirs under Lake Maracaibo. (The oil fields of the Maracaibo Basin include about 20,000 wells drilled under the waters of the lake.) This particular drilling platform required a long ride in a fast boat to reach it.

On a specific afternoon, I drove Chuck across the Lake Maracaibo Bridge to Ciudad Ojeda to receive the samples at an oil company dock. It was an extremely hot day, as usual. The cores had been frozen with liquid nitrogen, placed in a special, insulated box, and covered with dry ice to keep them frozen. A large, flat-bed truck was scheduled to meet us at a dock. I was mostly there as Chuck's driver and translator. He didn't speak Spanish.

The boat from the drilling site arrived carrying the box at around 5:00 PM, but the flat-bed truck hadn't arrived. The box weighed about a ton—too much for people to easily lift from the boat. A crane stood by to take care of unloading the box.

The crane operator was getting ready to lift the box from the boat. It was already past time for him to quit for the day, and he was in a hurry to get it over with. If he lifted the box and left it on the dock, we wouldn't have a way to lift it onto the truck later. If the cores sat on the dock overnight, the samples would thaw, which would mean that the entire operation of cutting the cores would end up as a costly waste—not to mention leaving a black spot on our company's integrity.

Chuck didn't know what to do. I looked around and spotted another truck. Two men were loading oil field equipment. I hurried over and offered to pay them if they would carry our box to Maracaibo. We didn't even set a price, but the driver—apparently noting my desperation—agreed to help. However, he explained that he and his helper had to make a number of stops first. I asked if they would let me travel with them to watch over the samples. He agreed to this, too.

Chuck said he thought the dry ice would last for several hours. More dry ice waited back at the lab. I handed him my car keys for him to drive back; he had never before driven in Venezuela—which could be a rather daunting adventure in itself. Once back in Maracaibo, Chuck was to explain the situation to one of the other managers and work with people to figure out how to get the box off the truck when it arrived after hours at the lab.

As I drove away with my two new friends, the original truck showed up at the dock, but the crane operator had already left. That truck left the dock empty.

We set out on a trip along the shores of Lake Maracaibo to all sorts of places I'd never seen before—and never much wanted to see again. We traveled as far south as Bachaquero, making several stops along the way to either pick up or drop off pieces of equipment. At a few spots, I put on an extra pair of gloves they carried and helped them to unload items despite my good clothes. We actually had a pretty entertaining time as we talked along the way between stops.

After a three-hour tour of drilling pipe yards and storage depots full of rusty equipment, we returned to Maracaibo at about 8:00 PM. Chuck had contacted the manager who rounded up the troops—about fifteen people from the various labs. Through sheer brute force and a little ingenuity (a ramp made from metal pipes), everyone manhandled the box from the truck and into the lab. The core remained frozen. As Shakespeare wrote, "All's well that ends well."

I gave 500 bolivars to each of the men from the truck. Their eyes went wide when they saw the amount, which at the moment, was the equivalent of around $110 dollars—quite a tip at the time. It was well worth the price for the way they saved the project—and the company's reputation. The rest of the analysis proceeded without further complications.

Perks

My travel opportunities with Core Lab began in the late 1970s when the company sent a group of young executives—including me—to a conference in Midland, Texas. It only lasted two days, but we got to fly, which for me was always a treat.

Whenever I flew anywhere and had my choice, I always preferred a window seat. In this way I sometimes learned a little about a new place while landing for the first time. I got to see many locations only from the air as I traveled from one place to another, such as the Island of Rhodes, the Amazon River, Mount Vesuvius, Cuba, and much of Syria. When flying internationally, I carried a small world map in my brief case to help identify the places I saw. Sardinia appeared most interesting from the air, and maybe someday I'll write a novel with this location as its setting.

Once, the company sent me to Los Angeles. I left DFW Airport really early in the morning and landed at LAX a few hours later, gaining two hours on the way due to time zones. My task was to carry a small (but heavy) box full of core samples to an oil company office overlooking the golf course of the Beverly Hills Country Club just so someone could select a few of them for future testing. After a taxi ride from the airport, I arrived much too early for the meeting. I wandered around Century City for a while (still carrying a box full of rocks), and I ate an early lunch at a Japanese restaurant.

In the afternoon after an oil company man selected a few samples, I headed for home, making a slight detour; I had a taxi driver drop me off at a sea food restaurant adjacent to a port full of pleasure boats north of the airport. I relaxed for a while and enjoyed a delicious meal. Still carrying the box full of samples, I then took a late-night flight back to Dallas, arriving early in the morning—after losing two hours during the return. I was in LA for less than a day, but this trip helped to inspire the locations for *Searching for Jennifer.*

In 1979, my first great travel opportunity arose. The company office in the east end of London decided to add a reservoir conditions lab. One of my bosses explained that the company needed people who could adapt to international travel, and it was time to see if I was one of them. While the trip was still being planned, I supervised the construction of a fully-equipped, sample testing oven. I also had to

John M. Moody

apply for a passport. Once the London office received the equipment, the company sent me to London for three weeks to train the person expected to use it.

As noted previously, I had read all the Sherlock Holmes stories. I read other British mysteries, too. For years previous to the trip, I had been enjoying plenty of British television shows and movies. They included *Monty Python's Flying Circus*, *The Fall and Rise of Reginald Perrin*, *Fawlty Towers*, the early James Bond films, and all sorts of mystery programs. Before my trip, I did research, too. I visited a library several times as I studied every book I could find describing London and its sights. Before I got there, I already had an idea of where everything was located in relation to everything else.

Late at night the plane departed from DFW Airport headed to Gatwick, south of London. After dinner on the plane, I looked out the window as much as I could, and over Indiana, I first saw the Northern Lights. I stayed awake until we began to cross the Atlantic, and a short time later I awoke to watch the sun rise over the fields of County Kerry, Ireland. (This experience inspired part of *Many Shades of Green*.) It was an all-night, non-stop flight.

At Gatwick, two people from the London office met my plane to drive me to the Tower Hotel. I had an excellent view of the Thames and Tower Bridge from my window. For me, it felt like about 3:00 AM, but it was around 9:00 AM, local time. I felt excited to finally be in London, but I was really sleepy by then, so they let me rest until the evening, when a group planned to take me out to eat. As I tried to sleep in the morning and afternoon, the hotel was testing a fire alarm directly outside my door, which kept waking me up. Also, the date was November 14, Prince Charles' birthday, and people kept firing cannon volleys at the Tower of London, practically next door to the hotel.

After dinner in the evening at the Dickens Inn near the hotel— a pub that supposedly Charles Dickens used to visit, which had been moved to its new location—I went back to sleep and enjoyed a restful night. By the next morning, I felt ready to face my task. I've used this process to counter jetlag on more than one occasion, and I described it in detail in *Many Shades of Green*.

I worked to do my job well during the day, but in the evening and on weekends, the time was my own. I took advantage of being in London to see everything I could, even though it was November and the days were rather short. Within two days I started walking to work just to see more sights and to get a better feel for the city. I also bought a special pass allowing me to ride the underground unlimited times throughout the week—and I certainly got my money's worth.

As I walked the streets, I had a trim beard, I wore a long, black, winter coat, and I carried an umbrella. I soon realized I didn't appear much different from Londoners as long as I carried my camera in a small plastic shopping bag. Tourists often approached me to ask directions, and remarkably, I knew the city well enough within only a few days to give good instructions as to how to get them to their desired destinations.

I recall one time in particular when I walked toward somewhere in the east part of town. A man stepped up and asked in a British accent for direction to the Tower of London. I knew exactly where it was from our location, but when I opened my mouth and told him, he promptly appeared rather shocked. He asked, "American or Canadian?" We spoke for a moment, and I briefly explained my reasons for being in London. Then he thanked me and complimented my sense of direction.

I returned to the Dickens Inn for lunch one Saturday afternoon when I was tired of eating in the hotel. (While I ate in a regular restaurant upstairs on my first night in London, they served a simple plate lunch in the pub.) Most of the long tables in the place were full of drinkers, but further away from the bar, I saw a spot where an elderly man sat alone, smoking and drinking. When I asked if I could share his table, he merely waved a hand in invitation.

It wasn't long before he began to talk, and I soon became aware that either his mind had been "dulled by drink," or it wasn't quite right in the first place. He began to tell me stories of being in the area to "dig around for Roman coins." It was true; the area nearby has Roman ruins, but I saw nowhere for a regular person to dig. Everything was covered by cement walkways and buildings except for the river and St. Katherine Docks nearby. Still later, he showed me his disposable, plastic cigarette lighter and began to explain how he thought it might be a good idea to drill a small hole in the bottom in order to refill it with fluid when it ran out. His stories were entertaining, but I ate the food on my plate as fast as I could and left.

I visited the British Museum one Sunday afternoon along with friends I met for the first time the same day. (I have an idea for a mystery modeled after some of these people.) I particularly recall the Egyptian mummies and the horse's head among the Elgin Marbles from the Parthenon. In one room, I spied the Rosetta Stone on display. It was mounted on a pedestal with a thick, plexiglass-like covering over the top to protect it. I stepped up close, and without anyone seeing, I reached underneath to touch the bottom of the stone; I risked it just to be able to say "I touched the Rosetta Stone." I viewed my action as symbolic. Years later, Mary Ann always seemed to enjoy hearing this story.

The Natural History Museum filled most of another Saturday, and I got to see some of the famous fossils I had read about. I felt pretty impressed with Westminster Abby, too, and I read a number of names in the floor whose reputation preceded them. I used to wonder if some church official purposefully forced tourists to step on Charles Darwin's grave by placing a gate leading to the rear of the building at this particular location.

Although my flight from Dallas to Gatwick followed a curved path known as the Great Circle Route, it also took advantage of strong jet stream winds. The return flight took a more round-about route to avoid these winds. In December of 1979, I felt fascinated merely to sit in a window seat to watch a different part of the world slip by below. Our jet first headed northward from Gatwick. At first, I couldn't see much. There were too many clouds. Then after a while, I observed a wide, clear part of the North Atlantic with floating icebergs. Shortly afterward, the pilot promptly announced, "Ladies and Gentlemen, welcome to sunny Labrador." I then looked down and saw a dark, desolate-looking, rocky coast.

Much of Canada was covered by clouds, as well, but occasionally I noticed snowy ground and forests with frozen lakes. Sometimes roads passed straight across the lakes. It was my first time to ever see such sights. I caught glimpses of Hudson Bay through the clouds, and at one point, I observed a beautiful sight; a red-colored jet (probably Air Canada) crossed our flight path perpendicularly some hundreds of feet below our jet as it headed east. As it moved, it flew just above a flat layer of white clouds causing a wake much like a boat might make over water. It would have been a good time to own a movie camera.

By the time our jet crossed from Canada to the US, the pilot announced that we would fly over Fargo, North Dakota. The sky was clear from this point until the end of the flight. We crossed North Dakota and South Dakota headed southward toward Dallas. The fields of the northern US looked like a patch-work quilt, but the land changed as we approached Oklahoma. I spotted the Arbuckle Mountains and Lake Murry—the lake being a landmark that appears pretty strange from high in the air. I also got a good look at Lake Texoma, Denison Dam, and Denison. From there on as we descended, I saw familiar territory.

Most of the people on the flight didn't seem particularly interested in the sights outside the jet's window, but I think I could have watched the changing land many times without feeling bored.

I returned from my first trip to London feeling fascinated with the place, but my travel opportunities were just getting started. Over the years, Core Lab sent me back two more times. On one trip, which lasted only two weeks, I visited one of the Thames gravel bars at low tide near Charring Cross Bridge, where I collected a bag full of old, broken artifacts and pieces of bone. I found pieces of clay pipes, parts of plates with the maker's mark on the bottom, and interesting pieces of rusty metal. I picked up a perfectly-good pair of German-made, stainless steel, hairdresser's scissors among the gravel, and I used them for years. In fact, I still have them.

I came back with some special souvenirs at times. On one trip, I decided I wanted a British police whistle. The idea came from my enjoyment of the Sherlock Holmes stories. I searched several shops for a few days when I had the chance, but without much luck. Then one day I found a small shop near the Charring Cross tube station. It sold all sorts of interesting goodies. I found a nice, new police whistle, and when I went up to the counter to make my purchase, the man said, "Hey, I've got an old one of those, too." He soon produced a used example marked "Metropolitan Police," and it even had a serial number. The price sounded quite reasonable, so I bought both of them—one to actually use and one to simply keep. I still have both of them. I used one of them to call children from recess when I taught during summers at a private school, and the sound it produces is just like I occasionally hear in old British films.

On another trip, I went for a walk early one Sunday morning, and I strolled south across Tower Bridge. Later, I turned left and returned to the north side of the Thames by way of the Rotherhithe Tunnel, which dates back to 1908. I chose the time because the traffic at that hour on a Sunday was practically nonexistent. In this way I avoided most of the toxic, vehicle combustion fumes. (And I wasn't alone; I encountered another man at about the halfway point traversing the tunnel the same as me, only heading the opposite direction.) I've driven or ridden in cars under large bodies of water a number of times, but it felt rather eerie to slowly *walk* under the great river.

During some of my London trips, I traveled out of town. I usually took a train, but once I took a "coach" (a bus) to Charmouth to stay the night in a bed and breakfast near a pebble-covered beach. I chose the location because someone years earlier described how I might collect fossils there, and I found some pretty good examples in only a few hours. The next morning I walked along a coastal path to Lyme Regis, which has historically been an important location for fossils. It was here where Mary Anning collected some of the first complete ichthyosaur skeletons and sold them to collectors to support her family. Many ended up in the British Museum (now the Natural History Museum). On my walk, I spotted a male Lady Amherst's pheasant; this is a species introduced into England from China nearly two centuries ago, but is now believed to be extinct in the British Isles.

At the end of one London trip, I had to travel to Bahrain, in the Persian Gulf. In the company's new lab there, I did the same thing as in London, which was to train someone to perform reservoir conditions test. I saw as much as I could, but my visit coincided with Ramadan. Some activities seemed more limited. I came back with an antique, copper, coffee pot as my main keepsake from this country.

The most interesting part of this trip, however, was the journey home. It was a time during the late 1980s when Middle Eastern terrorism was in full swing, and plane hijackings occurred fairly frequently. My trip took me across Saudi Arabia and Syria to Cyprus, where we landed only to drop off a few passengers. Then we continued to Athens to change planes for Barcelona, Spain, to continue on to Madrid. (It was a standard practice in my company to make a layover in some city for a day on the way home to reduce jetlag, so I chose Madrid.) I learned later that a hijacking took place on a flight from the Athens airport only two days after I was there. (And I actually noticed what I considered to be a lapse of security when I stepped off the plane; from an international flight, passengers were not searched before entering another departure lounge.) Even so, Athens appeared to be an interesting place. Years later, I used it as the location for part of my novel, *The Mighty Hand of Doom*.

In Madrid for a single day I did much the same as I did most anywhere I traveled; I tried to see as much of the city's sights as I could. I later used my short time in Spain as background for part of my novel *Into the Center of the Shadow*.

Venezuela – A Dominant Force in My Life

I mention Venezuela in this book more than I do any other country other than the US. It is because I spent nearly 17 years there. In the spring of 1980, I journeyed to Maracaibo for the first time to help train people in a new lab being formed.

Although I had traveled for Core Lab previously, I viewed this opportunity as my first company trip to a more exotic location—one where the native language wasn't English. (This was before I went to Bahrain or Spain.) I felt both excited and nervous before the trip. The actual journey was more complex than any I had ever taken. For one thing, someone in Core Lab at the last minute handed me a package to hand-carry, which they said was an electronic computer board needed to repair a piece of company equipment.

I flew first to Houston where I had to change planes—and terminals. It was my first hurtle, but I figured it out. As I traveled, I kept telling myself, "Take it one step at a time." I set my next goal as the next place I needed to be at a certain time, and once I reached the location, I started to plan how to get to the one afterward—and so forth. I successfully arrived at the Viasa Airlines check-in counter and received my boarding pass for a flight from Houston direct to Maracaibo. Then I found the correct gate.

The plane took off only a little behind schedule. I recall sitting next to an older man who worked for the American Can Company, and he told me all sorts of stories about his visits to Venezuela, which I later found useful. About a third of the way into the trip, I looked down and spotted a landmass. I later found out it was the Yucatan Peninsula of Mexico. I saw the Cayman Islands a while later. Another third of the way along, I saw Jamaica for the first time. Still later, I looked down and watched as we crossed over the Guajira Peninsula of Colombia, where we began to descend toward our destination. I also spotted a cloudy mountain, Pico Cristobal Colon, the tallest peak in Colombia. In later years, some flights I took flew directly over this snow-capped mountain, which appeared spectacular from the air at fairly close range. I felt excited to see all these places.

As I stepped down onto the tarmac, I recall how hot the late-afternoon atmosphere felt. Then we went through still more steps of the journey. I received a stamp in my passport. Then I collected my luggage. I carried it all to a customs line.

When my turn arrived, I didn't know enough Spanish to explain the box holding the computer board, so I tried to open the box to show the official. Someone at its point of origin had packed it really well. After I got the box open, I found a layer of bubble-wrap held in place by plenty of strong tape. I tried to pull away the tape and had trouble. I felt nervous because I really had no idea what the piece looked like, and I didn't know what the official would say when he saw it. I also knew I wouldn't be able to understand him no matter what he said.

After struggling with the tape, I finally pulled away a layer of bubble-wrap—only to find an equally resistant second layer. At this point, the man simply laughed. He let me exit customs without seeing what I carried. I suppose he thought I was honestly trying to show him the item (which I was), and whatever the item might be, it couldn't be harmful.

Outside, two Core Lab employees waited for me, both of them Brits. (The company hired a lot of English employees at the time for their overseas operations.) They loaded my luggage into a taxi and escorted me into town to a company "staff house." It was a hair-raising taxi ride, giving me my first taste of how Venezuelans in Maracaibo often drove recklessly. (In later years after the first economic crisis hit, the really poor drivers were weeded from the roads due to accidents; they couldn't afford to replace their vehicles.)

Different Lives in One

I recall telling my companions I felt glad to be there. I mostly felt relieved to have completed my day-long journey without any serious problems, then to find people who spoke English waiting for me at the airport.

When I handed over the computer board, they informed me that electronic parts were usually held up in Venezuelan customs for days because they rate a high tariff—and how lucky I was to have left the building with the replacement part actually in-hand. Fortunately, I never again had to carry an item of this type across an international border where it mattered.

I was only in Maracaibo for six weeks that first time. For my second trip in 1981, I went down as a lab manager and stayed more than three years. The last time I went was in 1987, and I stayed for more than 13 years. On the last occasion, the company gave me a fancy title of "Technical Manager for South America," but because most of the operations centered on work in Venezuela, the title really didn't mean much. It only sounded important. Anyway, being in Venezuela has probably dominated—or at least influenced—my life in one way or another more than any other factor.

When my company first sent me, I had no idea what to expect. I started working at an office in Maracaibo along a busy street, but years later the local manager built a new building on the far north end of town. I felt comfortable in both places, but as is the case with most transitions, it took some adjusting each time I went. For one thing, as I said earlier, I didn't speak much of the language the first time. My Spanish was limited to what I learned in high school and at the university, which many years after the fact didn't amount to much. To complicate matters even further, the Spanish that people speak in Maracaibo can be rapid, full of slang words and incomplete pronunciation, and often uses an antique dialect only heard in this region of Venezuela or sometimes in Spain. It took me about a year during my second trip to feel totally comfortable while communicating. Phone calls were by far the most difficult. If it hadn't been for a few bilingual locals and the Brits, I don't know how I would have trained anyone to do a job.

Someone once explained that Maracaibo is among the hottest major cities in the world. Many spots around the globe can experience much higher temperatures during certain months, but those regions also cool off during other parts of the year. In Maracaibo, the average temperature for the year tends to run high at around 92 degrees, and it doesn't change much from month to month. About the only time of the year when it feels slightly cooler outside is in late December and Early January when the highs cool down only a couple of degrees some days. And the locals refer to Maracaibo as "the land loved by the sun." It rains only rarely, and when it does, heavy thunderstorms full of wind and lightning are the rule. Maracaibo wasn't for everyone, but I learned to adapt—and I actually enjoyed my time there.

The food tasted great at the time (although as I presently write, food shortages seem to be common, so I imagine everything has changed). A restaurant named *Mi Vacita* (My Little Cow) on the east side of town once served thick, beef steaks on a large, wooden cutting board—and often the edges of the steak overlapped the dimensions of the board. Another dish found in most of Venezuela with regional differences was called *Pabellón Criollo*. It consisted of white rice, black beans, and shredded beef in a home-made tomato sauce. It was sometimes served with fried slices of plantains on the side with a fried egg on top. Another good thing about Maracaibo used to be its cheese varieties. Some restaurants served plates full of cheese slices as appetizers. As a fast-food or for parties, other restaurants cut pieces of cheese into finger-sized strips and wrapped them in a bread-like covering in order to fry them. These made great snacks.

The food was generally good most anywhere I traveled across the country, and during all those years, I had plenty of opportunities to find out. I recall a hole-in-the-wall sort of place in Guanare, toward the central flatlands, with the best roast chicken I ever tasted. Immigration into Venezuela from Italy following World War II had been strong, so many Italian restaurants I tried were truly excellent. In the eastern part of the country, a dinner of white cheese, flame-roasted beef, and cornmeal pancakes were my favorites. Once again, however, I suspect much of this has changed. When I wrote my novel *Wherever the Wind Will Take Us*, I mentioned some of Venezuela's troubles as background material, but since I published it, things have become much worse than I then described.

Core Lab's Maracaibo office once experienced a rather abrupt change of top management when a manager unexpectedly resigned. The home office quickly selected and sent someone to take his place, and because I was in the US on a vacation trip at the time, they also sent a vice president to evaluate the situation. The two men arrived on a Saturday and took rooms in Hotel del Lago—the city's best hotel, which overlooked Lake Maracaibo. Neither of the men had been to Venezuela before. One of them later described the following story.

On Sunday, with no one at the office, the men found they couldn't do much of anything. They decided to go out to the pool in the afternoon to relax, to enjoy a few beers, and to leisurely discuss future plans and operations.

Venezuela is famous for its beautiful women, and these men had heard rumors to this effect before their trip. Even so, as they sat at a patio table, both men couldn't believe the number of knock-out, young women dressed in swimsuits they observed lounging around the pool. Before long, one of them remarked, "Hey, this is a great country!" They were starting to believe nearly all Venezuelan women looked much the same. As it turned out, a Miss Venezuela beauty pageant was in progress at the hotel.

While working in Maracaibo, I often had to travel to other places, both inside and outside the country. As described earlier, many business trips took me to the opposite side of Lake Maracaibo. It is still possible to see the old towers of oil wells drilled in the 1940s. Trips to Caracas were most common for a while, but I also had to fly to Barcelona / Puerto La Cruz and to Maturin in the eastern part of the country. International trips took me mostly to neighboring Colombia, but I also traveled to Trinidad and Tobago, to Peru, to Brazil, and to Argentina for my company. And at each place, I saw and learned about as much as I could.

The Other Places

I once stopped in Cartagena, Colombia, on the way to Bogota. I traveled with a large group at the time on the way to a major meeting, and we had to wait for hours between flights. Someone suggested we load into a couple of taxis to find a restaurant. One of the Englishmen from my office commented, "That's fine, just as long as it doesn't have rats crawlin' 'round on the floor."

We went to a place that appeared pretty high-class, but while we ate, I happened to see a couple of rats scurrying around in the shadows of the tables. I kept my mouth shut.

While staying in Bucaramanga, Colombia, a group of guerillas blew up a natural gas pipeline, and I passed the fire the next day on the way to the airport.

On my way back from Peru, the plane landed in Quito, Ecuador. The Air France crew first announced that we would remain on the plane, but all of a sudden, I noticed some confused looks as they spoke among themselves. Then they told us we were all to leave the plane and head into the terminal. My first thought was of some sort of emergency. The flight attendants led us straight into the airport's gift shop—where nearly everyone bought something. Airport officials apparently ordered us off the plane merely to stimulate the country's economy.

The country of Trinidad and Tobago was one of my favorite places to go on business. I called upon many memories from there when writing *Wherever the Wind Will Take Us*. For one thing, the people there spoke English—sometimes. The islanders communicated among themselves using a special dialect only they seemed to understand. I recall once approaching a group of taxi drivers who spoke together at a taxi stand near the Trinidad Hilton, and I didn't understand a word of it. As soon as they noticed me, however, one of them turned in my direction and addressed me with a perfect British accent, "Would you care for a taxi, sir?"

The flavor of the place was nice in more ways than one. The population of the islands who were of East Indian ancestry made curries that usually tasted delightful.

I traveled to Tobago only once. A local company representative named Dave invited me to go with him one weekend, along with his wife and two friends. Our objective was to see some sea turtles hatching. The others had watched as a turtle dug a nest and laid its eggs during a previous trip; they tried to arrange their return to see the eggs hatch the night after we arrived. As it turned out, the eggs hatched the night *before* we arrived. We only saw a couple of stragglers that were inhibited from reaching the sea by objects in their paths. Even so, I got to see baby turtles for the first time before they were released into the sea.

Different Lives in One

I also had a memorable birdwatching experience on this trip. Dave described an elderly woman who owned a house a few miles from the beach-side hotel. She fed the birds each day at precisely 3:00 PM. Armed with the information, I walked to the place and arrived a few minutes early for the spectacle. She set out bottles a liquid food for a group of pretty little birds called bananaquits. I had seen these before, but I had never seen nearly a hundred of them at the same time. The woman invited me into her home, which was located on stilts. From there, I saw for the first time a bird now known as the Trinidad motmot. I saw it fairly close because the woman regularly fed it slivers of white cheese. The dining room of the house had large, open windows and doors, and large birds such as the rufous-vented chachalaca frequently flew through her house—in one window and out the other. It was quite a sight.

I attended a conference in Rio de Janeiro, Brazil, and my hotel faced Copacabana beach. The city looked beautiful in many locations, but Rio also holds what are described as the largest slums in the world. I made friends with a man selling fossil fish on the street near the hotel.

In Buenos Aires, Argentina, I stayed in a hotel within view of the symbolic obelisk on Avenue 9 de Julio. Later, I flew south by jet for two hours to the town of Comodoro Rivadavia. It was so far south, I happened to be standing on the sea wall one day when a penguin swam past. The airport there was the only place I ever traveled where passengers didn't routinely go through any kind of security screening for a commercial flight. It was an oil town where everyone knew everyone, so I guess they simply didn't bother to check.

I had plenty of chances to travel while in Comodoro Rivadavia. I even collected fossils while there from a hillside near the hotel. Trips on weekends allowed me to see a petrified forest and plenty of interesting wildlife, including wild llamas called guanacos and a colony of southern elephant seals, representing the world's largest non-whale mammals.

During the final week, the weather turned extremely cold. One day a local manager drove me far out of town to an oil rig where I sipped *mate* (a form of tea) with the drilling crew. My research before the trip told me everyone shares the drink from a traditional container made from a gourd by sipping through the same metal straw. In this way I wasn't surprised when someone took a sip and then passed it to me to do the same.

Changes

No matter where I traveled, however, I always returned to Maracaibo. I worked at Core Lab for a total of nearly 17 years, but the petroleum industry is in constant flux. Business will be excellent one year and bad the next, and the trend usually extends worldwide for prolonged periods. It reached the point late in 1992 when Core Lab no longer needed me. They laid me off.

For a day or so, I wasn't sure what to do, but almost immediately a Venezuelan petroleum engineering company heard I was no longer working at Core Lab. They asked me to come to work for them. I stayed there for a few months until one of the men I worked for formed his own company and lured me away to work for him. I found myself working on actual geological studies of petroleum reservoirs instead of supervising lab tests. The second company made me "Senior Geologist," and I remained there until almost time to return to the US in 2001.

Grayson, Again

By the time I returned to Denison, accompanied by Belkis and Mary Ann, my father had already passed away. My mother needed someone to help her at home. We all enjoyed some good years together until she also passed away.

I briefly worked in educational institutes for young children, but I felt I needed something else. As I looked for work, Grayson College came into my life again. I performed several jobs, but my favorite is what I'm doing now, which is to help college students develop their reading and writing skills. I've published all my novels since the time I started working at Grayson, and I'll describe this in greater detail later.

But first, it's time to look back at some more traveling. This time, it wasn't specifically for business; it was mostly for the fun of it.

My Life of Travel

Oh, the Places I've Gone ...

While I lived in Venezuela, I traveled a lot. Even before I lived in Venezuela, I went places with family and friends. It wasn't always for work, and many times I tried to go places where I might find fossils. At the time, I had the resources allowing me to do extra things and visit all sorts of locations. Fortunately, I also met people who enjoyed doing the same sorts of things, so we went on many trips together.

Going Places

On one of my first trips into the mountains of Venezuela, I stayed in a motel a couple of miles above a small town in Trujillo State known as La Mesa ("The Table," in Spanish). The motel sat on some of the lower slopes overlooking the town. This town probably got its name from flat lands nearby, some of which looked as flat as tabletops, but the entire area was surrounded by fairly-high, picturesque mountains. I modeled the small village of Mezet in my first three novels based on my visits to La Mesa.

But back to my story, I was doing a lot of bird watching at the time. I walked down the hill and stepped out the motel's front gate. I stood along the road not far from the gate with my binoculars hanging by a strap around my neck and my camera dangling from my shoulder. Whenever I saw a bird, I lifted the binoculars to try to make an identification.

About that time I looked down and spotted a small bird lying on the asphalt road. It was an American goldfinch. I noticed it was still alive, but it had apparently been stunned after hitting a passing car. I picked it up to look at it, but I didn't know what else to do with it.

All at once, a car stopped in the middle of the road (which had very little traffic). A man came hurrying out and said to me in English, "Hello! I'm a birdwatcher, too."

We talked for a moment. He introduced himself as Jesús, and he presented his wife, Olga. Jesús and Olga were out for a cool weekend in the mountains. They were from Caracas, but they lived in Cabimas at the time. Cabimas is a town not far across the lake from Maracaibo.

Jesús just happened to be a geologist working at Lagoven, one of the Venezuelan petroleum companies. He and Olga had both studied at the University of Texas—not in Arlington, but instead the one in Austin.

I showed him the goldfinch, which still breathed as it rested in my palm. We arranged to meet later, and they left to go to lunch (where they had been headed before they spotted me wearing my equipment). I ran into them several more times over the weekend, and later, we became good friends. We arranged to take trips to watch birds and to do other things during the next two years or so until Jesús was transferred to Caracas. During that time, however, I met other people through Jesús and Olga with similar interests—and with similar spirits of adventure. If I hadn't been standing on the road with a pair of binoculars hanging around my neck, I doubt I would have ever met them, and that chance meeting led indirectly to many wonder-filled adventures.

A few minutes after Jesús and Olga drove away that first day, the goldfinch stood up and perched on my finger. A moment later, it flew away to live its life, apparently unharmed.

Two good friends I met through Jesús and Olga were both named Jorge. Both were Venezuelans. One was another geologist who worked at Lagoven. The other was an entrepreneur who had studied forestry in the US; this Jorge was something of an amateur naturalist and adventurer. His wife, a medical student, was Olga's cousin. After Jesús returned to Caracas and could no longer go with us, the two Jorges and I used to go on trips into the mountains simply to visit places we had never seen before. Jorge the geologist usually served as our guide because he had more experience in the area. Those were exciting times, and I got to see many places with them I wouldn't have otherwise seen. In fact, I got to see places in Venezuela that most Venezuelans never saw.

Perijá – The First Overnight Trip

The two Jorges, Jesús, and their wives decided to take a trip into the Perijá Mountains, and they invited me to go with them. They arranged to stay overnight. It was my first trip deeper into the mountains, and it resulted in still another life-changing experience. Once again, Jorge the geologist knew the area and served as our guide.

We traveled first to Caño Colorado north of Rio Palmar. Pairs of large, mostly green, military macaws flew over us, making their noisy calls. As we climbed the canyon, we stopped and collected fossils along the way. Jorge showed me brachiopods from the Caño del Oeste Formation (Devonian), but he also spoke of trilobites. At another location, he pointed out plant fossils from the Campo Chico Formation (also Devonian). Later in this book I'll describe this area and some of its fossils in greater detail because it became an extremely important location when I later worked at a museum.

At one stop on a mountain trail along the way, we heard bellbirds. These small, feathered creatures make calls sounding like a hammer hitting a piece of tempered steel, and the calls are rather loud. It's not the sort of noise I expected to hear originating from several directions at the same time across a green-forested canyon. I use this experience and later ones when writing *Journey from Mezet*, and I describe a similar trip in *Into the Center of the Shadow*. Later, I spotted other birds I had never seen before, including the elusive, nocturnal oilbird.

From Caño Colorado, the trail dropped into the valley of the upper Rio Socuy. We ended up on the north side of the river. This is the location where we camped for one night. I spent that evening and much of the next day exploring—even while it rained at times. The tall trees standing nearby looked fantastic, and clouds hung in the mountains in many locations. It was a great place to take photos.

Not far away we visited a limestone cavern where I later learned that the passageways were quite extensive. Water flowed through some parts of the cave, and as we explored, I happened to step into an unseen hole, dropping almost completely under water. I barely saved my Pentax SLR camera from being ruined by holding it over my head until I was able to scramble out. Years later, I learned that the cave might be an important location for Pleistocene aged fossils, which I also refer to in *Into the Center of the Shadow*.

The trip seemed too short, and looking back, I guess this event inspired me more than any other. During this journey, I fell in love with the Sierra de Perijá. I was ready to go back as soon as I could, but it took me years to return to some of the same locations.

East Instead of West

Jorge the naturalist and I sometimes took off for weekends into the desert regions of Falcón State. At one spot in particular, we visited with a family on a small farm south of the town of Borojó. Jorge had made friends with this family when he discovered they were artists who worked with wood. They raised goats—which was about all they could raise in such dry, desolate, cactus-filled country—but nearly everyone in the family carved objects out of wood and painted them bright colors. This family earned extra money by placing their artworks in craft shops in Maracaibo, but Jorge and I thought it was more fun to visit them in person to see their work in the harsh environment where they produced it.

One Saturday while we paid them a visit, they invited us to sit down and have lunch. The rest of the family had already eaten, but they set two places at the table. They served soup containing vegetables and what looked like pieces of chicken still on the bone. As we ate, I lifted a bone with my spoon in order to remove some of the meat with my fingers (not an ill-mannered practice in such a situation), and when I examined the bone, something about it didn't look right. It wasn't like any chicken bone I had ever seen, and it appeared to be from a somewhat smaller animal.

I told Jorge in a whisper, "This looks a little like a dinosaur bone."

After a few minutes, one of the women entered the room, so Jorge asked, "What kind of soup is this?"

She answered, matter-of-factly, "Iguana."

Tucuco

While I lived in Venezuela the second time—between July, 1981, and August, 1984—I gathered as much information as I could on the Perijá region. I bought a book from one source describing ethnic differences among some of the Native American tribes there. From this book, I learned about the Yukpa and the Barí. These are two of the major tribes that once extensively occupied the region south of Machiques on the eastern side of the Perijá range. In the old days, the tribes were collectively known as the "Motilones." For many years, these two tribes were at war with each other.

Another geologist friend named Jhonny Casas (who will be mentioned in more detail later) once allowed me to read an old report from one of the first petroleum companies in the area where they described how natives armed with bows and arrows attack a group of oilfield workers, killing one of them. This took place in the 1940s.

The Catholic mission of Los Angeles de Tucuco was founded in 1945 near the base of the Perijá range at a point between Yukpa territory to the north and Barí territory to the south. The site was selected in an attempt to pacify both tribes. From early on, the Yukpa were more receptive to the church's efforts. The Barí, on the other hand, were much more resistant. In fact, some of the church's early efforts weren't at all successful.

My friend Jesús told me it would be worthwhile to visit the Tucuco Mission. It was fairly easy to reach Tucuco when I visited there for the first time in October of 1982. After traveling to Machiques, a person only had to turn southward along a back road to a certain junction and turn right to head toward the mountains. Some parts of the road weren't especially good, but it was possible to reach the location by regular car if a person drove carefully.

At the mission, one of the friars led me into a small museum. He described the differences in bows and arrows made by each tribe.

The main difference between the two types is in the construction of the various bows. While Yukpa bows are flat in cross-section, Barí bows are generally about a foot longer and stronger, being oval in cross-section.

Many of the arrows look much the same. They don't use feathers. Instead, the head is made from a carved piece of dark brown, hard, palm wood (from a type of palm with a spiny trunk). Most of the arrow shaft toward the rear, in turn, is made from a long, light-weight piece of dried reed. Once an arrow is fired from a bow, it is actually quite accurate because the heavier weight near the front of the arrow serves to pull the rest of the shaft along a fairly strait trajectory.

I occasionally saw and purchased Yukpa bow and arrow sets in markets in Maracaibo even before I knew what they were. Sometimes the modern Yukpa arrows had metal arrowheads attached. At the village of Toromo west of Machiques, I also bought a set of two arrows and a bow from an elderly Yukpa native. In this case the arrows had long, steel points made from old machete blades. (When I asked the man what he hunted with arrows so deadly, he answered "Tigres," or tigers—the name they give to jaguars. But he then added "… y hombres," or men. He appeared old enough to have participated in the war with the Barí tribe as a young man, but he might have also been merely joking.)

According to the friar, the Barí never used metal arrowheads. For years, I searched for differences in bow types in markets in Maracaibo, but I never saw a Barí bow and arrow set for sale there. The friar mentioned that the Barí rarely parted with them.

The most interesting display I observed at the Tucuco Mission museum, however, was a glass display case holding three broken, wooden arrow points. They had tags attached showing names, along with dates ranging from 1948 to 1950. When I asked about them, the friar described these as arrows removed from other friars' bodies on those dates. As I said, some of the mission's early pacification efforts weren't always successful.

Taxis and Planes

While working for petroleum service companies, I spent plenty of time in jet airplanes—or in taxis traveling to and from airports. Sometimes I traveled with other people from the companies where I worked, but often I traveled alone. As a result of these trips, I can share many stories dealing with my experiences.

I traveled to Caracas frequently. The flight from Maracaibo to Caracas was non-stop, but I usually had to take the earliest flight, the one leaving Maracaibo at 6:00 AM, to make an early meeting or a connection to another flight. To make sure everything would be okay when I travel so early, I needed to be at the airport by 5:00 AM. Because it normally took about 30 minutes to reach the airport by taxi, this meant I needed to be up at four in the morning.

A flight took about an hour to reach the main airport serving Caracas—the one at Maiquetia on the coast. However, Caracas sat in a high valley on the other side of the mountains. From the airport, it could take from 45 minutes to an hour to arrive at a petroleum company office. This meant I had to get up at 4:00 AM to make a meeting by 8:00 or 8:30 AM. Sometimes the meeting finished within 30 minutes or an hour. Then it was time to head back home if I didn't have another meeting scheduled at another company. The process went in reverse: a taxi from Caracas to Maiquetia, waiting in the airport for the flight to leave (which was often scheduled for the late afternoon because we didn't know how long the meeting would last), the flight to Maracaibo, the taxi ride home or to the office. Occasionally a meeting of only half an hour took all day when travel time was taken into account. Once I had to make two of these trips on two consecutive days, with a third trip later in the week. It could be tiring. I usually carried along a book to read.

When I traveled alone, sometimes the taxi drivers tried to overcharge me because I had the face of a "gringo." However, I later discovered that when I started up friendly conversations with them during the trips, they didn't try. On one trip before I felt comfortable with conversation, a taxi driver tried to charge me double for the trip in the morning, and I felt determined it wouldn't happen in the afternoon. I flagged down a taxi on a Caracas street. It looked like a pretty old car with an even older man driving. I asked the price before I got in; he set a fair one. I stepped into the back, and all at once I heard music that sounded familiar.

I immediately remarked to the driver, "Hey, that's Stravinsky's *Petrushka*."

John M. Moody

He answered, "Yes, it is! You Americans know a lot about classical music." It was sheer luck I happened to recognize those particular bars of music from that piece well enough to recall its name and the composer, but my time listening to classical music while working at Core Lab's Dallas office had apparently paid off. That trip ended up as the most pleasant I took from Caracas to the airport in all the time I spent in Venezuela. The driver and I enjoyed the rest of the piece and the following one—something by Beethoven that now slips my mind. He also restored my faith in taxi drivers.

When traveling to Barcelona / Puerto La Cruz, I first had to fly to Maiquetia and change planes for another half-hour flight to the airport in Barcelona. This meant four take-offs and landings in a day—and most often, the final flight from Maiquetia to Maracaibo didn't leave until about 9:00 PM. This made for a pretty long day.

On one occasion as I sat on the runway at Barcelona with a co-worker, ready to leave for Caracas, I promptly smelled what I believed to be burnt plastic—like an electrical cable had overheated or shorted out. The odor was quite strong and pretty characteristic. My co-worker smelled it, too, so we informed the flight attendant. The woman smelled something as well, so she got her supervisor to step back to our part of the jet. He apparently smelled it because within a couple of moments, the jet's captain also stepped down the aisle to see for himself. By then, however, with people passing back and forth, and with the internal air conditioning moving the air around, the odor had dissipated. The captain went ahead and took off. My co-worker and I worried about it for half an hour—our entire time in the air. The plane landed safely. We never learned the cause of the odor.

Once at the Barcelona airport again, an extremely heavy rain fell just before a co-worker and I were about to board a flight for Caracas. The jet sat on the tarmac near the gate, but a twenty-foot-wide river of rapidly flowing water blocked our way. The airline's solution was to back a flat-bed baggage truck to the terminal entrance and load the passengers on it to ferrying us across the stream. It worked, and I captured the moment with a great photograph.

While landing in Barranquilla, Colombia, the jet passed through a tremendous thunderstorm just before it touched down. The last few minutes weren't pleasant.

The airport serving Bucaramanga, Colombia, looked like someone had simply cut off the top of a mountain to build the runway. The planes that hadn't landed safely seemed to be piled up on a lower slope just short of where the cement began.

I didn't much care for my only landing in Medellin, Colombia, either, because the plane descended between a pair of mountains. Long before reaching the runway, the jet passed close enough to the rooftops of houses on a mountainside to see children playing in their yards and to identify underwear hanging from clotheslines. And I couldn't help recalling that Carlos Gardel, the famous singer and composer of tango music, died when his plane crashed into another plane on one of the same runways.

On the way to Bogota from Maracaibo, it was often necessary to fly to San Antonio de Táchira in far southwestern Venezuela. From there, a taxi took me and others across the border to Cucuta, Colombia, stopping first at border control offices so our passports could receive exit and entrance stamps. On one occasion when we reached the Cucuta airport, a major military operation was underway. As passengers watched, several Lockheed C-130 Hercules aircraft landed to rapidly unload men and equipment without stopping their engines before taking off again. Before long, the entire airport was full of Colombian soldiers, all armed to the teeth. They had even positioned tanks to guard the corners of the unloading area. It might have been part of an anti-guerrilla campaign.

The airport at San Antonio de Táchira was notorious for having a messed up departure schedule. When making reservations, they always showed an early flight that didn't exist, and the travel agent always booked our company's employees on it. When this occurred, a person normally had to sit in the airport for eight, boring hours until the next flight could depart. (The airport's piped-in, ambient music program ran for about an hour, and I once heard the same series of songs eight times consecutively as I waited.) After this happened to me the second time, I decided I didn't want to wait. I took a taxi to San Cristobal, about 25 minutes away. From there, I took what is called a "route taxi," which travels a specific route from one town to another. I caught one for Maracaibo. The trip took only six hours. I arrived home before the jet departed from San Antonio. And besides, I had an interesting time looking at wildlife, forests, and mountains much of the way. The only thing that bothered me was the man who sat next to me. For the entire trip, he tried to keep hidden—unsuccessfully—a 9mm automatic pistol. He might have only been an off-duty military officer, but who knows?

The Simón Bolivar Bicentennial

To celebrate the two-hundredth anniversary of the birth of Simón Bolívar, the country's liberator from Spain, Venezuela had been preparing and planning for years. For months in advance, many invited performers from other countries had been presenting free, public shows all over the country, all organized and paid for by the Venezuelan government. I attended a number of performances prior to the actual date of July 24, 1983, including Chinese and Russian dance and musical groups, the Moscow Symphony Orchestra being one of them.

For the actual birthday party, Caracas planned to go all-out, and a vice president of my company—also named John—had heard about it. He and I had a morning meeting in Caracas scheduled for July 25, so he decided we would travel to Caracas by jet on Sunday morning to observe the festivities. The idea sounded fine to me.

At the airport in Maiquetia, we observed a number of official jets from other South American countries. (By living in Venezuela for nearly seventeen years and traveling a good deal during that time, I encountered Venezuelan presidents from time to time. We sometimes passed each other along the highways around Caracas, or I saw them disembarking from planes at airports. Occasionally, I saw some of the men at a distance at election events before they became presidents. I even heard one of them give a speech once.) What we saw at the airport was only a small indication of what we would see later.

When we reached Caracas, it became obvious that something special was taking place. Traffic in and around the city was often congested, but not usually on a Sunday. After hearing what the cab driver had to say about the scheduled events, we dropped off our luggage at a company apartment in Parque Central and took another taxi to Los Próceres. This is a park where military parades are often held for official celebrations.

We arrived just before the parade began. I had seen these sorts of parades on television, but it was my first time to see one in person. Soldiers and sailors from all branches of Venezuela's military services marched past the crowds along with equipment such as personnel carriers, cannon, boats on trailers, boats with wheels, and tanks. (You're welcome!) At the end, representative groups of military aircraft performed fly-overs.

Most amazing, however, was the reviewing stand in the center. It held the presidents of Venezuela, Colombia, Ecuador, Peru, and Bolivia (the countries Bolívar liberated from Spain). Not only that, the vice president of Panama and Juan Carlos, the King of Spain—along with the men's wives and other dignitaries—were present, all in one place. Where else could we have been that day to see five presidents and a king? Although they were pretty far away, it was possible to take a photo with my camera using a telephoto lens. The king appeared much taller than the rest.

After the conclusion of the parade, John and I traveled to a Latin American arts and crafts exhibit where we saw products from nearly everywhere in South and Central America. Then we returned to the center of the city using the new "Metro" subway system.

As John and I went to dinner in the evening, some sort of official celebration took place at a theater bordering Parque Central. Security appeared tighter than I had ever seen, including snipers on the roofs. We ate dinner in the up-scale part of the city known as Sabana Grande, and afterwards, we decided to walk part of the way back to the company apartment. We encountered live bands all along the boulevard with people literally dancing in the streets. With the international flavor still in the air, it reminded me of the words from a Rolling Stones song.

Rio de Oro

No trip was as much of an adventure as our journey upriver along the Catatumbo and Rio de Oro Rivers to Boxi, a Catholic mission in the heart of Barí tribal territory. Once more, I traveled with the usual group—both Jorges, Jesús, and their wives.

A few weeks earlier the two Jorges, the wife of Jorge the geologist, and I traveled along the Perijá Highway south of Machiques to investigate the possibility of making such a longer trip. Rio Catatumbo is the largest river that enters Lake Maracaibo (from the southwest), and much of the lower areas are swamplands full of caiman and capybara. As the river flows out of the mountains, however, it is joined from the west by Rio de Oro (translated Gold River). Rio de Oro forms part of the border between Venezuela and Colombia. Near the river bridge, we engaged a man with an aluminum motorboat who agreed to take us a few kilometers upstream to a general store for a small fee. (In those days, I earned more money than any of my Venezuelan friends, so I always insisted on paying most of the expenses.) We soon learned that the general store actually stood on the Colombian side of the river, accessible most commonly by boat. The borders there were rather fluid, however. Sometimes the river changed course, cutting off pieces of one country or the other, so no one seemed to care about which country we ended up in.

When we returned to the Rio Catatumbo Bridge later in the afternoon, we asked about the possibility of going much further upstream to the mission over an extended weekend. He agreed, but it was going to take more than one boat to carry a group of the size we planned to have with us. He still told us it wouldn't be a problem. We worked out a price and set a date—a three-day, holiday weekend in November of 1983.

When the proper time arrived two weeks later, we traveled back to the bridge with the full group and supplies for three days. However, the man we spoke to earlier had changed his mind. We didn't have transportation to take us to the mission—at first.

My friends began to ask around. Finally, a man with a large, motorized, wooden canoe agreed to take us. The canoe had been made from a single, large tree trunk. It could hold as many as ten people and all our supplies. It actually worked out better because we all got to ride in a single boat. We only had to wait long enough for men to unload his cargo of plantains (bananas) onto a waiting truck.

We left the bridge at three in the afternoon and traveled up the river for six and a half hours, navigating a few shallow spots at times. As we entered the mountains, some locations displayed sizable waterfalls along the main stream. It turned dark around 7:00 PM, but part of the time we had a mostly full moon until it disappeared behind the clouds. We didn't reach the Boxi Mission until well after dark

(9:30 PM). However, Padre Gregorio and some nuns there welcomed us. They found places in buildings where we could hang our hammocks, and we turned in for the night.

Boxi Mission served the Barí natives of the entire region. (I use the past tense "served" because when I tried to locate the mission on the internet or through satellite photos, it doesn't seem to exist anymore.) The center of the mission was a soccer field with buildings facing it from some sides. The church stood on one end of the field, and the infirmary with the nun's quarters stood on the other end, closer to the river. The landing was a large sandbar. The location was on the southern edge of Sierra de Perijá National Park, which has to be the most remote mountainous forest of the entire range.

Extended family units (as many as a hundred people) used to live in large, wooden dwellings with thatched roofs. When it was time to sleep, everyone hung hammocks from the rafters. The missionaries tried to discourage this sort of communal living for health reasons and built individual block-and-cement houses for smaller family units to use in an attempt to "westernize" them. Even so, many families preferred to live outside the cement dwellings most of the time because they were too hot for the climate. In order to maintain the sense of community-under-one-roof, however, the church at the mission was constructed of brick with a sheet-metal roof in the same shape and style as their former communal dwellings.

The day after we arrived, we found plenty to do. Padre Gregorio guided us around and even took us in a boat upriver to show us their crop fields.

He also explained how the natives did spearfishing. They made long, narrow spears from the same dark palm wood as they used for their bows and arrow points. Then they stood in a place on the rocks where the river was fairly shallow. They placed only the tip of the spear underwater and waited for a fish to come within range. By placing the tip into the water, they were better able to judge the fish's position in relation to the point of the spear due to the refraction of light in water. Finally, they merely stabbed the fish at close range. One of the items I brought back from this trip was a fishing spear, and it still hangs on a wall at our home.

At one moment, some of the villagers started to get excited when the news reached them that a hunter was bring in a wild pig; he had shot it with an arrow. The type of arrow he used had a large, barbed, metal arrowhead (contrary to what I was told at Tucuco Mission).

These arrowheads are attached to the arrow shaft in such a way that if the animal doesn't die instantly but instead runs away, the arrowhead detaches from the arrow shaft. Due to a cord connecting the two, however, the running animal ends up dragging the arrow shaft through the underbrush. The arrow shaft tends to snag and slow down the prey—or stop it altogether through blood loss if the barbed arrowhead rips free.

When the hunter reached the camp, he had already cut the meat into large chunks and was carrying it on his back using a strap across his forehead. This allowed him to have hands free for climbing and for carrying his bow and arrows. He stopped long enough for Jorge the naturalist and me to take photos as he reached the mission.

I later took a photo of a young woman wearing an orange dress, but she also wore a necklace made of monkey teeth. She was one of the three wives of a chief we met named Simón. The church apparently tolerated this sort of practice because he was a chief with a lot of influence over his tribe.

While visiting with Simón at his home, Jorge the naturalist and I noticed the chief's bow and arrow set. It was the same type used by the hunter, complete with a special hunting arrow. We asked if anyone would like to sell us sets, and Simón assured us he would ask around.

Later in the afternoon, the Barí men put on an archery contest for our benefit, and we came up with several prizes for the winners. Padre Gregorio hung a rather small, paper target (about three by two feet) on one of the soccer goals; in the center of the target, he had drawn a circle about the size of a pie plate. The archers stood in a line about a hundred feet away down the field. The Barí are general of small stature, but it was amazing to watch how well these men could arch these bows made of such hard wood. Most amazing of all, however, was how many arrows hit the target's center at that distance. We had seven prizes, so the top seven shooters—those with arrows nearest the exact center—were able to choose, beginning with the first-place winner. (In some way, each man all knew which arrow was his.) The prizes were two knives, a meat fork, a new T-shirt, a pair of scissors, a machete, and a 50 bolivar banknote (worth about $4.00 US at the time). I brought most of these items to possibly use for trade.

The money ended up being the first prize chosen. Even there in the middle of nowhere, the natives had an appreciation for monetary value. The seventh man ended up with the machete. When we asked Padre Gregorio the reason, he told us everyone already owned one. It was "standard equipment" so close to the jungle.

My friend Jorge the geologist was a large, strong guy. Toward the end of the contest, one of the men allowed Jorge to try his hand at shooting an arrow toward the target, but when he pulled back the bowstring, the bow snapped in half in his hand. Jorge felt embarrassed for breaking the man's bow, but the Barí only laughed. Padre Gregorio assured Jorge that the man could easily make another one. I think they were mostly amazed by Jorge's strength.

After the contest, Jorge the naturalist and I began to ask if anyone wanted to sell us sets of bows and arrows, but at first they seemed reluctant. They especially didn't want to let go of the special arrows with metal heads—the ones they used for hunting. However, when they discovered we were willing to pay 100 bolivars (about $8.00) for a set, two people quickly came forward and seemed happy to sell. The next day another man also brought us a set, so the three of us who wanted them ended up with them.

That same morning the nuns had asked the wife of Jorge the naturalist (who attended medical school) to examine a pregnant woman. They said she was feeling pains. The Barí woman was supposed to be only seven months along. That same evening, we learned that Jorge's wife helped to deliver a baby girl. Apparently she experienced a different kind of adventure while the rest of us were running around the mission.

On Sunday morning, we packed after breakfast and took up a collection to donate to the mission. Then we said our goodbyes and started downriver. It had rained in the mountains during our trip, so the river held more water. And because we "went with the flow," the trip took much less time, even including a stop at one of the waterfalls to take photos; the trip back to the bridge took only five hours. We returned home the same evening. My part of the entire three-day trip (including purchases, food, some gifts, canoe rental, gasoline, and donations) came to only $127.

I thought a lot about this experience when writing my introduction to *Land on the Verge of Darkness*. Even though the location in my book is eastern Peru instead of western Venezuela, my research showed quite a few similarities.

Angel Falls

Jesús and Olga once again recommended this trip. They had taken it about two years before I went, but the landscape surely hadn't changed. It looked fabulous.

Angel Falls is reportedly the tallest continuous waterfall in the world, with a free-fall height of 2,368 feet. Below that level, the water continues to cascade over rocks for several hundred additional feet. It gets its name from a pilot name Jimmie Angel who first saw the falls from the air in 1933 and later brought it to world attention. It's truly a memorable place.

The first part of the trip was rather simple. Avensa, one of the Venezuelan national airlines, had built a nice hotel at Canaima, in Canaima National Park. The location was served by an airport large enough to accommodate a jet, and they regularly flew in tourists as part of a vacation package. I only had to make reservations, pay some money, and catch a flight from Caracas.

The resort-style facilities were situated along the Carrao River leading back toward a mountain named Auyan-tepuy. Angel Falls is located along the west side of a deep canyon of this mountain. This part of Venezuela has a lot of unique features, and a "tepuy" is the native name given to the high, mesa-like mountains in the area. These are the homes of plant and animal species unique to the area—some of them endemic to single mountaintops. The flat-topped mountains consist of very old rocks (geologically speaking) making up the "stable craton" of the South American continent—this means the part lasting longest without being eroded away. These are the lands Sir Arthur Conan Doyle wrote about in his novel, *The Lost World*, where prehistoric animals—including dinosaurs—were supposed to roam. The hotel was constructed with a view of two waterfalls with tepuys in the background, making it the perfect photo spot. Some of these landscapes appear fantastic; I found it difficult to believe they were not part of some fantasy landscape even while looking directly at them.

Different Lives in One

In order to see Angel Falls, people either fly over it by plane or travel up the river canyon in a canoe. The Avensa jet passed near it on the way to Canaima, but I sat on the wrong side of the plane at the time. I decided to see it by canoe, so not long after arriving at the hotel I made arrangements to go on a tour. Other than two guides and a friend of theirs who came along for the ride, the trip included only three tourists, including me.

After leaving a dock above the waterfalls nearest the hotel, we traveled east along the Carrao River in a motorized canoe, with Auyan-tepuy toward our right. The side facing us at times appeared like a massive wall of fractured, brown to orange colored rock, but a lush, green forest of tremendous trees grew up to the base of the cliffs across the lower areas. The cliffs are so high it is difficult to appreciate the scale without a proper frame of reference. Dozens of large waterfalls cascade down the sides of the cliffs in places, but most of the water falls only half way toward the forest (perhaps 1,000 to 1,500 feet) before striking the lower cliffs.

The canoe made good progress at first along the main river, but when we turned to enter the canyon along Rio Churun heading toward Angel Falls, the trip upriver became more difficult due to low water. For some of this part of the trip, my stomach didn't feel good due to something I ate the night before at the hotel, but the problem went away by the following day.

After a couple of hours climbing the river through the base of the canyon, we reached a small camp with shelters about a mile away from the falls. It was built on a small island called Isla Ratón (Mouse Island) at the intersection of Rio Churun and the smaller stream originating from Angel Falls, itself. The shelters had sheet-metal roofs and poles for hanging hammocks, but that was all. They were open-air. The guides roasted chicken over an open fire for our meal that night, and the meal tasted great.

To drink, they made Kool-Aid using the water straight from the river, and if anything, my stomach got better after drinking it. This is the only time I ever drank water directly from a stream, but someone once mentioned that the acid levels are high in this water from so many decaying leaves. Maybe not a lot of harmful bacteria can live in it. The water appears red under the right light conditions.

John M. Moody

We had an excellent view of the falls from the center of the camp. Angel Falls is taller than the rest of the waterfalls we saw because a collapse of the base of the cliff at that point leaves more room for water to fall without striking anything. I used a Super-8 movie camera and took a time-lapse shot of the falls over a number of minutes, which looked pretty interesting once I developed the film.

It rained hard during the first night. The river surrounding the island rose about two feet. However, the weather had cleared up by morning, and the water of Angel Falls had increased significantly. It sprayed outward with greater force as it fell.

Following breakfast, the guides led us overland and through the jungle to the base of the falls, and the trip took about an hour. When they noted the force of the water from the falls as it fell, however, they wouldn't let us go as close as they originally planned. The spray falling at that point was constant, making it difficult to take photos without getting water on the camera lenses.

We stayed for a while, but then they led us back slowly. Along our route, we encountered a "bird-eating spider," a variety of large tarantula said to be the largest type of spider in the world. The specimen certainly was large, probably measuring at least six and a half inches across without the legs stretched. In the afternoon, I wandered around taking photos near Isla Ratón. I captured one of my all-time favorite photographs, which is a view of a tranquil stream showing the transparent, reddish water and a partial reflection.

Our group started on our return trip the next morning. The higher water in the river made the trip go swiftly.

We made a couple of stops along the way back, and one of them was to pay a visit to man named Aleksandrs Laime at his small plantation on the south side of the main river. Mr. Laime was obviously European, but he seemed to be something of a mystery to the locals. He greeted us wearing only a loincloth held in place by a makeshift belt and with rubber boots on his feet. The guides before and after our visit told us all sorts of stories about him, some of which were hard to believe. In any case, he had been living in the area for more than 40 years as one of the area's first European residents. He was something of a hermit, living in little more than a shack made from poles, but it seemed to have a new, sheet-metal roof. He had explored much of the region on foot, and I even believe he served as a

Different Lives in One

guide for a man named Phelps who wrote the most complete guide on Venezuelan birds. When I spoke to him about birds, however, he claimed that undescribed species still exist in the area, which Phelps never observed. I recently found Mr. Laime described on a Wikipedia page.

Despite its condition, Mr. Laime's home was full of books, tools, hardware, and natural history specimens. His books were in several languages, including English. He had created a colorful, printed map of the area showing landmarks, and I purchased a copy. He claimed that his plantation was built on an old native camp, and the place had powers that were slowly healing his bad eyesight. When he told me, I wasn't sure what to believe.

After our return to Canaima, I took a room at the hotel again for the night. The next morning, I arranged to fly in a single-engine plane with several men to the diamond mining areas across nearby Rio Caroní at a mining town called San Salvador de Paúl. The diamonds are removed from thick sand deposits left over the years by the river. The miners do this by pressure-washing the ground and pumping out the water and sand, leaving behind only gravel, which they sort by hand.

We landed on a dirt airstrip. I saw the men working in one pit before we moved on to the town. San Salvador de Paúl looked pretty rustic, consisting of wooden shacks with sheet-metal roofs. It reminded me of an old-west town from an American cowboy film.

We entered a brothel (too early in the day for anything interesting to be happening). It was basically a large bar with plenty of tables, but it had little rooms along the side so couples could pair-off. I met with a man there who sold diamonds. I wanted an uncut Venezuelan diamond as a collector's item. I ended up purchasing two small diamonds displaying good crystal form, but the quality of each example was rather poor. Even so, it was an interesting experience to be buying diamonds in a remote Venezuelan brothel. After we made our deal, the man showed me a ring holding a faceted, cobalt-blue diamond of at least a carat in size, which he claimed came from the area. I drew upon some of these experiences when writing my books of the Mezet Trilogy and *Return to Nowhere*.

The natives in the Canaima area are of the Pemón ethnic group. I mention this because of something I noticed when leaving the hotel.

At the front desk, a clerk sent a local Pemón bellhop to collect my suitcase from my room in order to take it to the airfield for my Avensa flight back to "civilization." I accompanied the man as he did what the clerk told him to do. He finally set my bag on a cart, which was to be rolled to the jet after it arrived. Then the man simply turned and began to head back toward the hotel office. I had to call for him to stop so I could give him a tip. It just impressed me that he wasn't expecting anything extra for doing the job he was already being paid to do. I can't remember any other location in Venezuela—or anywhere else in the world, for that matter—where a bellhop didn't expect to get a tip.

I left early in the afternoon and was back in Maracaibo by the same evening feeling tired but pretty content with such an adventurous journey. During the trip, I also observed 16 species of birds that were new to me, along with a pretty, blue and yellow, venomous frog of the "poison dart" variety.

Stuck in the Middle of Nowhere

Along with a small group of adventurers (not the two Jorges or Jesús this time), I took a trip in August of 1984 to the Gran Sabana area of southeastern Venezuela. It was a trip full of interesting sights, but one part stands out in particular.

We had rented a Jeep for the trip, and we decided to drive from Kavanayen—one of the Catholic missions in the area where we were staying for the night—to a waterfall called Karuai Merú. It was reported to be a pretty location. A priest at the mission gave us instructions, so we set out early in the morning. We expected the trip to take only half a day.

We traveled through desolate country. Most of the terrain is covered with short grass with the only trees growing in valleys or canyons. When we had been on the trail for a couple of hours, we reached a spot where the dirt road divided. One branch took off toward the left along a low ridge, while the other went straight through a shallow depression. They both appeared to have had the same amount of traffic, so we drove straight.

All at once, the Jeep got stuck in some mud in the center of the depression. It only appeared to be a small patch, but we worked on trying to free the wheels for six hours without success. We tried all the tricks we could imagine such as placing cut up branches or rocks under the tires, but nothing worked. The vehicle remained stuck. We were on a little-traveled trail about fifteen miles from the mission by then, and we were just about to decide we needed to walk back to get help when we heard a noise. It was a helicopter.

We all started waving, and after a moment, someone in the craft spotted us. The helicopter circled once, and then it landed not far from the Jeep. The men worked for one of the large Venezuelan national corporations responsible for the massive hydroelectric installation near Ciudad Guayana. They tried to pull us out, too, but the Jeep still wouldn't budge.

However, they said they would fly to the mission and send someone with another vehicle to help pull us out. Sure enough, a truck from the mission arrived a little before dark, and several people had us out within five minutes with the help of a long piece of rope.

After I paid our rescuers a good tip, we quickly backtracked and continued along the high trail to the waterfall, which by then was only about two miles away. Then we returned to the mission by about 9:00 PM, making sure to take the high road again on the way back. I've never seen mud quite as sticky.

Different People

As I thought about some of the places I visited beyond work hours, I recall other trips to La Mesa and to Merida in the Venezuelan Andes. I've already described the part La Mesa played in my first three novels, but I also remember something quite minor, which left an impression.

While out sight-seeing, my companions and I sometimes stopped at a restaurant along the highway near Timotes, in Merida State, as the road began to climb the taller mountains. The place sat on a rise above the road, and it had its own parking lot. It was just about the only restaurant of any size in the area. Even so, it wasn't especially large. Although it had a limited menu, the food always tasted good, making it a regular stop.

On one stop early in 1984, a tall, thin waiter brought the menu, took the order, and served the food. For some reason, I noted him; I don't really know why.

In August of 1984, my company sent me back to Dallas. I worked there most workdays. I took company trips to London (twice) and to Bahrain with a stop in Spain—as well as several vacations to various parts of Texas, Oklahoma, New Mexico, and Colorado.

In 1987, my company sent me back to Venezuela, and some months after I arrived, I took another weekend trip to the mountains, stopping once again at the same restaurant. I saw the same, thin waiter. He gave me a menu, he took my order, and he served my food. But all of a sudden, I turned philosophical.

About three years had gone by since I last saw the man. There he was, working at the same job, doing exactly the same thing (which was nothing wrong). It was only I had done lots of different things during that same time period. I had performed complex laboratory tests on core samples, some of which exploded. I had traveled to all sorts of places. I had bought and sold a house and a car.

Why didn't I ask him how he did it?

On the other hand, I felt something similar once when I recognized a national security officer (DISIP or National Directorate of Intelligence and Prevention Services) in the airport in Maturin, Venezuela, during a company trip. He was an older fellow wearing the typical black uniform of his organization, and he was probably approaching retirement age at the time. His job was to hand-check luggage in search of drugs, weapons, or anything else a person wasn't supposed to take on a plane. (The Maturin airport was pretty small; it didn't have X-ray scanners or large, walk-through metal detectors at the time.) The officer carried a large, chrome-plated revolver, probably a .357 Magnum. I recalled seeing him doing the same thing (and carrying the same firearm) while gathering impressions at the same airport years earlier during my first visit. In his case, however, I had a different notion.

As an older guy involved in security at an airport, I wondered if he might have a lot of interesting stories to tell. And before he worked at that particular airport, what did he do? Had he possibly been in the military? What was his training in national security like? Had he worked in other locations, Caracas for instance? Why didn't I ask him?

And why am I describing these two men at all? These are just some of my impressions collected along the way. Isn't this part of what writing memoirs is all about?

While these two men had probably done well for themselves, making a living doing the same jobs day after day, I simply wondered if I would be able to work jobs like theirs for years without going crazy. Sure, people do it all the time most everywhere in the world, but I don't know if I could do it. Maybe this is partly the reason I became a writer. Whenever things turned routine, I made my escape to other worlds through books. And still later through my writing, I escaped into my own other worlds populated by familiar characters—all of which I created.

It is sometimes interesting to look closer at people you meet on your journey through life. Be friendly and try to get to know them. Although I didn't do this with either of these people, I've sometimes regretted the missed opportunity. I might have learned something new.

In both cases, however, I've designed book characters with these two men in mind. Of course, my characters are products of my imagination, but some of my books include people who are waiters (or waitresses), security guards (or police officers), and people in other occupations a person might encounter every day. In my opinion, their points of view make stories more complete.

Revolts

I lived in Venezuela during two attempts at armed rebellion. The first occurred on February 4, 1992, when Hugo Chavez tried to take over the government. The second happened on November 27 of the same year when a group of generals tried to do the same thing. Both were attempting to get rid of then-president Carlos Andres Perez, whom they believed to be corrupt.

When I drove to work on the morning of February 4, 1992, I found the streets rather empty, but I normally took back routes part of the way, so I didn't think much of it. When I arrived, some of my co-workers had heard the news. A lot of them had remained home. The person normally in charge of the office at the time (another American from the US) lived in an apartment building near a military base close to the University of Zulia, and he preferred not to leave his building because of the gunfire taking place at the base. (And I don't blame him one bit.) This left me in charge for the moment, so I told the workers who showed up to simply remain at the office until we knew it was safe to leave.

The company had a television in the conference room, so most of us simply sat and watched the events as the unfolded. During one moment, we stood in front of the company office and watched tanks roll by. The rebellion was quashed before the end of the day, and I sent everyone home. Even so, a lot of people were killed that day throughout Venezuela.

The revolt on November 27 was much like the first, only I noticed less military activity in Maracaibo. Once again I learned what was happening from co-workers after I reached the company office because I saw little indication of anything wrong on the streets. Again, we turned on the TV and watched. That time as someone changed channels, I saw the rebels on one channel claiming they were in control of the government. On the next channel, Carlos Andres Perez (appearing rather haggard) urged soldiers loyal to him to continue fighting. On a third station, I saw a cartoon from *The Super Mario Bros. Super Show!*

The main difference the second time was I was dating Belkis. She worked in another company's office adjoining the company where I worked, and when we left that day, I drove her all the way across town to make sure she made it home safely.

Looking back now, I find it ironic that Hugo Chavez was later pardoned for his crimes, and still later, he was elected president. And then after he got what he wanted, which was full control of the government, he made a complete mess of things.

Musical Concerts: "I was there!"

As I began to organize the chapters and smaller sections, I came across the part about musical concerts, and there didn't seem to be any good place to include it. Even so, music has played an important part of my various lives, so I must place it somewhere.

From a young age, I've always liked music. As I've already stated, my mother introduced me to classical music at an early age, but I've grown to like lots of musical genres, musical artists, and songs over the years. In McDaniel Junior High and at Denison High School, I played cornet in both their bands.

Different Lives in One

The first rock concert I attended took place in Denison as part of the Community Concert program. It happened sometime in the late 1960s, and I'm a little fuzzy on the name of the group, but I think it was The Box Tops, a group with a Top-40s Hit about this time. For a first concert, I suppose it wasn't bad, but I don't recall being impressed enough to run out to buy an album. A local Community Concert series over several years brought to the Denison area such famous names as Pete Fountain (jazz clarinet), Louis Armstrong (jazz and pop vocalist, and trumpet), and Al Hurt (jazz and pop trumpet). I remember seeing all three of these performers during different years, but I just barely remember the events after so long.

The first really big name in pop or rock I saw was Elton John. At the time, he had just grown to be popular worldwide, and he came to the Cotton Bowl in Dallas on August 18, 1973. If I remember correctly, the ticket cost $6.50. He was promoting his soon-to-be-released album, *Goodbye Yellow Brick Road*.

I felt quite impressed by the event. A group came on stage to play before the main event. The announcer said they were Elton's invited guests for the opening. It seemed to me they had a strange name, and years later, I could have sworn it sounded like "Queen." The now-legendary British rock group hadn't become popular at that date. Queen hadn't even released their first album by then. However, I've never been able to confirm if the group I saw was actually Queen or some other group. All I can recall about them is they weren't especially impressive. If it was the same group, they soon became much better than what I heard.

The second, introductory group was Steely Dan. After they played, I felt I hadn't wasted my money even before the appearance of the main attraction. They put on a great show with some music I had heard and much I hadn't. One song that still stands out is "Las Vegas."

Then the main event started. Elton John began to perform, and after about the second song, I started to feel a little disappointed. I don't know what it was, but I think he sang a song I already knew, and it didn't sound like I was accustomed to hearing it. I started to think, *At least Steely Dan sounded good.*

However, by about the third song of his program, I started to change my mind. To me, the performance sounded better and better the more Elton and his group played. It was the first time I heard songs that later became some of my favorites as soon as his new album came out, and I still like a lot of them. In particular, I remember the way "Funeral for a Friend" sounded with the ghostly bell at the beginning, and as Elton waited to start playing this number, his piano reminded me of a coffin with his head sticking out of it from the angle where I watched. "Bennie and the Jets" also stands out. When he announced "Saturday Night's All Right for Fighting," Elton said (and I probably paraphrase slightly), "I don't know if we've done this one on a Saturday night before." It really set off the crowd, but surely he exaggerated; the band had probably performed it a number of times on Saturday nights before reaching the Cotton Bowl.

As I left the concert, a hawker sold souvenir picture books of Elton, Bernie Taupin (Elton John's lyricist at the time), and the other musicians of the group, and I spent the last dollar in my pocket to buy one. I still have it.

My next big concert was in Fort Worth to see the Moody Blues. They've always been among my all-time, favorite groups, and I saw them at the Tarrant County Convention Center on November 3, 1973. They seemed to materialize on stage as if out of a cloud while playing "Higher and Higher," which looked pretty awesome from where I sat. I've often heard that live concerts rarely sound as good as the performers do in a studio or on an album, but I heard the group perform songs sounding much like they do on a recording. I felt pretty impressed. I especially enjoyed hearing Mike Pinder's Mellotron live.

About the only thing I didn't like about the concert was the fact that as soon as the lights went down, the auditorium filled with cannabis smoke. When the concert ended, a couple sitting on my right were so stoned out of their minds they didn't respond when those around them stood to leave. I had to climb over a seat to get to a row further down to reach the nearest aisle. I thought, *Why pay good money to come to a concert and hear a band like the Moody Blues if you're not going to listen?* They could have stayed home if all they wanted to do was get stoned. I left the convention center with a headache due to the smoke, and it felt good to breathe fresh air again.

During the late seventies, Six Flags amusement park in Arlington, Texas, held small, nighttime concerts to boost attendance. I saw Helen Reddy perform at one, and she did a great show. I saw the band Blood, Sweat, and Tears on another evening, and they sounded as good live as their recordings. I only thought it looked sad when during the final number for the band some of the audience was already leaving a one-of-a-kind, live performance to head to some other park attraction a person could see any time.

While living in Maracaibo, I took Belkis to see an outdoor Gloria Estefan concert held at a baseball stadium in March of 1992. It was Gloria's *Into the Light World Tour*, which she created following her recovery from a traffic accident that nearly killed her. The entire concert sounded excellent. We enjoyed hearing a number of favorite songs live, including "Here We Are."

One thing that impressed me most about this concert was the security measures. During the last part of the final encore while the musicians continued to play, I observed an SUV leaving the back of the stadium. Her security team had ushered her away before most of the crowd knew she was gone. No one bothered to announce, "Gloria has left the building."

Some Final Thoughts on Travel and People

I've actually stood in 14 countries so far, and I've looked down upon many more from the seats of aircraft. In addition, I've met or corresponded with people from dozens of other places. If there's one thing I've noticed, it's this; people everywhere are much the same. They hold the same values and want the same things. Sure, I've also encountered a few pickpockets, swindlers, and some outright thieves along the way, but most people want to be friendly and helpful if they find you're friendly toward them at the same time, regardless of if it's in Madrid, Manhattan, or Merida.

John M. Moody

My Life Among Weapons

If it Goes Boom, I'm Interested.

From a young age, I've been interested in weapons of all sorts, especially firearms, artillery, and aircraft bombs. The following stories are mostly weapon-related in one way or another.

Big Guns

Probably because of my father, I have been interested in artillery most of my life. I recall as one of my early memories the family vacation to Gulfport and Biloxi, Mississippi, which I previously mentioned. I was about three or four years old. We took a tour boat to Ship Island and to Ft. Massachusetts located on its eastern end facing the ship channel. I saw my first, very large cannon there, which I much later learned is a post-Civil War, 15 Inch Rodman (firing a cannon ball 15 inches in diameter). A group of young people were climbing and sitting on its massive barrel, and I wanted to go climb on it, too, but my parents wouldn't let me. I was wearing shorts, and they explained that the barrel sitting under the sun (and painted black) was simply too hot. At least that was what they told me to keep me off.

As a youth, our family vacations were usually trips from Denison, Texas, to Columbus, Mississippi, where my parent's families still lived. On the way, we usually passed through Greenwood, Mississippi, where a small, Civil War cannon sat in a park along the side of the highway. It rested on a cement slab facing a river. At some time after I first began to pay attention to it, I understand that someone stole this artillery piece, but it was later recovered. It was always a high point for me to see it as we passed swiftly by.

Later in life when we weren't in so much of a hurry, we used to stop so I could examine the Greenwood cannon up close. As a young teen, my parents started to let me take photos of any cannon we passed. By high school, I had amassed quite a collection of color slides showing cannon and other military weapons.

When I was around 11 years old, my mother drove my sisters and me to Saltillo, Mexico. Along the way, we stopped for breakfast at a café in Laredo. A building on the property had on display in a window a used brass fuze from the top of an artillery shell. I asked a waitress if I could buy it, and she sold it to me for $2.50. During the same trip, I spotted an artillery shell in pretty good condition that was on display in the window of a pharmacy in Saltillo. With someone's help, I asked if they would sell it. They agreed. I paid $20, which at the time was a small fortune for someone of my age, but I had started to mow lawns by then. These were about the earliest items in my collection, and I later found that both of them date to around 1911. I feel lucky to still have them.

As a teenager, I felt quite impressed when we once made a stop at Ft. Sill, Oklahoma, to visit the military base. They had a nice museum with plenty of artillery-related items inside, and it gave me a chance to observe more types of cannon than I had ever seen up to then along its "Cannon Walk." I took pictures of many at the time.

One of my favorite cannon models was the "disappearing gun." These are cannon once used as coastal guns near most major harbors and ports in the United States. During the visit to Fort Sill, I saw a beautifully-machined scale model of one of these in a display case, and I didn't know if any of them still existed. Then many years later I took a trip to Fort Pickens, Battery Cooper, near Pensacola, Florida. I finally got to see a smaller example, and I thought it looked great.

On one trip, our family passed through Vicksburg, Mississippi, to see the national battlefield park, but I was too young to remember much about it. Later, when Belkis, Mary Ann, and I were in the same area, we returned to Vicksburg so we could all see it, and I felt pretty impressed. I ended up taking a lot of photos there, too. Unfortunately, Mary Ann was too young to remember much about it. Someday maybe she'll return to see the park again as I did,

I sometimes found cannon in unusual places, but whenever I had a chance, I stopped to examine and photograph them. I stumbled across a number of interesting examples of artillery pieces in Colorado when I attended college there for a semester.

After I returned to live in Denison after a long time away, I visited Sherman, Texas, ten miles to the south to photograph a small, 70mm Japanese gun on the courthouse lawn. Oddly, this gun sat in the same spot for years. I used to see it when my family drove through Sherman on the way to points further south. Even so, I never had a chance to see up close until the last few years.

Still later, my friend Keith told me about a French (US) 75mm gun from World War I that sits in front of a VFW post in northern Sherman. I was especially pleased to learn about this one because my main interests at the time revolved around the developments of artillery during the time period from the American Civil War through World War I.

I later became more interested in collecting artillery shells and related items, so each time I found one at an antique store or at a garage sale for a reasonable price, I usually bought it if I could afford it (and as long as it didn't cost too much). Over the years, I learned quite a lot about military ordnance in general, and I've used this knowledge in stories on occasion. In my first romantic mystery novel, *Brass Puzzle*, the female protagonist's father collected inert artillery shells and related items. This plays a small—although important—part of the story. In fact, the puzzle referred to in the title was made from a brass, 105mm howitzer case, and I used the proportions of an actual shell case to accurately describe the dimensions of the puzzle pieces. Later in the story while the principal protagonists are searching for clues, one of the "hints" is artillery related. In a later story, I describe how another main character takes shelter in a stone tower while terrorists shoot rocket-propelled grenades at him.

I'm still interested in items of this type, and I've connected with other men through the internet over the years who share similar interests. I've used items from my collection for historical displays at local events, such as during Civil War Days at Frontier Village in Denison.

Long Shot

As a teenager, I was a member of a local gun club for a few years. I used to go with friends to shoot guns at a range a few miles east of Denison. I learned a lot about firearms during this time because a couple of friends were serious enthusiasts.

The club leased enough land to have a "trap range" for shotguns where people could shoot at flying clay pigeons, but they also had a rifle range. It measured about a hundred yards long and had a dirt back-stop. Further away behind the backstop, the forested land was generally empty of people for miles as it sloped northward toward the Red River. Normally, if someone shot too high and didn't hit the dirt backstop, the bullet hit the oak trees behind it.

One Saturday I was with a friend shooting a variety of guns at targets. One gun in particular was a post-World War II Spanish 8mm Mauser. I had just seen a show on television where a man carried a similar high-powered rifle with one hand as if like a pistol, ready to shoot it while he carried something in his other hand. I spoke about the show with one of my friends, wondering if it was possible to fire a rifle in such a manner without the gun's recoil being too much to control. My friend said, "We should try it." (When he said "we," he meant "you.") I loaded the chamber with a cartridge and took it in my right hand, just like the actor on the television show had done. Then I raised my left arm in front of me to block the gun in case it rose toward my face. I pointed it downrange and pulled the trigger.

The gun fired, and it didn't rise or "kick" badly at all. The only problem was when I fired the rifle, the muzzle pointed too high. The bullet left the barrel traveling over the backstop and over the trees, alike. We heard the high-velocity bullet's crackling echoing as it traveled across hills and valleys for miles while breaking the sound barrier.

I didn't try any tricks like that again. It was a chilling sound, and I thought of this incident many times while writing, especially when working on *Brass Puzzle, Wherever the Wind Will Take Us,* and *Land on the Verge of Darkness.*

A lot of my memories relate to this shooting range, and I'll describe a few more.

John M. Moody

Exploding Gun

I once went to the gun range with a friend who owned a .22 rifle that worked through a pump action similar to some shotguns. This rifle had a tubular magazine under the barrel that held eight or ten shots. I can no longer remember much about it now, but it might have been a Harrington & Richards. I mostly remember the gun being pretty old. He said it once belonged to his grandfather.

My friend loaded it up and let me fire it. I sat on a wooden shooting bench and took aim downrange. I fired the gun and pumped in another round. Then I fired again and did the same thing.

On about the third shot, I pulled the trigger, but at first I thought nothing happened until I realized something had struck me in the forehead. I didn't hear the gun go off, but I soon discovered I couldn't hear. My friend came over to me appearing rather concerned, but as I watched his mouth move, I couldn't hear his words for a short while. Then all at once a loud ringing began to grow in my ears. I had what is known as "telephone ears." This is a condition that occurs when the ears are recovering from a sudden, loud noise.

The cartridge had exploded toward my face. The entire base of the shell case separated from the rest, and a small piece of brass hit me in the forehead hard enough to break the skin and embed itself there. (I dug it out in front of a mirror after I returned home in the evening.) The tubular part of the cartridge case remained stuck in the chamber of the rifle, and if I remember correctly, the lead bullet was lodged somewhere down the barrel.

Other than the nick in my forehead, I suffered no ill effects. My hearing returned completely within only a few minutes after the ringing subsided. I'm only glad I was aiming the rifle downrange at the time. If my head had been a little higher, the piece of brass might have hit me in the eye.

I used some of this experience in *Journey from Mezet* when the main character—Marc—has an experience with a sudden, loud noise.

More Old Guns that Weren't Really Old

Both Keith and one of my other friends named Pat enjoyed shooting "cap and ball" revolvers. They were modern reproductions of guns used either during the Civil War or by gunfighters in the old west before cartridge weapons became more common. We fired these types of guns at the gun range at times or much later, on a local farm.

It was messy work to load and clean the guns, so I never took much of an interest. Also, I thought of them as somewhat dangerous. The cylinders of these revolvers often held six shots, one for each chamber. To load a chamber, the shooter had to measure out a certain amount of black powder and pour it into the bottom. Then a spherical, lead bullet of the proper diameter is pressed on top of the powder using a special part of the revolver, itself. Pat usually loaded grease into the top of the cylinder over the bullets because he said it might be possible for the flame from one shot to ignite the powder of one or all of the other cylinders if nothing is in the way to block it, such as the grease.

The "cap" refers to a percussion cap. It is a small, copper igniter that is placed at the rear of the chamber. The gun's hammer hits this cap to set off the powder, and when the gun is fired, loads of white smoke follow the bullet out the barrel with a loud roar. Loading a gun such as this is not a rapid process, and I understand that some of the old-time gunfighters carried extra loaded cylinders to change out in case of emergency.

Luckily, we never had a gun explode in our hands, but occasionally Pat's revolver was unreliable. Either a percussion cap was bad, or the tiny opening into the chamber was blocked. It's rather unnerving to aim a pistol and pull the trigger to have nothing happen.

Along those same lines, we sometimes met other shooters at the gun range, and it was a common practice to "trade shots." In this way I got to fire all sorts of guns I might have never had a chance to shoot. Once I fired a .444 Marlin, which was about the highest powered high-powered rifle I ever had a chance to fire. It had quite a kick, and as a younger man, my body mass at 140 pounds wasn't large enough to absorb all the recoil without it giving me a slight bruise on the shoulder.

On another occasion, a man brought a flintlock pistol he was in the process of building. He had the gun put together, but he hadn't done any finishing to the wood. He asked if I would like to fire it, and I thought it would be an interesting experience. These guns are usually single-shot affairs, and if I'm not mistaken, his used a .60 caliber lead ball. (For anyone who doesn't know much about guns, this means the bullet measures *more* than half an inch in diameter. As guns go, this is rather large by today's standards.) To set off the black powder in the gun's chamber after it is loaded, a small quantity of black powder is placed in a "pan" next to a small hole leading into the chamber. To set off the powder in the pan, the gun's hammer holds a piece of flint, which makes sparks as the hammer falls after the trigger is pulled. This system was "state of the art" about 300 years ago.

The man loaded it for me, and told me how to stand when firing it. He explained that a person should position his body parallel to the line of fire for there to be less chance of serious injury in case something goes wrong. This was news to me, but I didn't "chicken out."

When I pulled the trigger, the hammer fell and made sparks. This set off the powder in the pan with a flash of smoke in front of my face. Then I guess I waited a full second before the flame reached the black powder in the chamber, finally firing the gun with still more billowing smoke. It had a pretty large kick, but the delay after pulling the trigger while waiting for the gun to fire wasn't pleasant. I did it once and can describe it to my readers, but once is enough.

We're Hunting Watermelon Today

During my visits to the shooting range, we tried shooting at a variety of targets over the years. I had always heard that shooting a watermelon with a high-powered rifle could be interesting, but I had never seen it done.

One day a couple of friends and I decided to give it a try. It was during the summer. We went to a grocery store and purchased the largest watermelon we could find. It was of the round variety and measured about 18 inches in diameter.

I believe we used a 7mm Mauser. We usually fired cheap, old, military ammunition with solid, copper-jacketed bullets, we brought along a single round of soft-point, hunting ammunition. One of us bought it for five cents in a pawn shop on Main Street in Denison.

No one else was at the gun range that day. We set the watermelon on a stand in an elevated position, with the dirt backstop behind it. The others wanted me to take the shot. I loaded the rifle, aimed, and fired from about 20 feet away.

The watermelon disappeared in a cloud of pink, watermelon vapor. Then pieces began to rain down all around me. Except for the melon's base, still rested on the stand, the largest piece was about the size of my hand. We cleaned up most of it before we left that day, but afterward, the local fauna probably enjoyed a real treat.

Confrontation on Main Street

An old building housing a used furniture store once sat on the southeast corner of Main Street and Tone Avenue in Denison. This was cattycornered to a convenience store I used to frequent. The old building was torn down years ago to leave only a vacant lot. At night, especially during the warm, summer months when I wasn't in school, I often walked around—sometimes with friends and sometimes alone.

On one night, I just happened to be passing in front of the furniture store heading east toward downtown when I noticed a car parked in front of the store. An older teenager was doing something near the open trunk of a car, and as I passed, I spoke to him. I might have asked if he was having car trouble. I feel sure that whatever I said wasn't spiteful or unkind or taunting; this simply wasn't the sort of thing I would have done because I'm not that sort of person and wasn't back then, either.

For some reason, he took what I said the wrong way. He pulled a rifle out of his trunk and pointed it at me—right there on Main Street. Then he threatened me with it, telling me if I didn't move on, he would shoot me. It was fairly dark at the time, and the traffic was practically non-existent. And I was alone.

I felt more surprised than afraid. Even then I knew that if a person merely pointed a gun at someone in a threatening way, it was considered assault with a deadly weapon. Even a hand in a pocket that might be a gun accompanied by a threat carries the same charge. If a perpetrator happened to be caught and convicted, he or she could be put in prison for as much as two years. I learned this by being associated with friends who knew about guns.

John M. Moody

This is not to say I wasn't afraid. I had already been shooting guns for a number of years by then, so I knew what a bullet could do to a person. After all, I once shot a watermelon.

For some strange reason, however, I didn't want to let the guy know I felt threatened. I viewed him as a bully, and I hated it when bullies picked on kids they saw as weaker. At the time, I felt that showing fear would be worse than not doing it. I could have been making a bad mistake, but I chose to hide my emotions.

I recognized the rifle as a .22 caliber bolt action. I stood my ground and remarked in a friendly manner, "Oh, I see you've got a .22."

He stared at me for a moment, but when I didn't move, he simple lowered the gun and returned it to his trunk. I then turned and walked away, hoping he wouldn't pick it up again and shoot me in the back. He didn't, and I looked back a moment later to see him getting into the car. He drove past me, but I don't think he saw me because of some trees.

The incident has remained among my memories. I found out I might not only be braver, but stupider than I previously imagined.

Being on the Receiving End

True soldiers who have faced combat or policemen who have faced gunmen in shoot-outs probably view my little stories as minor incidents, but they seemed pretty serious to me at the time—serious enough to include them.

While on a field trip with the Texoma Rockhounds, I recall a time when a large group of us were traveling together on the way to hunt for early Native American artifacts around Stillwell, Oklahoma. (I've described this area in more detail in other parts of this book). Someone decided to investigate a plowed field along the way. It sat just southeast of a major river bridge near Webber's Falls. The field wasn't fenced, and it didn't have any crops in it at the time. I believe I was about 12 years old.

All the cars pulled off along a side road, and everyone left their vehicles to see if the field showed any traces of early artifacts. We had all moved off to couple of hundred yards away from the vehicles when all of a sudden I heard a strange noise. It sounded like a loud pop followed by a buzz that changed pitch, abruptly ending somewhere nearby. Then I heard the same thing again. Finally, someone figured out that a person near a pickup truck had pulled off the road, left his cab, and was shooting at us. The noise was from the discharge of a low-powered firearm (perhaps a pistol of some kind) being fired at long range, and the bullets were striking the ground only a few feet from where we walked.

I recall being afraid after someone told us what was happening, but I also remember I didn't panic. I stayed with one of my sisters as we moved out of the field toward one side. In the meantime, the person simply got back in his truck and drove away. He was apparently doing it just to have fun. It wasn't much fun for the rest of us.

I've also drawn upon this experience in some of my writing.

The Thompson SMG

Ever since I was pretty little, I've been interested in machine guns—as young boys who grew up as I did usually were. I played "army," and my pretend weapon of choice was often an automatic weapon. Even so, I might have taken my interest further than most people as I grew older. I was most interested in the Thompson sub-machine gun, the famous "gangster gun."

Whenever I saw a picture of a Thompson in a book or magazine, I always stared at it for a long time. In the barber shop in downtown Denison where my parents sent me to get my hair cut, I used to look for a specific copy of a hunting magazine that never seemed to get thrown away. It showed an advertisement where a gun dealership sold deactivated Thompsons for $99. As a young boy, however, the amount was a small fortune. Even so, I began to collect Thompson information and photos wherever I found them. I usually discovered the photos in old magazines, and I recall finding a photo of a masked Irish Republican Army soldier holding a Thompson. The memory of this photo helped to inspire my plot for *Many Shades of Green*. The action for about half this book is set in Ireland and involves revenge dating back to "The Troubles."

I soon learned that the gun came in different models. One was the kind they often showed in old gangster movies. The other was the kind I saw in movies depicting World War II.

While I was still in high school, someone published a history of the Thompson and its development, and I saved up enough money to buy a copy.

As I wrote earlier, I did a good bit of wood carving while growing up. I eventually carved my first, full-sized Thompson, which I painted to look superficially like a real one from far away. Encouraged by this, I carved others until my models looked much like real guns up close. My best wooden Thompson was good enough to fool law enforcement, as one of my later tales will illustrate.

One day while waiting for a class to begin at Grayson County College, I stood at the front of the classroom, idly drawing a picture of a Thompson on the blackboard. Another student named Keith (the one I mention several times earlier) just happened to be passing and spotted it. He entered the room and asked me about it. I told him I was interested in these guns, and Keith said he was, too. We arranged to meet later and compare notes. This started a friendship that has lasted for 45 years. Looking back, this was another of those serendipity moments in my life.

Keith studied art, but he enjoyed a lot of other interests besides guns. He is what I would consider to be an expert on gangsters and gangster movies. He also has an amazing ability to watch a movie and catch mistakes, such as the types of weapons or other props used in films that were from incorrect time periods. He should have had a job in the movie industry as a prop master because he would have been good at it. He's also a great artist, and I will speak of this later.

When Keith learned I carved Thompsons out of wood, he immediately said he would pay me to make a couple of them. I carved one gangster gun and one WWII gun for him, and we even bought authentic wooden parts to make the guns appear more realistic.

Keith was working on a gangster movie to be filmed in Super-8mm. He needed weapons, and my wooden Thompsons exactly fit the bill. He worked with my example and his to have two of them for some scenes. He worked on his film for a couple of years and finally finished it. I thought his finished product looked great.

I eventually moved away for years at a time, but Keith faithfully kept in contact, often sending me news about these guns and many other subjects, as well as some of his activities. He soon became a gangster reenactor, and a group of like-minded people joined him. For a while, they used the wooden gun I carved, but he eventually saved up enough money to buy a registered, legal, fully-functioning Model 1921 Thompson. He soon converted it to fire blank cartridges, and the group's shows were extremely popular at certain town festivals. I watched them do a show in downtown Denison once in front of the Hotel Denison, and the crowd easily numbered 500 people. They performed at a Bonny and Clyde festival in Louisiana several years in a row, and they reenacted the final ambush of these two criminals at the actual location where it took place.

I once returned from Venezuela on vacation not long after he bought his sub-machine gun, and he took me out to a farm to fire it. He loaded up a fifty-shot drum magazine and told me to "empty it," which I did with pleasure. It was like a dream come true to finally be able to fire one of these guns after studying them for so many years.

Keith took a favorite photo of me with his gun. It shows me looking along the sights while firing it. The camera captured three ejected cartridge cases suspended in mid-air next to the gun, showing I was firing it fully automatic.

After a number of years, Keith ended up selling his Thompson. While it had been expensive to buy, by the time he sold it years later, the price for one of these guns had increased exponentially. It ended up as a good investment.

The Oklahoma Highway Patrol Story

Years ago, the Denison Police Department used to routinely send patrol cars to park across the street from the house where I grew up to watch for people running red traffic signals up the street. One day during my later high school years when I was manufacturing wooden guns, I pulled up in my car in front of my house. I had my best model of a Thompson sub-machine gun wrapped in a blanket on the back seat of my old, green 1955 Chevy. A police car sat a few feet away. The officer behind the wheel appeared rather bored, so I decided to show him my handiwork—only I knew better than to simply pull it out. I decided to warn him first.

I stepped across the street and said to the officer, "Hello. I made a gun. Would you like to see it? It's in my car."

He later said he thought I might have made a zip-gun and worried he might have to confiscate it. He responded, "Maybe you'd better leave it there, and I'll walk over to take a look at it." I led him to my car, and when I opened the blanket and showed him, he seemed truly impressed. He picked it up and began to examine it enthusiastically.

We talked about it while still standing in front of my house, and I eventually asked him if carrying it around would get me into any trouble. He explained that as long as I didn't point it at anyone or use it to threaten anyone, it wasn't illegal to carry in my car.

A couple of years later, I got my summer job working for the Katy Railroad. One Sunday afternoon in July when I was returning to my job after a weekend, I set my wooden Thompson in the shelf just inside the back window of my car. I wanted to show it off. Then I left home, heading for Tulsa.

About two-thirds of the way into my journey, I passed a mobile unit of the Oklahoma Highway Patrol. Two officers had pulled over a speeder. I rolled right past them, doing the speed limit (I always drove within limits.)

Only a moment later the same patrol car was on my tail with its lights flashing. I calmly put on my turn signal and pulled onto the shoulder. While one of the officers remained near the rear of my car (my green, 1955 Chevy again), the other officer stepped up to my open window. (I kept my hands on the steering wheel the entire time.)

As he approached, I said, "Oh, I guess you noticed my gun. Would you like to see it?"

He responded in a no-nonsense manner, "Just step out of the car. I'll get it."

I did as he ordered, and stepped to the rear of the car to watch. As he lifted my wooden Thompson, I saw the look of relief on his face when he discovered how light it weighed.

He removed the gun to show his fellow officer. Then he reprimanded me for a moment, saying it was dangerous for me to be driving around with the gun on display. He said, "You never know how many people in '55 Chevys might have just robbed a bank. You might find someone who'll shoot first without asking next time."

I then told them what the policeman in Denison said about carrying it in my car as long as I didn't point it at anyone.

One of the officers appeared thoughtful for a moment, and then he told me, "Well, yes, he's right. Even so, it's not a good idea." I agreed not to do it anymore.

Then they started asking me questions about it. I told them I sometimes carved them to sell, and they thought I had done a pretty good job—good enough to fool them for a while, at least. They eventually let me hold my model while we talked as we stood on the shoulder between the two vehicles for a few more minutes. I held it by the rear grip with the buttstock resting on my hip so the gun pointed skyward—just like I might have held an actual "Tommy Gun." At the time, I wore jeans and a black turtleneck. I imagine people on the busy highway traveling past might have believed I was an undercover officer.

After a few more minutes, they let me go, and I never displayed my Thompson in the back window of my car again.

Jeep-Jacking

I've earlier described my two good friends in Venezuela who were both named Jorge. While I lived in Venezuela the second time during a period of about three years, Jorge, the naturalist, bought a bright yellow Jeep.

The three of us took a trip into the northern Perijá Mountains. We traveled along the lower Rio Socuy, and at one stop, we took the time to shoot a 9mm Beretta automatic pistol—a weapon Jorge with the Jeep carried for protection. (Some parts of Venezuela could be dangerous, and 4-wheel-drive vehicles were often targeted for carjacking by local gangs. As a businessman, Jorge also carried cash on occasion. For these reasons, my friend carried a gun. He had the proper papers, making it perfectly legal.)

We were on our way back to Maracaibo. We needed to stop for gasoline. It was a Sunday afternoon, and the first place we found open was in a town some distance northwest of Maracaibo. When I looked, I noticed the town was called Los Cuatro Bocas (The Four Mouths).

Who can say why it ended up with such a name? When my friends noticed where we were, they became wary. They told me the town didn't have a good reputation when it came to security.

I sat in the back of the Jeep with the equipment we carried. The gas station had a lot of people milling about. As someone pumped gas for us, I listened to my two friends in the front as they watched a group of men toward one side. Then Jorge, the geologist, promptly said, "They're coming toward us." My friends felt certain the men were going to try to steal the Jeep.

Jorge, the naturalist, told me, "John, hand me the pistol."

Feeling a good deal of concern, I reached into his pack and extracted the Beretta, handing it to him over the seat. He pulled back the slide and loaded a cartridge into the chamber.

Just then, the man pumping gas finished and told my friend how much to pay. Jorge paid and didn't wait for his change. Jorge immediately started the Jeep. Just as the group of men reached the passenger's side window, Jorge quickly drove away. We all felt relieved.

A few months later, I traveled with Jorge the naturalist in the same Jeep to another location in the desert on the east side of Lake Maracaibo. That time his wife decided to go with us. During the trip, she dug up a small, live cactus from the side of a dirt road to take home. After the trip, they dropped me off at my place and headed for home. It was already dark by then.

The couple lived in a nice apartment complex on the eastern side of Maracaibo. The parking lot had a fence with a gate, and the gate usually remained locked throughout the night. That night, however, someone had left the gate open.

As soon as Jorge pulled into his parking space and turned off the Jeep's engine, a man pointing a gun appeared as if out of nowhere beside his window. He ordered them to get out.

While Jorge complied with the gunman's demands, his wife said to the stranger, "Please, sir, allow me to get my cactus."

While the gunman held my friend at gunpoint, Jorge's wife calmly reached over the activated an anti-theft device on the floor of the Jeep as she picked up her plant. Then she also stepped out onto the parking lot, cactus in hand.

The gunman entered the Jeep and started it. Then he quickly drove away. The anti-theft device was of a kind that allowed the Jeep to travel about a block before the flow of gas to the engine was cut off. The Jeep soon stalled. The gunman got out and ran away. Jorge got his Jeep back.

John M. Moody

My Life as a Fossil Hunter

Plus Some Other Details

Early Years

As a child, I was interested in fossils, as most children are even these days. When we lived in Denison after moving up from Dallas, my family returned to Dallas pretty often. My mother still visited friends near our old home, but it seemed we used to visit the fair grounds for the State Fair of Texas each year. Sometimes even when the fair wasn't in progress, I recall visiting Fair Park in Dallas. When we went there, I liked the Science Museum, and in the gift shop, my parents sometimes bought plastic, toy dinosaurs for me. I think I had all the different kinds before we stopped going so frequently. Using these toys, I once built a diorama of a prehistoric scene at elementary school for a science project.

I've already described how being in the Texoma Rockhounds influenced my interest in fossils, and I used to regret I never pursued a university-trained career in paleontology. However, I now believe my "paleontological life" actually turned out better by following the other twisted path it took.

Fossil Dinosaur Tracks near Gen Rose, and a Puzzle

My parents took our family to Glen Rose, Texas, when I was only eight or nine years old. This was several years before Dinosaur Valley State Park opened in 1972. We saw the single dinosaur track that had been mounted into the gazebo near the courthouse, but along a road out of town, they spotted a sign at a farmer's house offering access to tracks along the Paluxy River. I believe this location was somewhere up-stream from where the park is today, but since I was so young, I might be mistaken. Anyway, the farmer only charged my father a dollar to take us across his land to the river to see some of the tracks. Unfortunately, the water level was high, but we still observed large tracks in the water at several locations. He also pointed out the spot where R. T. Bird of the American Museum of Natural History collected a long section of tracks in 1938 showing a sauropod and a theropod walking along similar paths. Today a section of these tracks is on display at AMNH with dinosaur skeletons mounted near them. I got to see them during a paleontology convention in 1996.

But back to the farmer, the man was pretty old. He had been living on the farm when the tracks were removed. As we were leaving, he gave me a puzzle he made from fence wire. It was one of those that use a trick to separate and rejoin two elaborate loops of wire. It's actually pretty clever, and it kept me entertained for quite a while as we continued to travel that day. When we returned home, I put the puzzle away somewhere, but I came across it from time to time. I found it once more when we moved back from Venezuela the last time, and I now display it on a wall among other antiques. As I write these words, the puzzle is more than 55 years old.

Since my first trip to Glen Rose, I've visited Dinosaur Valley State Park several times, and I think it's great that Texas has set aside a place for people to see actual dinosaur tracks in the river.

More Tracks

When I was a student at Colorado School of Mines, our geology class took field trips to several areas around Golden. On one trip, we stopped at an outcrop near the road where it was possible to see some small dinosaur tracks. I captured photos of them.

A couple of years later, I returned to the location, but someone had taken a chisel and removed them all by cutting around them.

In the late 1970s, I read a newspaper story about a man along the South Bosque River in Texas who discovered lots of small dinosaur tracks on his property. They were in the limestone of the river bed, similar to those near Glen Rose, only these were from much smaller animals. He found them during a severe drought some thirty years earlier. At that time he never told anyone. When I read the story, central Texas was once more suffering from drought; the river on this man's property had dried up completely again. However, he decided to tell people—including the newspaper reporter. I traveled down from Dallas with a group to see the tracks.

The man charged a dollar per person, but he explained that initially, he hadn't charge anything. He had to start charging so only people who were serious about seeing the tracks would come. He merely gave the money to a young person in his family for helping to escort visitors. (People were going down by themselves and doing damage to the tracks and to his property.)

The tracks were well worth a dollar to see. In a pretty small area, I observed hundreds of small tracks. Most of them were only six to eight inches long. It looked like the dinosaurs were engaged in a dance-off. I measured some of the sets and drew pictures in my notebook. When it rained again, they were covered until the next drought.

Finding Things

I've been finding things most of my life. The first thing I recall finding was an Easter egg. My family took me to a community Easter egg hunt at Kiest Park in Oak Cliff, Texas, sometime before I was seven years old. Unfortunately, we arrived late, and groups of children like swarms of locust had passed through the park ahead of me. The egg I discovered was a candy one in the hollow of a tree. It had already broken open and was covered by ants. My sisters wouldn't let me touch it. Since then, I've done considerably better, and over the years, I've trained myself to find things.

My father enjoyed searching for—and especially finding—early Native American artifacts. As a child living in Dallas, I remember him having a handful of nice artifacts he collected at various places over the years, but later when I asked him where they came from, he no longer remembered. One of them was a "paleo point," probably dating back to more than 10,000 years. Another was a nicely shaped dart point that was manufactured from a clear quartz crystal. (I had this example in mind while writing part of the plot for *Shards of Time*.)

During the early 1960s—a time when the level of Lake Texoma was historically low—an older acquaintance of my father once drove me to Mill Creek Flats along the Texas side of the lake (Grayson County) to hunt for "Indian Arrowheads." The low water elevations had exposed areas along the shore that were not often seen. For some reason, my father couldn't go that day. He might have been working on a weekday during the summer. It wasn't the first time I went out searching, but it was the first time I found a complete artifact. I felt extremely proud that day.

Later, my father and I sometimes returned to Mill Creek Flats or to other places around the lake when the water was still low. We also collected artifacts from other places around Denison, normally farmer's fields west of town. Some of the artifacts we found were small arrowheads called "bird points," which I learned later in life represent true arrowheads. Most of the larger points are actually "dart points," which were said to tip spears thrown with the help of an atlatl. Occasionally, we also collected scrapers and knives, even drills or awls chipped from stone.

While at Mill Creek once, I was searching for artifacts near the foundation of an old building, one that had previously been covered with water. I found a small, thin black disc. It looked like a coin. It had a faint image of a six-pointed star on one side, so someone who saw it suggested it might be a coin from Israel. After I returned home, I cleaned it and found it to be a US 3-cent silver coin dated 1853.

I used to go on trips to collect artifacts with Keith Richardson, an older friend who owned a car before I did. On a beach in Oklahoma, I found a gold, Denison High School ring holding a polished blue stone. If I remember correctly, the date on the ring was from the early 1960s. After I learned that high schools and universities might be able to determine the names of rings' owners using initials engraved inside, I sent the ring to the high school. The same thing happened about a year later on the same beach when I found a gold university ring with a red stone and sent it off. I later heard through a note of appreciation from this ring's owner that he had lost it the summer after his graduation, which had been several years earlier. The ring appeared as if he lost it the same day I found it. I guess it gave him a nice story to tell, too.

On field trips with the Texoma Rockhounds, we often visited locations where it was possible to collect rocks, minerals, artifacts, and fossils. Two general locations that come to mind were the Stillwell area of eastern Oklahoma for artifacts and the North Sulphur River area of northeast Texas for both artifacts and fossils. I generally collected a lot of both. North of Stillwell I collected dozens of nice artifacts during a two-day outing, and the items included not only dart points but stone knives, hatchet heads, hoes, scrapers, and other tools. In the river on the best day I can remember, I collected twelve complete dart points, and one of those was a paleo point. Also, I picked up loads of fossils, mostly incomplete mosasaur vertebrae. The mosasaurs were swimming reptiles that lived during the Cretaceous Period, and the ones from the North Sulphur River probably dated from 70 to 75 million years old.

And by the way, I once spotted a Native American dart point from a moving vehicle. I was in a university van traveling along a dirt road south of Alpine, Texas, during the Geology Summer Field Course mentioned previously. That time I merely spoke out to say, "Hey, I just saw an arrowhead!" Most of the people didn't believe me, but the professor stopped and allowed another student who sat next to the door to go back to pick it up as I pointed out and described its location from the open window. Sure enough, he came back amazed as he handed it to me through the vehicle's window where I still sat. It was a complete example. The other students talked about it for the rest of the afternoon.

While on the same college field trip to West Texas, our class stopped near an old fort. I discovered cartridge cases for a 45-70 rifle on a rocky hill overlooking the fort. Some of them dated from 1886.

I earlier described discovering a broken dinosaur limb bone in Big Bend National Park that might still be there.

Somewhere along the way I found I was constantly looking down in search of artifacts or fossils. As a result, I started to find money. Most of the time I only found coins; occasionally I was lucky enough to find paper money.

I've found almost countless coins over the years, and I still find them. It has turned into something of a hobby, and now I keep records. Nearly everywhere I go I'm looking down, searching. Pennies are always the most common, but I come across dimes fairly frequently. Nickels show up less than quarters for some strange reason. Maybe not as many people carry them in their pockets.

Parking lots are the most common locations where I find coins. I imagine when men pull their car keys from their pockets or when women dig out something from their purses, they accidently extract coins, which fall to the ground. People either don't notice or they don't want to go to the trouble of picking them up. I also find coins at my feet when checking out in stores, but occasionally, I encounter coins in some pretty odd places. They seem to be just about everywhere, and I often wonder how much money might be simply resting on the ground around the world at any given moment.

I've found coins and occasionally paper money in countries other than the United States. I think I've picked up coins in nearly every country where I've traveled, except perhaps for Ecuador, Aruba, and Greece, where the only time I was actually on the ground was walking from planes through the terminals and back.

Brazil was quite a prolific country for finding coins when I was there back in the late 1980s. They were suffering from run-away inflation. As a result, the money rapidly turned less and less valuable until some coins became practically worthless. When people received coins as change following a purchase, they often threw them on the ground so the extra weight wouldn't wear out their pockets. Over about a week, I collected a large bag full of big, shiny coins along with a few small-denomination banknotes. I once mentioned to Dr. John Maisey of the American Museum of Natural History that I find coins all the time. John is a fossil fish expert who visited me in Venezuela while we worked on a project. He told me, "I do, too." He has done work in Brazil and described how he always picked up a lot of coins there during his visits, but he also finds them wherever he goes. He explained it is apparently a characteristic of good paleontologists because they are constantly searching the ground for fossils—even while walking on city streets and across parking lots.

As I stated, I've started to keep track of the money I find, and I do it for a calendar year. Some years have been better than others. It probably depends on how much time I spend looking, but it might also be a reflection of the local economy. Here are some examples of my statistics: 2016 - 191 pieces valued at $8.74, 2017 – 168 pieces valued at $6.78, 2018 – 155 pieces valued at $10.18 (one of them was a five-dollar bill).

I once spotted a small wad of bills at the end of a line where people were paying for an event at a ticket window. I picked up the bills, which amounted to about $12. I couldn't very well announce "Hey, who lost some money?" because everyone might have made a claim. Instead, I waited off to the side to see if any of the people missed the money when he or she reached the window. Then I would know who lost it. However, after the last person went up and paid, no one seemed to miss the dropped dough. After that, I stuck it into my pocket.

Years later the same thing happened to me in Venezuela. I spotted a 100 bolivar banknote on the floor behind a short line of people paying in a restaurant. At the time, 100 bolivars was worth about $23. The third and last person in line—a woman—went up to pay, and I watched her suddenly go into panic mode when she searched through her purse. I immediately stepped forward and asked her if she lost the bill, which of course, she had. She thanked me.

I once found $5 in a median between lanes of traffic, which I was able to keep, and I found another $5 on the sidewalk about a block from where I lived. Over the years, I've discovered a number of one dollar bills, but once while driving, I spotted a one-dollar bill as it blew across Camp Bowie Boulevard in Fort Worth. I was able to pull into a parking lot to pick it up. The person I was with at the time couldn't believe I spotted it the way I did from a moving vehicle.

However, my daughter, Mary Ann, has me beat. Once when she was no more than nine years old, she found a wad of paper money while we shopped at Walmart. The amount turned out to be about $30. I decided, *This will be the perfect opportunity for teaching her the rewards of being honest.*

We stepped up to a sales lady (with Mary Ann standing right beside me), and I said, "My daughter just found some money. It looks like about $30."

The sales lady said only, "I need to call security."

Within a couple of minutes a uniformed security guard stepped up, and I repeated the story. I handed him the bills, and he turned away, carrying them with him, leaving my daughter and me simply standing there. No one took our names. No one even told my daughter (or me) "Thank you." Failed lesson; I felt extremely disappointed with the way they handled the situation.

As Mary Ann and I walked to our car, I told her, "I'm going to give you $30 to spend any way you wish." She had fun spending it.

Lake Texoma Fossils

One of the first locations where I ever collected fossils is on the Texas side of Lake Texoma just above the water release gates of Denison Dam. This area is only four miles north of Denison, where I grew up, and it is easy to reach. Unfortunately, the years haven't been particularly kind to this location. Most of the Cretaceous outcrops have been covered to prevent erosion. While the limestone produces ammonites, echinoids, and mollusks, a thin layer of dark gray shale once produced shark and fish teeth, as well as dwarf ammonites and mollusks. My father once collected an interesting fossil fish from these same beds. The fish was open toward the top as if scavengers had feasted on the body, but on the other side, which would have been resting on the ocean floor, the scales still rested in an orderly fashion. Further around the lake toward the west, some of these outcrops are still exposed, but new laws prohibit the collecting of certain fossils in some areas.

Some years back I wrote my second article for the Dallas Paleontological Society, which was published in their monthly bulletin for July of 1988. I describe my impressions of this location as a "Famous Fossil Locality." I wrote several of these articles during subsequent months.

Many parts of the Texas shore of the lake where limestone and shale are exposed still produce fossils, and in more recent years as part of her education, I took Mary Ann to see if we could still find anything. We collected some fossils, but it simply wasn't as good as before with regard to the quality of specimens.

On one of these trips with Mary Ann, we stopped at a location near a boat dock, and I had a morbid thought; I wondered what she would do if I happened to die while we were out. One thought led to another, and I soon had an idea to write a murder mystery addressing such a scenario. It wasn't too much later when I wrote the book and published it as my "Denison mystery" because most of the action takes place in this area. I call it *Shards of Time*, and it has been a popular book among my local fans.

The Pawpaw

Pawpaw Hill stands just east of Denison as a person drives out of town along Texas Farm Road 120. Most people may not even know its name anymore, but that's what people called it when I was a teenager, as well as many years earlier. Back about a hundred years ago when some of the geological formations in Grayson County were first being described, the geological strata forming much of Pawpaw Hill were named after this location. The Pawpaw Formation is thicker in the Denison area than it is further south. In the Fort Worth Area, the entire formation is only between about 12 and 25 feet thick. Even so, it's full of remarkable fossils.

While I was a geology student at the University of Texas at Arlington, I had access to their fossil collections. One day while I rummaged through the cabinet to learn about local specimens, I encountered a small box containing lots of pretty, tiny fossils. A label on the box gave a location, and I set out one day to see what I could find there. I identified the location, and it still produced plenty of fossils. I collected some that day, and over several years while I lived in Arlington, I often drove over to Fort Worth to search for more. I tried to return often, especially following heavy rains, and almost always I found outstanding specimens. My research showed these fossils to be nearly 100 million years old.

As I continued to search, I also discovered additional locations, and some of them were quite productive for a while. Some were in areas where construction was taking place, and one pretty good location now has an apartment complex sitting on top.

I often felt pretty amazed by what I found. The fossils were usually tiny, but the preservation was excellent. I found mollusks of several types, as well as ammonites and echinoids. Shark teeth, fish teeth, and fish bones turned up occasionally. I even found starfish remains in one location. The pieces of these were from several individuals, and I eventually collected parts of at least four species.

Most amazing to me, however, were the crustaceans. I collected several species of crabs, and maybe also shrimp or lobsters. Some partial crabs still have eye stalks, and I found one that still had parts of legs attached. They were of several body shapes and characteristics ranging from narrow to wide and smooth to ornate.

During the early 1990s, the Texas Highway Department or the federal government began to build a bypass for US Highway 75 in the western part of Denison. They made a series of large cuts through several formations. One of these is where Texas Farm Road 120 crosses US 75 near the Denison Walmart. During construction, they exposed some of the Pawpaw Formation that no one had ever seen before. My father went to collect fossils here several times, and he took me there while I was home on vacation. The mollusks still displayed a mother-of-pearl covering, which would have been part of the original shell. We also collected shark's teeth, and he found a small lobster. It was nearly complete.

Unfortunately, the area is now covered again, but it can be worthwhile to check the areas nearby during future construction projects. Who knows what a person might find by only looking down.

Some Pretty Amazing Locations

The Texoma Rockhounds during the 1960s used to organize frequent field trips to the North Sulphur River in Fannin, Lamar, and Delta counties of Texas. Following each big rain, new fossils washed from the river banks to mix with the river gravel. From what I understand, the river once meandered tranquilly across the flat prairie until someone got the idea that if they cut a straight channel, the water would run off faster. I guess it worked for a while, but in the process, the rapidly flowing water began to erode the banks until they were dozens of feet high in many areas. Still, this meant it also eroded out lots of fossils, and we used to pick up bags full on each trip. For a while, some of these locations near bridge crossings were among my favorites when it came to collecting fossils. The river gravels also produced Native American artifacts, as I've already mentioned elsewhere.

On a lot of weekends I used to travel with my father to hunt for fossils at certain river locations. In a single day, we could easily return home with 15 or 20 pounds of interesting fossils, mostly mosasaur bones. These were great times to share with my father.

For one trip, we traveled to the river along a really muddy road right after a rain. The car got stuck in the mud after it slipped to one side, but he decided to just leave it, hoping the land would dry out enough during the day for him to get it free. We went ahead and hunted for fossils by walking the rest of the way to the river. In the afternoon after we carried our accumulated treasures back to the car, he discovered that the car was still stuck just the same as before. He carried a set of snow chains in the trunk, and I had to lie down in the mud to get them onto the back tires. I was a complete mess, covered nearly head to foot in mud, but I successfully installed the chains.

Luckily, it worked. He was able to free the car and drive out of the location. Even so, I had to sit on a piece of newspaper for more than an hour with the mud drying on my skin as he drove us home. It wasn't very comfortable, but I didn't care; I had my fossils in the trunk to study after I got cleaned up.

Over the years, we collected many fossil reptile bones. Most of them were from several genera of Cretaceous mosasaurs, including *Clidasties, Platecarpus*, and *Tylosaurus* (the big one now made famous by a movie). Also, we collected plesiosaur bones, along with fish bones and teeth and shark's teeth of many varieties, both large and small. My father once collected a large plesiosaur limb bone in two parts, recently broken, which he glued back together to make a really nice, complete specimen.

Some of the most amazing fossils were coprolites, or animal "poop." Some of these contained fish scales. A lot of these simply look like rocks unless a person knows what to search for, so not a lot of people collected them (unless it's for some other reason). Marine turtle bones turned up occasionally. Other common fossils back in the old days included Pleistocene teeth and tooth fragments from mammoths, mastodons, camels, and bison.

I once found a jaw section of a mosasaur that ate shellfish. This animal is called *Globidens*. The section of jaw has four, bulb-like teeth still attached, and I was very careful with it. Years later, a researcher from SMU in Dallas asked to borrow it, and somewhere along the way, it ended up in the collections at SMU, but it's probably better this way if it is such an important example. Over the years, I've ended up donating other parts of my collection to SMU for study, as I will describe shortly.

A Stop Along the Road

One day Core Lab held a management conference at an American Airlines training center between Arlington and Euless, Texas. I lived in Arlington at the time, so it was an easy location for me to attend. I normally had to drive much further to reach my regular job in Dallas each day.

I left with plenty of time to reach my destination, and when I knew I was nearly there (too early), I decided to stop along the side of State Highway 360 for a few minutes to look for fossils. The location was one I already knew from my time as a university student at UTA. The spot sat just north of the Trinity River. I had stopped there on a university-sponsored field trip at least once, and Dr. Dodge, one of my professors at UTA, had done field work in the area.

I initially picked up a few invertebrate shells from a shale member of the Woodbine Sandstone, but all at once I found a partial tooth. It didn't look like a fish tooth, and I thought it might be a plesiosaur tooth. The tip was broken, but otherwise, it was in pretty good condition. I put it in the car, and continued on to the conference, which lasted a couple of days.

As soon as I could, I returned to the location and started to collect pieces of fossilized bone. I saved each piece I found, and I returned often each time the area experienced a heavy rain. I found bone present on the east side of the road, but a small strip in the median also produced fossils at times, as did a road cut on the west side just north of the river. The fossils all originated from the same bed of gray shale. Over a period of a couple of years, I amassed quite a few nice bones, and I sometimes found that fragments from one trip connected to pieces found on other occasions to make more complete specimens. Some of the bones were those of turtles, and I later figured out that most of the teeth I collected were from crocodiles. One tooth happened to be quite large. I removed it from the ground in nearly a hundred fragments, but I carefully collected everything I saw and was able over several days to reconstruct it into a rather nice specimen. It would have come from an animal of monstrous size.

Then one day I discovered a strange-looking, small fossil I couldn't identify. It appeared to be some sort of tooth, but it was worn flat on one end. Over a time span of about a year, I collected half a dozen others, which were very similar to the first one, and I even found a larger portion of a tooth with serrations along one edge.

I sometimes visited the libraries at UTA and SMU to search for fossil identifications. My research was rather haphazard, but I learned a lot. One day I happened to open a journal volume showing a jaw section from a hadrosaur (plant-eating) dinosaur, and all at once I recognized that some of my fossils were individual hadrosaur teeth that had probably worn down short enough to fall out while the animal fed. I also believe that the larger tooth fragment was from a dinosaur, possibly a large herbivore with serrations along the edge, like illustrations of *Iguanodon* teeth from the Natural History Museum in London. I even found a small vertebra from what looked to me like a dinosaur—certainly not from a crocodile.

On one trip, I observed that construction work was in progress near the fossil locality. I returned often, and some of the earth moving began to turn up even more fossils for a while until the area began to experience a long period of drought. As the work continued, the highway department slowly began to cover over one of my favorite localities, and before long, I couldn't find much of anything. I still saved everything I collected over the time period, but I didn't believe anyone would ever collect more fossils there.

In one of my "Famous Fossil Localities" articles (mentioned previously), I wrote about these teeth when describing the location (which by this date had been covered completely with cement). Dr. Dale Russell, a well-known paleontologist, wrote to me suggesting I should show these teeth to experts to see what they thought about them. Paleontologists at the time didn't believe that hadrosaurs lived during the geological time period I wrote about. I was living in Venezuela by then. I allowed *The Fossil Record* to publish Dr.

Russell's response to my article. Then I wrote a letter to a paleontologist at SMU, giving all the facts and inviting him to take a look at my fossils, which I kept at my parent's house while overseas. I explained that I could show them the next time I returned on vacation. I never received a response, so I simply forgot the idea it for a while.

After I returned to the US in the mid-1980s, I heard that a hadrosaur skeleton had been discover at Lake Lewisville northwest of Dallas, which wasn't far north of where I found my fossils. It was from the same age of rock as my fossils. I contacted Dr. Louis Jacobs at SMU and invited him to look at the collections, of which I had access again. Lou and Dale Winkler visited my house a couple of days later and confirmed my discovery—years after the fact. I gave Lou a photocopy of my letter to SMU, and he couldn't believe that no one had ever responded. That same day I donated the most important fossils from the highway location to SMU for their collections.

During my third stay in Venezuela, I started to hear news about the Arlington Archosaur Site, which was being organized by my old school, UTA. It seems they had received permission to excavate on the river plain below the highway where I used to find my fossils, and they were finding all sorts of excellent specimens using volunteer labor and university funds. I don't know if the area is still active, but I know they collected a lot of nice species. When I was collecting fossils from along the road, each time I walked down in that direction, I never saw much more than a grassy slope, so they must have done a real good job of excavation. As it turned out, they found fossils despite my fears that none would ever be found again.

Dallas Paleo

Between my second and third times living in Venezuela, I learned through Charles Finsley of the Dallas Museum of Natural History that a group of fossil enthusiasts were thinking about forming a club to help the museum and to promote paleontology in general. When I heard this, I thought it sounded like a good idea, and I recall how excited I felt while driving across Dallas that evening for the group's organizational meeting. I viewed it as an important event, and as it turned out, I was right.

That night through a show of hands, we formed the Dallas Paleontological Society, and everyone there at the time was noted as a charter member. I attended meetings regularly, and I made a lot of friends there. Then about a year later, I had to return to Venezuela the third time. Even so, I changed my address and continued to be a member, receiving their news bulletin, *The Fossil Record*, regularly whenever my parents could forward them. Later, as I already described here and there, I began to write articles for the bulletin whenever I thought I had something important to say. For a while I wrote the "Famous Fossil Localities" series where I described places I knew pretty well, describing the fossils that could be collected there. The last two of this series described Venezuelan Sierra de Perijá fossils of all sorts, and I later wrote about other museum work, which I will describe in detail further on.

I once went on a long fossil hunting trip with my father and one of my father's long-time friends, R. C. Harmon. R. C. took us to some of his favorite location for invertebrates near his home in central Texas. On the last day, he took us to a farm where we were to find a type of clam in the Austin Chalk of Bell County, Texas. I stumbled across a pretty large section of mosasaur jaw that had weathered out of a creek bank. I carefully collected it and later took it to the Dallas Museum of Natural History. I explained to Charles Finsley that there might be more of the same animal in the rock below the surface.

Charles, my father, and I returned to the same location to explore, and as we dug down, we soon encountered another bone. We spoke to the land owner and received official permission for the museum to dig, and two weeks later, we returned with a large group of volunteers to excavate whatever we could find. One bone led to more, and we soon had a large block containing fossils exposed. For part of the work, we used equipment from the museum where a gasoline generator ran a pneumatic pump that operated a small jackhammer. I gained experience using this equipment for a while, as well as most anyone who wanted to give it a try. Over a weekend, the group extracted a pretty nice block of rock containing a partial skull. I owned a Super-8 movie camera at the time, and I made a short movie showing the process, which I still keep at home.

While I was still in the Dallas area, the society had the idea of inviting famous speakers, and during a conversation with the person in charge after a meeting, I suggested for them to invite Dr. Edwin Colbert, formerly of the American Museum of Natural History in New York. Dr. Colbert was once called "Mr. Dinosaur" because of a popular children's book he wrote on the subject, and I had just read another of his books, *A Fossil Hunter's Notebook*, which is what gave me the idea. The man in charge took my suggestion seriously and called Dr. Colbert to see if he might be interested. Fortunately for the club, he thought it sounded like something he would like to do as long as he could bring his wife. They told him it would be fine, and the society paid for his trip. I believe SMU also sponsored some of the event once they learned he was interested.

He gave a great speech, and we all got to talk to him at times. My mother took a picture of me sitting next to him, and I still have it. I also had him autograph my copy of the book that brought him to Dallas on this occasion.

Later, the society invited other well-known paleontologists, some of whom I had also suggested early on, but by the time they came, I was already in Venezuela for the third time.

The Dallas Paleontological Society is still going strong, and they are heavily involved with area discoveries, which often end up in local museums. I feel pretty glad I raised my hand that night to vote in favor of the society's formation.

My First Venezuelan Fossils

While I worked at Core Lab in Venezuela, most people knew I was interested in fossils because I spoke about them often. A few local people working there also shared my interest—although not as fanatically. One of these was a man named Guillermo. He was a geological technician who worked in the company's lab and sometimes in the field. One day Guillermo suggested for us to visit a location where we might be able to search for ammonites. He made all the arrangements with a friend of his named Merlin who worked for the country's energy and mines ministry.

On November 29, 1981, they drove me to see the Cretaceous outcrops at La Luna Quarry near the La Luna Formation's type locality (where the formation had originally been described by geologists). It wasn't a long trip. Merlin drove a suitable vehicle belonging to the ministry, and on the way, we stopped at a ministry office near Villa de Rosario to pick up a rather large hammer and a shotgun, "just in case." Then we proceeded straight to the quarry.

Guillermo soon collected two ammonites in poor condition, but I didn't find much of importance along those lines. Later, Merlin told me, "There really aren't any good fossils in Venezuela."

Even so, I began to examine a shale bed in the lower quarry face, and I soon discovered a string of fish vertebra (14 in all) along with a piece of a fin, which I took with me at the end of the day. Both Guillermo and Merlin appeared surprised when I showed them the fossils and explained what they were.

After years of collecting fossils in Venezuela, I heard many people with the same opinion as Merlin. Everyone always seemed surprised by the fossils I found. Looking back, I now believe that few people found good fossils in Venezuela because few people were looking for them. Even so, I had days when I didn't find much, as my next story will illustrate.

Attack of the Killer Bees

After I returned to Venezuela the third time for an extended period, I decided to take a trip to the area around Carora in Lara State to look for fossils. Through some of the geological information I collected over the years, I learned that several geological formations of Cretaceous age are present on the surface around this town. I had even spotted some promising rock outcrops during road trips through the area, but I was never able to stop to take a closer look. Based on my research, I expected to find ammonites.

It was a Saturday, and I planned to take advantage of being there by staying in a motel overnight to return to Maracaibo on Sunday afternoon. I arrived in Carora at about 10:00 AM. The area around Carora is dry and hot, so I thought I'd have a great day exploring.

A bypass for the highway had been built directly south of town a few years earlier, and the construction exposed some interesting beds of rock. I stepped out of the car (a Toyota Corolla), and I locked it, taking along my usual fossil collecting equipment and other items. I walked across a flat area consisting of rock fill removed from the nearby road cuts. I attempted to reach an exposed natural outcrop of weathered, grayish rock I observed in the distance. I was near the edge of town, which spread out for a distance below me toward the north.

I climbed down a rocky slope and turned left to reach the outcrop. I soon found that most of the rock was slightly altered by metamorphic processes to where any fossils I might find would be extremely difficult to extract from the rock. Even so, my realization didn't stop me from continuing my search.

I soon reached an area where the gray rock was exposed at my feet, and I hadn't been searching for more than two minutes when I stepped under a spiny, scrub tree to reach another spot. As I did, I looked down just ahead of me and saw an eroded hole in the rock about eight inches in diameter. I immediately noticed some bees flying around it, and I decided to back away so as not to disturb them.

By the time I backed under the tree again, a bee stung me. Then right away, another one hit me. Within a few seconds, I had bees buzzing all around me, and I had been stung a number of times. This was my first encounter with the famous Africanized bees that escaped from Brazil. I hope it will be my only encounter. I had heard about them. By that date, they had reached the southern US.

I couldn't think of anything to do to make them leave me alone, so I dropped everything and decided to simply place more distance between them and me. I ran up the slope and across the flat, rocky area to get to my car, which sat about a hundred yards away. The bees followed me the entire distance, stinging me as I ran.

I finally reached my car and managed to unlock it. I got inside, and at least one bee followed me in before I could close the door. It stung me, too.

I didn't know much about bees and even less about "killer bees," but I felt pretty dreadful as I sat there trying to decide what to do. I mostly believed I was about to suffer some sort of reaction and die there on the spot. As I mentioned, I had heard stories.

For a few minutes, I simply sat there, trying to regain some calm. After about 15 minutes, I started to feel a little better. My heart rate began to slow, and I decided that maybe I wasn't going to die after all. The stings still hurt, and the locations of the stings began to swell, but I figured it was something I could tolerate.

Even so, I felt extremely disappointed that my fossil collecting trip had turned into such a disaster as soon as it started.

Also, I took stock and realized I had dropped everything as I ran, including my camera (a Pentax SLR with a special lens), my fossil collecting bag, my rock hammer, my notebook, an ink pen I had been carrying for six years, and most importantly, my passport. I especially needed to get the passport back if nothing else. I had let go of most of these items only about 20 yards from the hive.

After about thirty minutes, I opened the car door to go back and retrieve my lost items, and the bees were still there, waiting for me. I got back in, trying to decide what to do.

For hunting fossils, I usually wore a long-sleeved shirt, and I normally kept the sleeves rolled up to my elbows. That day was no exception, so I rolled down the sleeves and buttoned them, also raising and buttoning the collar. I managed to get out of the car and open the trunk to remove some items, but the bees continued to buzz around, and another one stung me.

From my trunk, I removed a red, nylon jacket with a hood, a billed cap, and a large rag. Then I returned to the driver's seat, started the car, and drove quickly up the shoulder of the highway for about 200 yards. At that point, I waited for about 15 minutes as I made preparations and started to remove bee stingers.

I only imagined that the bees were hanging around for reasons unknown, and if I moved the car, they wouldn't sense me there anymore and would leave.

I put on the jacket. I tied the rag around my face like a bandit. Then I put on the cap and raised the hood to cover my hair, my ears, and the back of my neck. In this way I only had a tiny slot exposed, which allowed me to look out from under the bill of the cap. With my hands in my pocket, I showed practically no exposed skin.

I started the car again and backed up along the highway shoulder, but I didn't stop the car in exactly the same spot. I parked about twenty yards from the former location.

When I stepped from the car, my trick worked. No bees awaited me. I walked back to the slope and descended, recovering everything I dropped. Even then, however, as I reached the spot, bees came out to greet me. Still, they could no longer sting me directly, and I returned to my car without suffering any further harm.

Once I reached the car—along with a few bees that followed—I got back in, started it, and drove away, never to return. But that isn't the end of my story.

I decided I wasn't going to let the incident ruin my trip completely, so I searched for other locations to explore in the afternoon. I found another outcrop further down on the other side of the highway, and I searched in vain for fossils. After a while, a bee started to buzz around angrily. I soon left this location for another much further away—a couple of miles away, at least. The same thing happened there; I soon encountered an angry bee, although the newcomers never stung me. Afterward, I spent much of the day driving along roads I saw on my map while seeking new locations, but I later decided I felt too tired and too ill to continue. The bee stings were still rather swollen.

I went to a motel in Carora and checked in. I bought dinner, which I ate in the room, but later at night, I found I couldn't sleep. I think I had developed a fever. At about four in the morning, I packed and checked out to begin my drive to Maracaibo. I was back by about seven-thirty.

As I examined myself later and continued to remove stingers, I discovered 49 locations where bees had stung me. I never went to see a doctor, and within a couple of days, I felt fine. I don't think I've been stung by a bee since then—wasps, yes, but not any more bees.

A few days later when I went to clean out my car, I discovered a dead bee (without a stinger) on the little shelf near the car's back window. I saved it and placed it in a plastic photographic film container along with a little cotton. I still have it. I taught at a private school during summer months for a few years, and I always took the bee along for a show-and-tell as I told my "killer bee story," which was a favorite among some of the children.

Years later, I watched a British-produced nature show about Africanized bees. I still lived in Venezuela at the time. It explained that each time a bee stings a target, it leaves a scent or a pheromone to tell other bees where to attack. I still had this scent on me as I continued to search for fossils that afternoon. For this reason, I had angry bees following me around the rest of the day. I'm just glad they weren't angry enough to attack.

John M. Moody

My Work at MBLUZ

I feel fortunate to have worked at the University of Zulia's biology museum. It is better known in Spanish as "Museo de Biología, La Universidad del Zulia," or by the acronym "MBLUZ." While working at the museum, I got to see places most Venezuelans—or most everyone else—could only imagine.

As a matter of fact, good fortune—what people call "luck"—actually played a part in me working at the museum. On July 12, 1990, Alfredo Perez, an MBLUZ student who was interested in the biology of modern-day fish, stopped by my office at Core Lab. He learned about me through a micro-paleontologist whom I sometimes spoke to at one of the Venezuelan national oil companies. If Alfredo had never dropped by that day, I might have ended up with a far different life.

Alfredo had heard about some fossil fish I collected in the Perijá region, and he wanted to see them. I invited him to come to my home on a certain night, and he asked if he could bring along a small group of visiting researchers. I agreed.

Several researchers from the US came to my house, and I showed them my Venezuelan fossil fish—along with a few examples I bought on the streets of Rio de Janeiro, Brazil. Alfredo then told me he had some other people he wanted me to meet, and we made the arrangements.

Tito Barros joined Alfredo during a visit a few days later (July 20). They showed me some slides and described trips they had taken on foot into the upper reaches of the Sierra de Perijá. I showed them my small collection of Venezuelan fossils, which also included Devonian plants, brachiopods, and trilobites, along with some Cretaceous ammonites. That same evening, they asked if I might be interested in working as the curator for their paleontology section at the museum. I told them I would. I said that if I worked there, I would donate my collections to the museum.

On my first trip to the museum on July 28, I met Professor José Moscó, the museum's director, and he extended an official invitation to become the museum's paleontology curator. I also met for the first time Angel Viloria, the museum's entomologist. I am still in contact with Angel.

Professor Moscó needed a copy of my university diploma and a few other documents, but I took a vacation trip to the US in October, which gave me the chance to get everything I needed. As easy as that, I was part of the museum staff, although I was there without pay. They called it "*ad honorem.*" Most curators were the same as me except for the full-time professors. Later, they extended me the title of "Invited Professor," which sounded great when I told people.

Curiously, the paleontology section only existed in name before I arrived. It had been part of the overall plan for the museum since the institution's formation, but they had never found anyone who knew enough about fossils to become its curator. The museum lacked not only a curator, but it also lacked fossils for its collections. However, my experience over the years with the Texoma Rockhounds and collecting in various parts of the world had been pretty good teachers. I started with no collections of note, but my personal collections from several years in the country became the nucleus. Some of the paleontology section's first catalogue numbers were my Perijá fossil fish.

Whenever I could, I continued to add catalogue numbers, and I had no trouble finding students who wanted to go on field trips to help me make collections. I used my famous, white Jeep. (A lot of paleontological studies in Venezuela would never have taken place without this noble piece of equipment. As I understand it, a man in Caracas now owns the vehicle. He has restored it and keeps it in a garage all the time as a collector's item.)

I always paid for gas and lunch to take along. Sometimes they bought breakfast for us along the road, often in a town west of Maracaibo known as La Concepcion. Students of many biological disciplines were always looking for a chance to get out of town and into the mountains, and most of them didn't have access to vehicles.

(As an added note, I describe a similar field trip in my novel, *Into the Center of the Shadow*. In my writing, I even included an off-hand reference to me. In 1998—according to my story—some students discuss a "*yanqui*", or a North American, as being in charge of the paleontology section at the university museum in Maracaibo.)

Alfredo Perez was with me when I rediscovered the Devonian fossil fish locality in Caño Colorado Sur (described later in more detail). Other students were there when we first visited the Inciarte tar

John M. Moody

pits. Several of the museum staff went to Cerro Pintado. Ascanio Rincón was a student when he became my main assistant at the museum, and we went on plenty of field trips together over the years.

The staff members other than Alfredo and Ascanio with whom I had the most contact at MBLUZ were Angel Viloria (butterflies and insects, but a little of everything), Tito Barros (reptiles and amphibians), Rosanna Cache (birds), and José Moscó (fish). I also occasionally worked with Miguel Pietrangelli (plants). It was an excellent, scholarly group to work with.

I became deeply involved with the museum, and I made friends there with everyone with whom I came in contact, especially with the other curators. Occasionally, individuals from outside the museum brought rocks they had found, which they wanted me to identify. I always thanked them for coming in to see me, regardless of if the "dinosaur bone" they brought just happened to be an interesting-shaped rock. A few people even invited me into the field to see fossils in situ, and I always had a good time talking with them. On some occasions, petroleum company geologists came by on special tours to visit the museum, and I made new friends this way, too. I sometimes traveled on field trips organized by other groups as a representative of our museum. I presented courses at times through the museum, and I participated in conferences sponsored by the university. Most importantly, I helped to published studies on new discoveries that no one had previously observed. I describe some of these later in greater depth. A few of these studies went a long way toward changing people's views of paleontology in Venezuela.

I remained at the museum as the paleontology curator until May of 2001—more than 10 years—until Belkis, Mary Ann, and I moved to Denison. The socialist government in Venezuela was beginning to put the country in steep decline, and the process has continued until the whole place seems about to fall apart. Belkis and I believe we left at a good time for Mary Ann's sake.

During the time I was at the museum, I catalogued 5000 specimens, but I left a lot of work to be done. A good deal more than half of the catalogue numbers were from the Inciarte tar pits, which during my last years in Venezuela tended to dominate much of our activities. The following sections describe some of the things I did while at the museum.

Evolution

During my first years at MBLUZ, the faculty asked me to teach a course dealing with an introduction to paleontology. I had a few months to prepare, and I did a lot of work to make it as complete as I could. By then, I had donated the greater part of my personal collection of fossils to MBLUZ as reference materials, and those included animal types from around the world. I designed the course to discuss everything from the history of the science to fossil types, from modes of preservation to lab preparation. I drew upon much of what I had learned about fossils over the years, and I supported my lectures with information from books on the subject, which I had accumulated since my own student days. I also included a discussion of evolution, and for my lecture, I drew upon two examples I noticed during my travels.

One example came to mind during a trip to the Sierra de Perijá. I stopped my Jeep once to observe some birds near a small herd of cattle. All at once, I noticed a tiny cow. It might have been merely a calf, but if it was, it was about half the size of a normal calf. I took a photo, which I later used for my lecture to illustrate how certain people have erroneously believe over the years that Charles Darwin's theory states "The strong will survive." I pointed out that in the case of the tiny cow during a drought, the smaller animal might have an advantage over its larger companions because it consumes less food. It might survive where the larger ones would not. It's actually "The most adaptable will survive" to possibly leave behind offspring.

The second example comes from my observations of a certain species of bird called a black-faced grassquit. These little, feathered creatures don't particularly draw people's attention. Their color is dull, olive green with the male being slightly brighter, but the male also has a black patch that extends from the face down to high on the chest, giving them their descriptive name. I used to watch these birds all the time from the terrace of a second-floor duplex where I lived in Maracaibo, and it got to where I could recognize the characteristic call made by the male of the species.

This species is found along the northern coast of South America and on many of the islands of the Caribbean. Interestingly, however, these birds are not observed on the island of Trinidad, which is closest to the Venezuelan mainland. Even so, they can be observed on the island of Tobago, which is much further away. They probably populated both Trinidad and Tobago at one time, but they later died out on Trinidad for some unknown reason.

During my trip to Tobago, I spotted a male black-faced grassquit on a telephone line, so I watched it for a moment like seeing an old friend. Then I heard it make its call. It sounded nothing like the ones I heard in Maracaibo. It caused me to realize the species had undergone the processes of evolution. The Tobago birds had been isolated from the main population for so long, they developed a different call. If by chance a Tobago male happened to be sent to Maracaibo (or vice-versa) and called out in search of a mate, the local females might not respond. They wouldn't hear the characteristic call. The Tobago birds were in the process of becoming a different species. Darwin strikes again!

I believe these were perfect examples for the course, and they meant more to my students because I presented them as first-hand experiences. I didn't have many students, but they all did well in class and made good grades.

Dead Animals Again - MBLUZ

While working at MBLUZ, I decided we needed a reference collection of modern animal bones, but whenever I was out on a trip and saw a road-kill in good condition, I made collections for other departments to add to their catalogues, too. My students and I stumbled across a few surprises.

Once near the bridge across Rio Palmar close to Villa de Rosario (Perijá), I stopped to collect an owl early one morning. It happened to be a spectacled owl, but it died (probably after hitting a moving vehicle) grasping a flycatcher in its talons. I viewed it as an important discovery, perhaps worthy of an ornithological journal note. However, after I went to the trouble to take this set of specimens to the taxidermy lab, I later learned that one of the students stole them. I don't know if the professor ever got them back in good condition.

I was collecting fossils in the Rosarito stone quarry near Villa de Rosario once when I encountered some dried owl pellets (regurgitated stomach contents). Earlier near the same location I observed a barn owl, so this bird probably produced them. I spotted bones in the pellets (from previous meals), and back at the lab, I carefully extracted them to determine the owl's diet. Several skulls were present, including one of a tropical "fishing bat," a somewhat rare species. Our local bat expert, one of the students, was quite pleased to add it to his collection.

On one field trip, a group I led stopped to collect a desiccated fox carcass in order to remove whatever bones the remains still possessed. We didn't imagine the bones would serve any use other than as comparison specimens. After some of the students cleaned the skull, the animal turned out to be a type that had never before been noted from the region. The museum's mammal curator considered the find important. As we discovered later with fossils from the area, a person never quite knew what surprises he or she might find by merely examining dead animals along the side of the road.

Devonian Plant Fossils

Not long after I bought my white Jeep in Maracaibo in 1988, I began to return to the Caño Colorado area of the Sierra de Perijá. This is one of the same areas I visited with a group of friends during my first extended stay in 1983.

As the dates above show, by not having access to a four-wheel-drive vehicle, it took me years to return. Some of the roads had changed by then, but when the workers cut new trails, they exposed a lot more fossils. On one of these trips, I collected a nice set of well-preserved plant fossils of Devonian age from the Campo Chico Formation.

I began to communicate with people in the US. One of them was Dr. Lou Jacobs of Southern Methodist University in Dallas, who already knew me from my days collecting fossils in the Dallas area. Lou referred my letter to his wife, Dr. Bonnie Jacobs. She is a paleobotanist. Before long, Bonnie passed the information to Dr. Diane Edwards from the University of Wales, Cardiff, who contacted me. Dr. Edwards is a well-respected researcher who deals principally with early fossil plants. In her correspondence, she sounded delighted to find someone in Maracaibo who might possibly help one of her PhD students named Christopher Berry. (Dianne had visited some of the same plant fossil locations in Perijá about two years earlier. While she recognized the potential, she didn't have the means or resources to send a person alone to undertake a detailed project. Chris Berry, with my support, was her solution.)

At this point, I must also mention Jhonny Casas. Jhonny was a geologist working for Maraven at the time, and we had made friends somewhere early on because of his interest in fossils. Jhonny also joined us on many of Chris' field trips, and we both helped him to do what he needed to do. All the trips we took were in my Jeep.

Jhonny and I first met Chris at the airport in Maracaibo on March 7, 1990. His suitcase didn't arrive from Caracas for another week, but other than that, Chris had a successful trip. Between the three of us, we worked out the geology of the study area while Chris selected specimens from the fossils the three of us collected.

I made one major, geological contribution to Chris' study by using my knowledge of structural geology. Chris had found plant fossils in certain locations, but nothing seemed to match as he moved along an outcrop. We found marine fossils in places where they didn't seem to fit in.

One day as we stood there staring at the outcrop, I had a revelation and promptly said, "I think I've just figured it out. There's a major geological fault cutting the formation down the middle." I showed them my evidence and drew a small diagram. All at once, everything fit just right. The locations of the fossils then made perfect sense. (I made high grades in my structural geology and field geology courses.)

Chris collected fossils, made cross-sections, and drew maps off and on until April 1. He returned to the UK on April 5 after a stopover in Caracas to meet some officials in Maraven who graciously helped him to transport his specimens, thanks to Jhonny. He went away quite pleased with what he found. He successfully earned his PhD through his work with Venezuelan Devonian plant fossils.

After this trip, "Dr. Berry" returned to Venezuela three more times. During part of his trip in 1995, Diane Edwards returned with him to examine the locations again. In 1998, Chris brought Craig Harvey who was working on samples of microfossils from some of the same locations where Chris did his initial study. On the last trip in February of 2001 (not long before Belkis, Mary Ann, and I relocated to the US), Chris returned with another student, Susan Hammond, also from Cardiff University in Wales.

Once during an email correspondence with Chris, I casually asked how Dianne was doing. The answer came back, "As a matter of fact, she's having tea with the queen today." As a woman of science and a well-renowned expert in the field of paleobotany, she had been invited to Buckingham Palace for some special event.

A few months after Chris left Venezuela the first time, I made a return trip to Caño Colorado. Along the roadside, I found a rock containing some nice examples of one of the fossils Chris collected for his study, but I noticed that the specimen in hand contained fertile structures. I collected the sample and carried it with me. Then I packed it and mailed it to Chris to include in his study if he wished.

He later described his surprise upon receiving the box and realizing the importance of my discovery. Chris and Dianne later scientifically described it as a new species, *Anapaulia moodyi*, which they published in 1996 in the *Review of Palaeobotany and Palynology*. I felt proud to have a fossil named after me, even though all I did was pick it up from the side of the road. Since that time, the same species has been reported from the Devonian of Morocco.

When Chris once spoke of the fossils he studied from the Campo Chico Formation, he said, "We've got more Devonian plant species on one hillside in Venezuela than are known from the entire state of New York where they are more famous." He might have been exaggerating at the time, but I think he was trying to say how pleased he felt studying Venezuelan Devonian plants.

Devonian Trilobites

Trilobite fossils have been known from Venezuela's Devonian collecting areas for many years. I think they were first mentioned in 1926. Even so, they were never fully studied.

As I wrote earlier about my first trip to the Sierra de Perijá interior at Rio Socuy, my geologist friend, Jorge, spoke of trilobites being collected from the Caño del Oeste Formation. When I began to seriously collect fossils in the area, I discovered several nice trilobites in pretty good condition, which I eventually placed in the MBLUZ collections after I began to work there.

I'll later say more about the Cretaceous fossils we collected from the Perijá mountain front, but during this time, I made contact with John Maisey of the American Museum of Natural History in New York. When John came to visit, he brought his fiancé, Maria da Gloria Pires de Carvalho, who just happened to work at AMNH with trilobites. When Gloria saw the Perijá specimens, she appeared excited and wanted to study them. She found we had three new species, which she published in an AMNH Bulletin with me as the co-author. About all I added was information on the geology at the location.

When the time came to name the species, Gloria asked me for suggestions. A Venezuelan government geologist working in Merida named Oscar Odreman had published a short report mentioning the trilobites, and I had heard he did a lot of good work with fossils in the past. I suggested we name one of the species after him. Gloria agreed, and Venezuela now has a *Rhenops odremani*. I got to send him his first copy of the publication as a surprise.

Plenty of Old Fish

During Chris Berry's first Devonian plant expedition into the Campo Chico Formation, we found another odd fossil—again from along the side of the road. It was an impression shaped a little like a horn, which we first believed to be some sort of invertebrate. After examining it several times, however, we decided it might be a Devonian fish spine. Chris recommended we tell someone. We bought a tube of silicone adhesive at a hardware store in Maracaibo, and we cast an impression, which Chris forwarded to Dr. Gavin Young of Australian National University at Canberra.

Gavin mailed me some of his publications a couple of months later. One paper on fossils from Antarctica showed similar spines. Gavin later told me he believed our report was a new location for these fossils, but the news was nothing earth-shattering. The papers he sent described a variety of other fish fossils from his study area.

I responded by forwarding some information about the Venezuelan Devonian. One of the reports mentioned fossil bone fragments from what was supposed to be a much younger formation (Caño Indio Formation – Mississippian age) along a branch of Caño Colorado known as Caño Colorado Sur. He expressed curiosity about these fossils, and I wrote back telling him I would see if I could find the location again whenever I had a chance.

A few months later, Alfredo Perez and I took a trip for the first time to Caño Colorado Sur. We parked pretty far downstream along Caño Colorado near a general store, and we began to walk. At the junction with Caño Colorado Sur, we turned upstream and climbed the stream channel. We continued all the way to the outcrop of a formation I knew to be of younger age, and on the way upstream, we didn't encounter the fossil bone locality previously described.

Then we worked our way slowly downstream again, checking each outcrop. About halfway back to Caño Colorado, all at once I spotted a small, black piece of bone in a dark gray outcrop along the edge of the channel. I informed Alfredo, and he responded from a few feet away, "Here's some more." We had located the correct spot.

At first, the fossils didn't appear particularly impressive, but the more we examined the outcrop, the more fragments we spotted along a strata of hard, gray rock several feet thick. But then I spotted a nice-looking, small bone with texture on the outer surface. It had a particular shape, and it looked like something I had seen before. The fossil just happened to be imbedded on the corner of an outcrop, so I used my rock hammer and collected it. We also collected a few other small samples of bone, and we made our way slowly back to the Jeep without seeing any other outcrops containing fossils.

After I returned home, I reexamined Gavin's Antarctica study, and right away I recognized that the bone I found matched closely to a bone from a primitive, Devonian, armored fish called *Bothriolepis*. I had inadvertently discovered that the bones were not of Mississippian-age Caño Indio Formation at all; they were actually from the Devonian Campo Chico Formation. I took a photo of the fossil and sent Gavin a photocopy of the picture I used for comparison from his own study. Then I waited for a few weeks to see what he might say.

When I received a response from Gavin, the first word on the top of the page was "Wow!" Gavin later described his reaction upon receiving my news. He said he was working at the university when he read my letter and took a look at my photo. Then he set them aside and went into a lab to do something not particularly important while he pondered the implications of what he just read. For Gavin, the news happened to be quite "earth-shattering." *Bothriolepis* had never been discovered in all of South America or in Africa, although it was a pretty well-known genus from Devonian formations throughout the rest of the world. At the time, no one could explain its absence from two complete continents. In his letter, he said he needed to travel to Venezuela to see for himself.

In November of the same year, I returned to the location alone, and I collected a number of samples. However, I soon discovered how difficult the project would be to carry large amounts of rock from the fossil location all the way back to the general store. I sat down to rest on my way back, trying to decide how we could attack the problem, but as I sat, I glanced down and spied a discarded plastic bottle. I wondered how a plastic bottle had ended up in such a remote location. I studied my surroundings, and I soon spotted a path leading from the south bank down to the stream. I followed it a short distance and encountered a "rancho," a small hut. No one was living there, but beyond it, I found a trail leading upward. I carried my rock samples containing fossils with me, and I climbed until the trail passed through a cultivated field to reach a dirt road. It was a road I once traveled along the south side of Caño Colorado Sur.

I left my collections along the side of the road, and I walked easily downhill to reach my Jeep. Then I drove the Jeep back up the same road to pick up my heavy bags full of rocks. I marked the spot in my mind. This one little detail saved us a lot of trouble later and allowed us to move excavation equipment in and a lot more samples out with little trouble. Later, I was able to drive my Jeep right down almost to the creek, and from there we only had to walk upstream for about twenty minutes to reach the outcrop.

During the summer of 1992, Gavin Young arrived in Venezuela, and the museum was prepared to receive him. Professor Moscó had arranged for us to buy a lot of good quality hammers, chisels, and other equipment, which stayed at the museum when we were finished with our project. (We used the equipment off and on for the entire time afterward while I was at the museum.) A lot of students participated in the project, and not only did we transport people in my Jeep, we also used a Toyota belonging to the University of Zulia. On some nights, we camped near the general store, hanging hammocks in an abandoned building nearby. We cooked over charcoal at night, and the collecting progressed rather well.

Different Lives in One

On some days, we took the vehicles up the road to Chris Berry's locations where Gavin's trained eye pointed out the impressions of fossils we had never noticed. Gavin showed us that the best way to study some of these was to make latex impressions and to coat those with a light colored powder, bring out the contrast. He taught me the tricks, and I made impressions for years afterward to ship to him through the mail.

On other days, we collected along Caño Colorado Sur. It was hard work, but it ended up extremely rewarding. Gavin recognized a number of species, including some bones he had never seen before. In the formation besides *Bothriolepis* (the armored fish), we had primitive sharks, bony fish, another primitive group called "spiny sharks," and a lungfish, which Gavin noted from a single scale. He pointed out the interesting fact that we found a lungfish from the Devonian (265 million years ago), and South America still has a species of lungfish.

On one afternoon, some of the students told me they had carried away some samples, leaving Gavin at the location when they left. When they returned, they found him excitedly and enthusiastically pounding on the outcrop with a hammer and chisel. He had just found a "baby" *Bothriolepis* in near complete condition, and he was looking for more. This fossil was perhaps the prize specimen of the entire trip, although I view the discovery of the coexisting fauna as the most important information. About a year after we found our *Bothriolepis*, Gavin told me about the discovery of the same genus in Africa. Devonian vertebrate faunal distribution had to be re-evaluated on a world-wide scale.

Gavin returned to Australia carrying along actual fossils and a lot of latex casts in order to take photographs and to study them further. Then for a while, we simply kept things quiet until Gavin could work up a publication. (Even so, at least one Maracaibo newspaper published a story, and Jhonny Casas wrote something with Gavin, Chris Berry, and me as co-authors.) Finally, Gavin received a grant to travel to Germany where he did a lot of the preparation work on some of his samples. He eventually published a major paper with me as his co-author. In it, Gavin described a new species of *Bothriolepis* as *Bothriolepis perija*, but he also described a new genus and species based on fragments. It is now known as *Venezuelepis mingui*.

During the time of our field work, the Venezuelan government was in the process of building a dam across Rio Palmar downstream a few miles from Caño Colorado. It was said that when this dam begins to fill, it might cover—or at least cut off—access to some of the Devonian localities, especially those along Caño Colorado Sur. At the time of this writing, I don't know if this ever happened or not. By the time I left Venezuela in 2001, the country was in decline in a lot of respects due to government mismanagement, but since then it seemed to get much worse from what Belkis and I heard. Only time will tell if anyone will ever collect Venezuelan Devonian fish fossils again. I certainly hope so.

The La Grita Dinosaur Project

A research paper published in 1993 described dinosaur fossils collected a number of years earlier from the vicinity of La Grita, Venezuela, in the Venezuelan Andes. A later report spoke of one species similar to a turkey-sized ornithischian (plant eater) found in southern Africa, but little else was known about them.

On a trip in the Jeep with Belkis to La Grita once, we stopped at a number of spots along the way to see what we could find. The area was near the small town of La Quinta, and an important geological location sat nearby where the Jurassic La Quinta Formation was first described.

At one location, we drove up a side road to examine a small road cut. I parked the Jeep at a wide spot along the dirt road, and we walked back while examining the outcrop. I soon found what looked like a plant fossil and what I believed to be some fossil fish scales.

Belkis—who explored just ahead of me—all at once asked, "Hey, John. What's this?" She pointed to a perfect digit bone, most likely from a small dinosaur's foot. And nearby, the rock was full of bone fragments. When I glanced down, I spotted some broken pieces of plaster of Paris. We had stumbled upon the earlier dinosaur locality.

Belkis and I collected a number of bones we could see on the surface, and as we removed pieces of rock, we found more bones underneath. I decided we needed to return with more people and better equipment.

As I began to dig into the rock samples back at the museum, I encountered not only bones but teeth, and some of the teeth were from a different kind of dinosaur—a carnivore, most likely a theropod. This indicated that the location might be even more important than previously believed. I eventually wrote a journal paper to report the theropod teeth. This was another first for Venezuela and only the country's second type of dinosaur.

On January 8, 1994, Belkis and I returned to La Grita with Ascanio Rincón and another student, Victor Hugo Gutierrez. We spent four days working at the location. We cut away around a large section of rock, collecting part of the formation as we did. Then we encapsulated the cut-away section in plaster of Paris to take back to the museum intact. I also took notes on the geology at the site, and I eventually figured out that the dinosaur location doesn't match the beds of the formation on the other side of the canyon because probably a major geological fault separates the two.

The rocks we collected, along with the people and equipment, were heavy enough to bend the flat springs over the Jeep's real wheels. I eventually had to have them bent back the other way at a mechanic's shop.

Afterward, the project remained on hold for a while. We had plenty of samples, and I prepared a few fossils to put on display in the public part of the museum, but little major work was done on them as other projects took this one's place when it came to results.

A couple of years later, professors at Belkis' old school, Colegio Universitario de Maracaibo, invited me one day to evaluate some fossils the students collected near La Grita. The location they studied wasn't far from the other locality, but they hadn't collected in the original location. As I examined the fossils, they showed me a fragment of a large, blade-like tooth, but it wasn't enough to tell for sure. I told them I thought it might be part of a carnivorous dinosaur tooth.

Then they showed me a strange-looking lump of rock. I used a binocular microscope and recognized bone grain across the broken end. I told them I believed it to be a good portion of a dinosaur limb bone. They let me take it to try to clean the surface with some of my tools at the museum, and I uncovered the upper end of a dinosaur femur (leg bone). The piece of the bone looked similar to that of a dinosaur from the late Triassic of Argentina. I estimate it would have been a fairly large animal when compared to the ones we collected years earlier. This dinosaur might have stood six feet tall. The professors seemed quite pleased with their discovery, and they decided to go back a few weeks later with all the students. They invited Belkis and me to go with them and even paid our expenses.

It was a good trip. They found a few more fossils, but the most important was another tooth. One of the students broke open a rock and found part of a tooth inside. The student excitedly called me over to see it and showed me both pieces. However, I noticed a small section from the center of the tooth had popped out. We searched the slope for the missing fragment, but we never located it.

They let me work on it to see what I could do. Luckily, the student had saved both parts of the broken rock, and the impression of the missing portion of the tooth was still present on both halves of the rock. I solved the problem by mixing an amount of commercial epoxy with some finely ground charcoal. Then I filled the empty space, stuck the pieces back together, and let the epoxy set. (The tooth was shiny black, so the black epoxy matched very well.) Then I carefully dug down to the tooth's surface and to the epoxy from one side, exposing one entire side. Except for its larger size, the tooth's overall form appeared quite similar to the ones I described in my paper on theropod teeth. When I returned the tooth to the school, they were happy with it, too.

Years later, a Venezuelan paleontologist I used to work with, Marcelo Sánchez-Villagra of Universität Zürich in Switzerland, decided to describe some of our museum's La Grita fossils, and the collection of authors on the team reported a new species.

Cretaceous Fish

Fish from quarries along the Sierra de Perijá mountain front were among the first fossils I ever found in Venezuela. As stated earlier, I collected several nice specimens from the La Luna Formation before I ever went to work for the museum. Over the years, we found a lot of important fossils from this formation, as well as from the

Machiques Member of the Apón Formation of the Rosarito Quarry west of Villa de Rosario in Zulia State.

Some of the fossils in the Apón Formation could be pretty spectacular. The Machiques Member consists mostly of shale with limestone lenses embedded. Apparently a dead animal on the ocean floor helped to create a protective coating that millions of years later transformed into one of the lenses. No one seems to know exactly how or why this happened, but pretty often these lenses hold some kind of fossil. Along the edges, it was sometimes possible to observe part of a fish, but not always. The lenses are often under pressure because when a person strikes them just right, they tend to explode in several pieces—which isn't the best for the fossils inside. Also, the freshly broken lens fragments smell like crude oil. This formation and others above it, like the La Luna Formation, serve as the source rock (origin) for much of the petroleum under Lake Maracaibo. We found not only fish and other vertebrates; we also found several species of ammonites. Occasionally I discovered strange creatures in some lenses, which I later decided must be squid fossils. The semi-soft body tissue had been preserved in the rock. This sort of preservation is unusual.

Sometimes the fossil fish were preserved in three dimensions, similar to those John Maisey of the American Museum of Natural History studied from the Santana Formation of Brazil. When I invited John to come take a look at our museum's fish, he decided they were important enough for a scientific publication. He did the descriptions and identifications while I did the geology again, and he let me be the first author, which surprised me considerably. We reported a number of fish in Venezuela for the first time, including one named *Vinctifer* that John had worked on in Brazil.

After our first publication was complete, Belkis and I were out looking one day when I spotted a nice looking limestone lens I decided to break open. Unfortunately, it exploded, but to my surprise, we saw a fish we had never before seen in the formation. It looked like a sunfish in body style. We gathered up all the pieces, and because we were about to make a trip to the US to visit my parents, we carried them along, where I mailed the pieces to John from Texas. He soon reported it to be a new species, and he once again published the description with me as his co-author.

I wish I could have lived near the quarry because I would have returned regularly to look for more fish and other interesting fossils. The ones we found were truly remarkable.

For the first Cretaceous fish study with John Maisey, I had already recognized teeth in the La Luna Formation from the Cretaceous shark *Squalicorax*, similar to fossils I used to collect near Denison while growing up. When John saw them, he agreed with me, and the information was included in our first publication.

Years later in 2017 Jorge Carrillo Briceño, a Venezuelan paleontologist who works with Marcelo Sánchez-Villagra, did a study on shark teeth from several locations in western Venezuela, and he re-examined the MBLUZ collections as part of his investigation. He found that the La Luna teeth differ enough from others to describe them as a new species, which he named after me as *Squalicorax moodyi*. At that point, I had two fossils named in my honor, a Devonian plant and a Cretaceous shark.

Jorge and Marcelo ended up writing nice things about me in books on Venezuelan fossils, which I will note later.

Cretaceous Surprises

Fish weren't the only vertebrates to be found in the La Luna and Apón Formations. The La Luna produced a few traces of animals that were probably from plesiosaurs (aquatic reptiles), but we found additional examples of "higher life forms" in the Apón Formation mixed in with the fish.

One day early during my numerous trips to the Rosarito Quarry west of Villa de Rosario, I came across a sizable limestone lens containing some sort of large, round bone in the center. I took it home and spent many hours removing the limestone matrix. It ended up being an ichthyosaur vertebra about six inches in diameter (in other words, from a pretty large animal). One interesting detail I noted, which I described in a short publication, was the fact that one side of the vertebra has a double rib connection (such as is found in the body area of the animal), while the other side has only a single connection (which is normally found along the tail). I used to joke that maybe the animal was unbalanced and swam constantly in circles. At some point later on—and not far from the first discovery—I collected another vertebra that could have come from the same individual, although the second example was somewhat damaged.

Still later, Belkis and I encountered a partial ichthyosaur skeleton in a different part of the quarry. We collected everything we could at the time, but there seemed to be more of it in the limestone. (This time it wasn't associated with the limestone lenses.) However, before we could return, the location was destroyed by the quarrying operations.

I went collecting one day and found a small limestone lens. When I hit the rock with my hammer, it broke a bone in half, which I could see in cross-section. My experience hunting fossils in the North Sulphur River in Texas paid off, however. I recognized from the grain of the fossil bone it was from a reptile instead of a fish. As is often the case, a tiny fragment flew out when the rock broke, and I never could find it. Even so, I used the same trick as I did with the broken dinosaur tooth from the La Quinta Formation. The impression (mold) of the missing bone fragment was still present as part of the rock. I mixed some epoxy to use as filler, but this time I used ground cinnamon as a coloring agent to match the color of the bone. I filled the gaps and stuck the rock back together. Then I dug down through the limestone using an electric engraving tool to expose the bone and the epoxy on one side. The end result looked really good. The bone was from the hip of a Cretaceous sea turtle.

On another trip, I escorted an American geologist who was new to Venezuela to see the Cretaceous formations. Our last stop was at the Rosarito Quarry, and it was getting late in the day. Along the quarry road, I spotted several small limestone lenses. Someone had tossed them into a muddy patch. I didn't want to take the time to break them, and because they were small, I merely tossed them into the back of the Jeep, where they rolled around all the way back to Maracaibo.

When I returned home in the evening, I unloaded the Jeep. Then I carried the limestone lenses to the backyard to wash off the mud. I took a good looked at them before I tried to break them open. All at once I saw a pair of eye sockets staring back at me. The surface of the limestone lens displayed the skull of a sea turtle.

I eventually let the group at SMU in Dallas study this fossil, but the person doing the work for some reason left the project, and it stood idle for years. Long after I returned to the US, the university still had the fossil, but little had been done to prepare it. I mentioned it to Jorge Carrillo Briceño, and he became interested in the possibility of working on it. He informed Marcelo Sánchez-Villagra, and they made arrangements to transport the skull to Switzerland. I also told them about the hip bone and gave them the catalogue number. They made arrangements through Tito Barros at MBLUZ to obtain this specimen, too. As of now, they are about to publish a study, and I just learned that this species will also be named in my honor. It will be the third fossil with my name attached to it. Based on the age of the rock formation, this sea turtle is not the oldest known, but it is among the oldest (perhaps as much as 110 million years old).

One day at the same quarry I spotted three small, isolated bones protruding from a limestone bank. The spot was difficult to reach, but I perched on the side of the bank and started to remove the fossils. Two of them appeared to be small fish fragments that were unidentifiable, but the third looked pretty different from anything I had seen at the quarry. It was also in much better condition. I prepared the bone on one side and believed it might be some sort of strange turtle bone again. As before, I could already tell it wasn't from a fish.

In 1996, I carried a photo with me to a convention at the American Museum of Natural History in New York where I found Eugene Gaffney, the museum's turtle expert. He took one look at the photo and said he didn't think it was a turtle bone. He said, "I think you should show this to Alex Kellner."

Dr. Alexander Kellner of Museu Nacional in Rio de Janeiro, Brazil, said, "I think this is a pterosaur bone," (his specialty), and he wanted to do a paper on it. After I returned to Maracaibo, I mailed the fossil to him, and he prepared it further, publishing it with me as co-author in 2003. It is Venezuela's first reported pterosaur.

An Interesting Helicopter Ride

Late in February of 1992, I received word that a documentary crew from the Venezuelan petroleum company Maraven wanted to do a short exposé on MBLUZ. I believe Angel Viloria set it up through some of his contacts. They wanted to take our museum's staff into the field and video us engaged in typical activities. Maraven sponsored these sorts of shows often. We all thought it might be fun.

On February 29 (1992 was a leap year), I put together some equipment, and the film crew escorted us to various places for their shots. They drove me to La Luna Quarry and followed me around for a while as I pretended to hunt for fossils. For one scene, they showed me opening a limestone lens containing a fossil fish I brought with me just to have something to show. They did the same thing with some of the others: José Moscó collected fish in a net in a local stream, Rosanna Cache watched birds, Angel caught butterflies, etc.

They put us up in a motel in Machiques, and the next day, March 1, they arranged for a small helicopter to fly us high into the Perijá Mountains to do more filming. It was my first helicopter ride.

I wish to point out here that the town of Machiques—from where our flight began that morning—is usually pretty warm and humid during the day. It probably sits only a few hundred feet above sea level. However, when I heard what the film crew had planned for us, I started to think about how much the temperature drops with increases in altitude. I had brought along an extra long-sleeved shirt, which I threw into my collecting bag at the last minute to use as a jacket if necessary.

They flew us in pairs, and most of us carried along some equipment. The helicopter pilot flew us up in three groups, and we traveled for quite a distance. We also flew pretty high. It was a great view. I saw Cerro Pintado fairly close for the first time toward our north for a moment. (This mountain was already important for our museum, as I will explain later on.) I had no idea where we were when the pilot dropped us off and flew away. The air in my lungs felt thin. The plan was to leave us for a while and come back to pick us up in the afternoon. Our group for the flight included José Moscó, Miguel Pietrangelli, Rosanna Cache, and me, plus the two-man Maraven film crew. Angel allowed the rest of us to fly on ahead. The helicopter for the three trips flew full. I believe he planned to join us on a fourth flight with the film crew's producer later in the day.

We all began to walk around and do our thing in the morning as we explored our environment. The guys with the camera sometimes followed and captured their shots. The weather felt cool, but after living in Maracaibo for years, it was a pleasant change. A large mountain peak with a burned top stood to our west not far away, and we were above the timber line. The vegetation I saw was mostly tundra-like plants, and all of these details should have given me something of a clue as to our location. I figured we had ended up well above 10,000 feet.

Around noon, the mountain began to cloud over. All at once one of the cameramen guessed that with so much cloudiness at our location, the helicopter wouldn't be able to pick us up in the afternoon.

While we waited, I decided to climb the side of the flat-topped mountain nearby to look at the geology. I thought about climbing to the top, and I figured I could have made it in about 20 minutes. About half way up, however, I spotted a few plant fossils. They weren't good enough to identify, but I thought they might be Devonian. It might have been a good place to do a little more exploration. Even so, I decided at that point to wander too far from our group's make-shift camp because I always thought there might be a chance for the helicopter to pick us up. For this reason I didn't continue all the way to the top of the mountain. I later learned it was the highest mountain of the Perijá range called Cerro Plano with an elevation of nearly 12,000 feet above sea level. I missed my chance.

We were on the east side of the mountain, and the clouds closed in. As expected, the sun disappeared completely long before nightfall, and the weather began to turn cold really fast. The temperature soon dropped to around freezing, with some wind to increase the chill.

We had a little food, consisting of some saltine crackers and small cans of tuna. We had brought along a little water, too. One of the cameramen smoked, so he had a cigarette lighter, but there above the timber line, we didn't have any wood to burn. Someone dropped a little lower before nightfall and brought back part of a small, dead tree trunk, but it wasn't enough to keep the fire going all night. Then someone else suggested that stalks of a dry, bamboo-like plant growing a little below our location might actually burned pretty well. We all went down and gathered arms full of these stalks, but they burned rather rapidly. We had to keep the fire small to try to make it last all night.

Poor José, who was older than the rest of us, had come on the trip wearing a short-sleeve shirt. After all, we left behind a warm climate in Machiques in the morning and expected to return in the afternoon. I still felt cold after I rolled down my long sleeves, but when I saw how he was suffering, I let him use my extra shirt. I had also brought along a little newspaper for wrapping samples, so they used a little of it to start the fire, and we used most of the rest to line the insides of our clothes. (I remembered this trick from watching old movies about homeless people in New York City.) We also tried to use clusters of dead grass for extra insulation. Even so, it wasn't nearly enough. We clustered around the small fire for a while, but then we tried to sleep. It felt mostly too cold to sleep on the bare ground.

I recalled a story my geologist friend Jorge once told me. He did his geological field training for his college on a mapping project in Perijá for a ministry office of the Venezuelan government. They flew groups of students by helicopter into the mountains, let them do their work, and then picked them up in the afternoon. In this way they constructed pretty good, large-scale, geological maps of the Perijá range.

Jorge described one day when the helicopter dropped them off and left them near the top of a mountain. When the leader of the group took a look at his base map, he discovered that the helicopter pilot had dropped them off at the wrong location. They were on the wrong mountain, and it would be impossible to reach the correct location without days of difficult travel. This meant that when the helicopter went to pick them up in the afternoon at the correct location, the group wasn't going to be there, and no one might realize what happened. From their location, it would also take them several days to descend to the nearest location in Venezuela where they could make a phone call (pre-cell phone days).

However, the Colombian border sat a short distance away, and due to the shape of the mountain range, the Colombians had developed much of their side of the mountains, making plenty of roads. From the top of the mountain, the team observed a settlement in Colombia not far below. To solve their problem, they simply crossed the border and walked down to the village the same day, where they called for help and got the problem all sorted out. For this reason, I figured if the helicopter didn't pick us up the next day, we could simply walk westward into Colombia, the other side of Cerro Plano, and reach help nearby.

Rosanna was rather short and petite. As night closed in, I noticed her shivering uncontrollably. Based on stories I read, the best way to stay warm under such conditions is to share body heat. Miguel and I sandwiched Rosanna between us. We put down a little newspaper and reclined on the ground, back to front, with our feet near the fire to stay warm. Every so often we all three turned around to face the opposite direction. It worked pretty well throughout the rest of the night, but I don't believe any of us got any sleep. José mostly sat close to the fire, and he said he was doing pretty well when we asked. The film crew also clustered around the fire and talked, continually tossing bamboo stalks on the fire throughout the night until they ran out.

After dawn arrived, it was light by 7:00 AM, but our location still appeared completely clouded over. We no longer saw the nearby mountains. We couldn't even see the lower areas nearby where we had gathered dry bamboo the previous afternoon. It started to get a little warmer, however. I packed my things, and we waited. We were out of food by then, and no one had much water left. Around 9:00 AM, the sun finally broke through the clouds at our location.

Not long afterward, we heard a helicopter approaching. The pilot landed next to our camp, and he quickly loaded in Rosanna and me. He flew us only a short distance—about half way down the mountain to a point below the clouds. Then he dropped us off in the middle of nowhere, heading back rapidly for the top. We guessed he was trying to get everyone off the top of the mountain before the clouds returned, and he would eventually returned to pick us up. Rosanna and I waited quite a while, but he eventually returned for us after he got the others away and back to Machiques. Then he flew us down to an old airstrip northwest of Machiques where he left the aircraft to use the restroom. Finally, he flew us back to town where the others were already waiting. As a result, my first helicopter ride turned into a total of four rides between take-offs and landings. It all seemed rather exciting and worth remembering—once we lived through it.

A few months later, the short episode about our museum appeared on television all across Venezuela. It ran weekly over a period of about a month during a Maraven-sponsored, evening program that was pretty popular. Thanks to the film editors, we all appeared quite professional. There was no mention of getting trapped on a remote mountain at night in the cold.

Cerro Pintado

The project to collect fossils from a cave on the top of Cerro Pintado turned out to be one of our longest running projects while I was at MBLUZ. It was a real logistical challenge.

Cerro Pintado is a high, limestone-capped, flat-topped mountain in the Sierra de Perijá range forming part of the border between Venezuela on the east and Colombia on the west. It is occasionally visible from as far away as Maracaibo on a clear day—but days are not usually clear enough in this part of Venezuela. Between Maracaibo and the mountains, some dry areas are present, which tend to produce dust on hot, dry, windy days. Most of the time, however, the visibility problem involves humidity, haze, or just plain clouds.

I recall the first time I ever saw the mountain as I boarded a jet at the airport in Maracaibo. I felt impressed by the view. The horizontal layers of limestone stood out clearly—even at more than eighty miles away. On a few trips toward the mountains early in the morning, it was possible to see the mountain, and when I did, I usually stopped to take photos, as rare as the spectacle seemed to be.

For a few weeks in the mid-1990s, I worked on a petroleum study in a 10-story building in Maracaibo. It was located on Ave. 4 (known as Bella Vista). During morning and afternoon breaks, I often walked up eight flights of stairs for exercise to reach the roof. It was a great view from there. I could see the bridge across Lake Maracaibo and lots of other landmarks on most any day, but I couldn't normally see the mountains. However, I took a trip to the roof one clear day and spied Cerro Pintado, as well as the entire northern part of the Perijá range. Cerro Pintado was about 90 miles away at the time. (I referred to this view from the building when writing my first novel, *Journey from Mezet*, where a young boy leads the main character named Marc to the top of an abandoned building to see the mountains—but it's too late in the day for Marc to see them. I also make a reference to Cerro Pintado as some of the characters pass it along its northern side while traversing the mountains later in the book.)

Over the years, I became pretty captivated with this mountain, and I believe Angel Viloria shared my fascination. This is why I felt pretty pleased when in March of 1993 the other curators at the museum invited me along on a biological expedition to Cerro Pintado from the Colombian side.

The mountain is full of depressions and caves. The sides are rather steep all the way around, with cliffs several hundred feet high observed from east and west. Just to reach the base of the mountain from the Venezuelan side is not an easy thing to do, but from the Colombian side, it is possible to drive a four-wheel-drive vehicle to within a few miles of the mountain's base.

Angel had made contact with a Colombian conservationist group known as "Friends of Pinta'o." Some of their members agreed to lead MBLUZ scientists to the top by way of a route they knew. It would be a difficult climb, but it could be done in less than a day from an initial point at the base of the mountain.

We packed some supplies and equipment, and we left Maracaibo in a university Toyota. We entered Colombia through Maicao, and at the border checkpoint, the officials didn't recommend we continue our journey when they learned of our destination. They claimed it would be too dangerous. However, Angel explained that we were to meet up with local people, and we would be all right. They stamped our passports and let us through. We advanced until we reached Villa Nueva, arriving in the early afternoon. We met one of our hosts there named Luis Guerra, and we traveled into the mountains to the end of the dirt road, where we stayed the night under a shelter.

From there the next day, we loaded our packs on some mules and walked on to a modest hacienda near the base of Cerro Pintado. The views along the way were spectacular. The hacienda belonged to Enrique Nuñez, who was to lead the group up the mountain the following day. Members of our group had observed condors in flight on Cerro Pintado not long before, and as we studied the mountain from a distance, I observed three very large birds in gliding flight near the summit, which couldn't have been anything other than condors. No other gliding birds in the region approach them with respect size.

In the afternoon as we rested, Enrique pressed some fresh sugarcane juice into glasses, and I drank about half a small glass. I also ate some soup that night, which was made there at the hacienda. I don't know which one did it, but I felt ill during the night and didn't get much sleep.

The next morning I still felt seriously ill. I headed toward the base of the mountain and started to climb with the rest of the group, but I felt so ill I had to turn back to the hacienda alone while the rest of them continued the climb. I made my way slowly back and went to bed in one of the shacks. I didn't wake up until the next morning, and I still didn't feel in top condition even then. In the afternoon when I felt a little better, I explored around the hacienda. I stayed another full day and night, and at times, I helped around the hacienda as I started to feel much better.

On the following afternoon, the group returned. They had spent most of their time exploring the top, and at night, they slept in a cave. During the hours of darkness one night, they lowered Angel into the lower part of the cave where he discovered some bones. They soon showed them to me. Angel had collected a pair of large humeri (upper arm bones, left and right), a radius (lower arm bone), and a rib fragment from a ground sloth the size of a large bear. They also brought back some other smaller bones, some of which might have been modern. Later, I learned that the cave is known as "Bone Cave," but not for the fossils; instead, it had been named by early spelunkers for some deer bones they encountered near the cave's mouth. The cave sits on the Venezuelan side of the border—just barely.

Another day later we packed the bones as carefully as possible, considering their size, and loaded them onto some mules along with the rest of our baggage for the trip to where we left the university vehicle. This allowed us to walk faster.

On the way back, however, Angel stealthy pointed out a man carrying a rifle who watched our group from the top of a hill. My companions speculated that he might be a member of a Colombian guerrilla group. We pretended not to notice him, but our route was about to take us in his general direction. We worried that he might be about to intercept our party at the top of the next hill. But when we reach the top, he was gone—to our relief.

We made our way to the Toyota and continued right away along the dirt road down the mountain. We stayed in Villa Nueva that night, and later, during dinner, Luis Guerra told us a story.

When we showed up several days earlier, he worried that as a citizen of the USA I might be targeted for kidnapping by the local guerrilla group. After we left on foot for the hacienda that first morning, he paid a visit to the group's commander and said something like, "Hey, we've got a group of Venezuelan biologists doing a scientific study on Cerro Pintado, and we'd appreciate it if you left them alone. Oh, and by the way; they have a Canadian with them." The local leader agreed to his request, but he had apparently sent a man to watch us as we returned to the university vehicle.

I felt extremely lucky. For days I'd been simply hanging around the hacienda in the company of a caretaker and a couple of young children—much of the time, feeling pretty ill. I had been carrying my passport in my pocket the entire time, and it would have only taken a man pointing a gun at me to figure out I was actually from the US. Some US citizens captured by Colombian guerrillas stayed in their control for years.

We returned home safely the following day, but after that incident, I knew I could never travel back to the area in the same manner. But if so, how was I going to get to the top of Cerro Pintado to look for more fossil bones? As it turned out, it took me more than four and a half years to finally get there.

At the museum, we decided the best way to return to Cerro Pintado would be by helicopter. However, it was too expensive for us to pay for one at the museum. Then someone suggested we get the Venezuelan Army to fly us there. It sounded like a good idea, but they needed to be approached in just the right manner.

Before long, the university dean in charge of the department governing the museum's activities assigned Professor Cesar Vargas to act as a liaison between the University of Zulia and the Venezuelan Army. Cesar was always very helpful. He set up meetings whenever he could find people willing to listen to us, and a couple of times I gave slide presentations in front of groups of army officers and state legislative officials. I sometimes used the Colombian guerrilla story as a way to stress how impossible it would be for the museum's resident paleontology curator to return to Cerro Pintado through Colombia, and army officers fully agreed with me. The people we spoke to usually sounded interested, but we missed out a couple of times when we showed up and found circumstances had changed or officials had changed plans without letting us know in advance. I barely missed meeting the Governor of Zulia on one occasion when he decided to travel by helicopter from an army base instead of by limo, leaving just as we arrived.

I knew we needed help in identifying the sloth, so I wrote to Dr. Greg McDonald of the US National Parks Service. I later discovered that Greg was the perfect person to know when dealing with some of our projects. He possessed the ability to identify most any type of animal based on a single bone or a reasonably large fragment. (Greg told me a story about someone trying to "stump" him once by asking him to identify a penguin bone, but he passed the test.) He even visited our museum once to examine our initial Cerro Pintado collections, and after studying them for a few minutes, he explained that our sloth once broke its front leg, but the bone healed. However, as it mended, the sloth had favored its other front leg, which eventually developed arthritis. He told us all this using only three bones of the four bones we had at the time. He took with him the rib fragment to use for Carbon-14 age dating, and he determined the animal lived just over 14,000 years ago, falling into the time period only 4,000 years before most of the Pleistocene megafauna went extinct.

On October 7, 1997, after nearly four years and seven months of making contacts without much to show for them, Cesar arranged a meeting between several of us from the museum and Brigadier General Manuel Antonio Rosendo, commander of the Venezuelan Army's 11th Infantry Brigade. His office was located at a military base practically next to the university. (General Rosendo later became famous for refusing to carry out Hugo Chaves' order for Venezuelan troops to fire live ammunition at protestors.) The general told us that the next time they launched one of their anti-drug campaigns into the Perijá Mountains, we could hitch a ride to the top of Cerro Pintado. We thought this news sounded great, and a date was soon set.

On the morning of November 26, 1997, we loaded up and left the museum parking lot in a university bus to travel to Machiques. Five of us from the museum were on the trip, along with two others whom we had arranged to come along. We continued on to Hacienda Los Andes, where the army had set up their base camp. This was a large hacienda the army used often for similar operations because it had an air strip. We soon met General Jesús Poggioli, who was in charge of the field campaign. He basically told us "We'll see if we can let you go, but it will be tomorrow." He explained that the clouds were already below about 8000 feet, and we had to travel to above 10,000 feet. After our museum's experience with the Maraven film crew, I perfectly understood.

We crossed our fingers and returned to a national park station for the night. Bright and early the next morning, we were back at the army camp. They decided to let us go. They had two French-built "Super Puma" helicopters operated by the Venezuelan Air Force, and a group of 12 Venezuelan Special Forces soldiers led by Captain Niño loaded into the front aircraft. We scientists and explorers soon loaded into the second one.

I could hardly believe it was finally happening, but unfortunately, they could only let us stay on the mountaintop for one day and night. We had to fly back to the army camp the next morning. Still, it was much better than we ever had previously.

Before the flight, a soldier mounted a large machine gun near the side door of the helicopter and loaded it. One of my friends took a great photo of the soldier behind his weapon with me sitting calmly behind him. Then they instructed us that when the time came to land, we needed to unload heading toward the front of the craft so the pilot could see us, but we had to make sure not to touch the machine gun as we climbed out (to prevent an accidental discharge, I suppose).

Both helicopters took off, and as with my earlier helicopter rides into the Sierra de Perijá, we had a great view. Almost before I knew it, we were flying over Cerro Pintado, which appeared really rocky and stark below. I spied large, eroded crevasses from the air.

The first helicopter identified a good landing site and tossed out a green smoke grenade to mark it, Then the soldiers landed and took protective positions around us just in case. After all, they were in the middle of an anti-drug campaign. The first helicopter took off, and we landed right behind it, unloading rapidly and carrying more equipment than we would ever need. Then the second helicopter took off, and they both flew away, leaving us to our fate.

Soon we set off to look for the cave. I saw ice on the ground—to give some idea of how cold it had been the night before. The cave wasn't far away over a ridge, but we had to walk the long way around to reach it. It sat in a depression—not obvious from most directions. Water flowed into it, but a larger, dry entrance opened a little higher.

Once we reached the cave, the army went in first to make sure it was safe. Inside, I saw a short upper cave, but on the right side, it had a deep sinkhole about 12 feet deep where animals could have easily fallen in the dark. The soldiers used a set of night-vision goggles, and later, they let me use them to see if I could find any fossils in the upper part of the cave. (I recalled this experience when writing *Wherever the Wind Will Take Us* after Ginger and Lee are attacked by pirates.) People had been camping in the upper cave off and on (including our own museum's curators some years earlier), and the army found evidence showing someone had stayed there only days before. They speculated it might have been some of the people who cultivated opium poppies in fields further down the mountain's slopes.

Our group divided up and started to explore. Most of my friends from the museum did scientific work outside the cave, but several of us explored the lower cave in search of more fossils, including Ascanio Rincón, Tito Barros, and a local explorer from Machiques named Leonel Lanier, who was a good friend of our museum. The lower cave extended along a twisted, sometimes narrow path. Water flowed toward the cave's interior.

I wore tall, plastic boots, but the water was pretty deep in spots. I soon had boots full of water, which didn't help much with regard to hypothermia as the day progressed. Still, as my legs heated the water, it served as thermal insulation.

Almost immediately, we began to spot bones, large and small. At first we only marked the fossils using flags in order to collect them later, and Tito and Leonel helped a lot by making measurements of the bones' locations throughout the cave for later cataloguing.

At a spot about 275 feet into the lower cave, we reached a point where the cave dropped sharply, and the water was such that we would have needed diving equipment to continue safely. We didn't go any further.

Ascanio had moved on ahead of me near the pool at the end of our trail, and he began to explore underwater with his hands. He discovered two skulls there, one of a small species of deer, and one from a wild pig of the type seen commonly at lower elevations. He also found some sloth vertebrae that had been fused together by arthritis. All these fossils were caught among the rocks.

I held back as I searched slowly, and all at once I spied a strange shape in a gravel bank on the right. When I looked closer, I noticed tooth sockets. I had found the skull of the ground sloth where Ascanio already passed, but I could see how he missed it. In most cases, the bones we collected were loose on the surface. This skull rested up-side down, embedded partially in the gravel. While one side of the skull lacked teeth, the other side still had them, although they were somewhat broken. Still, it wasn't bad for a fossil that had been transported more than 250 feet from where the animal fell and died—14,000 years ago.

We used carbide lamps on hardhats, and my lamp wasn't working especially well. At this point Tito went off to see if he could do something about my lamp, so I sat and rested next to the sloth skull for a while. (Ascanio had already headed toward the surface with the fossils he collected.) I carried a backup flashlight, but I didn't want to use up the batteries. I turned it off.

I sat alone in complete darkness for a few moments, and I found it to be a memorable experience—something of a "Zen" moment. I had visited a number of caves and dark places before, as my previous stories describe, but in retrospect, I view this time as quite special. There I was, after years of trying to get there, in the deepest part of a cave at above 10,000 feet on the Venezuelan-Colombian border. I sat in the dark next to the skull of a 14,000-year-old animal, now extinct, listening to the tranquil sounds of water flowing beside me. It felt rather surreal.

Once Tito returned with better light for me to use, I gingerly removed the skull by digging away at the gravel all around it. The gravel had been in place a long time, but the skull finally came out without damage. It still held gravel inside the brain cavity, but I simply left it there for more leisurely extraction under better light conditions.

Some months before our trip, the camera I had been using for years stopped working. It was the same one I dropped during the killer bee attack. I managed to hold it above my head to keep it dry once when I stepped into a deep spot in a water-filled cave near Rio Socuy. I had taken thousands of pictures with it over about 16 years. I found another camera body that worked with the lenses, but it had problems, so I didn't fully trust it. A couple of days before the trip when we found out the chances were good for the trip to actually take place, I bought a new, compact, fairly-fancy camera. As I held the skull right after I removed it from the gravel, I loaned this new camera to Tito so he could record the historic event on film. However, the camera had a factory defect. The internal sensor that read the ASO speed of the film wasn't functioning. All my photos of the trip taken with that camera were black when developed—except for that one historical shot. For some strange reason, the darkness of the cave combined with the flash made the image register on the film. This photo now appears in a book written by Jorge Carrillo Briceño, which I will refer to in more detail at the end of the following section.

We collected nearly 50 fossil specimens to add to the 11 the museum already had. I consider the sloth skull to be the most important prize of the trip, although we encountered the bones of several other rather surprising animals, including the hip bone from a species of giant capybara (rodent). We also found the bones of a few small animals, including a bat bone and part of a frog cranium. If I remember correctly, I even discovered a small bone inside the sloth skull when I removed the gravel from the brain cavity. Some of the bones may not be as old as those of the sloth, but they could all provide valuable information on the fauna at the location over the years through Carbon-14 testing if anyone ever wants to spend the money. There's no telling what other fossils might be discovered if someone ever has the opportunity to spend more than a single day searching for them.

We collected and packed all the bones for removal from the lower cave, and once in the upper cave again, I carefully wrapped and re-packed everything in boxes for transport in the helicopter the next morning. I had worked nearly all day in the lower cave, and I really felt cold. Even after I changed out of my wet jeans and socks, and got into my bedroll, I laid there shivering with my teeth chattering. (I used this experience in my novel, *Land on the Verge of Darkness*, when Wendy gets caught in a downpour on a cold night.) Even on the top of the mountain the time when the helicopter couldn't pick us up, I don't think I felt as cold as I did on Cerro Pintado that night inside the cave.

The next day we packed and carried everything to the helicopter landing site. We had to wait a while, but some of the others explored the area nearby. Tito captured a frog for the herpetology collection at the museum during our wait, and he later described it as a new species.

When the helicopters arrived, I made sure the box holding the sloth skull was loaded before we took off. The flight back to the army base camp went without a problem. The Special Forces soldiers, while they at first might have looked upon our project with a little reserve, were quite helpful, and before we left the top of the mountain, we were all good friends. I wasn't able to maintain contact with Captain Niño, but Tito paid him a visit once during a trip. I very much appreciate what Cezar Vargas, General Rosendo, General Poggioli, Captain Niño, and the Venezuelan army and air force did for us—even though the trip took more than four and a half years to organize and lasted only one day. We couldn't have done it without them.

With the specimens cleaned and catalogued, I informed Greg McDonald that we had the sloth skull, and he immediately expressed an interest in describing it scientifically because he believed it to be a new species. In 2013, Greg, Ascanio (who now works for the Venezuelan equivalent of the US National Science Foundation), and Timothy Gaudin described the sloth remains as a new genus and species, *Megistonyx oreobios*, or "greatest-claw mountain-life" because of its characteristics and high-mountain habitat.

The Discovery of Fossils in a Venezuelan Tar Pit

I wrote most of the following information in October of 2014, and rather than try to write it again and forget something, I'll simply leave most of it as I wrote it with a few updates and additions. Jorge Carrillo Briceño, whom I wrote about several times earlier, referred to it when he produced a 2015 publication, which I describe at the end of this section. This may be the most important paleontological discovery I ever made.

When the Tar Pits Project began in 1996, I had served as curator of the Paleontology Section at MBLUZ since October of 1990. I continued at the same post until May of 2001 when I returned to live in the United States. Previous to the Tar Pits Project, our museum dealt with Devonian plants, trilobites, and fish, Jurassic dinosaurs, Cretaceous fish, marine reptiles, and a pterosaur, and Pleistocene mammals from cave deposits, all collected in Venezuela. My wife, Belkis, who was a technical geologist, often accompanied me on field trips. Ascanio Rincón, a student at the time, served as my assistant in the museum, and he also went with me (or occasionally by himself) on many field trips over the years. While working as a geologist with petroleum service companies, I learned long ago that Venezuelan oil wells in the early days of the industry were "spotted" (located) and drilled on the basis of nearby natural asphalt seeps at the surface. Even so, I had never heard of or read about fossils from Venezuelan tar pits.

The full story of the discovery of the first recognized Venezuelan tar pit fossils really goes back to just over a year before the actual discovery took place. In October of 1996, Belkis and I attended the Society of Vertebrate Paleontology convention at the American Museum of Natural History in New York. I had been corresponding with Dr. Greg McDonald of the US National Park Service on other projects at the museum. At that moment, I had never met Greg in person, but in a correspondence, he told me he would be at a poster session on a certain night at the convention. I stood near the main entrance of a very large room at the American Museum while trying to read the name tags of all the convention participants who entered. Richard F. Wheeler of the George C. Page Museum of Rancho La Brea Discoveries also stood near the entrance. His poster displayed photos of the La Brea tar pits, and we started to talk while I continued to read name tags. Remembering the oil seeps in Venezuela, often called "menes," it occurred to me to ask him if any fossils had ever been collected from Venezuelan natural asphalt deposits. Richard had never heard of any.

I later met Greg, and over the next few days, I asked him and other paleontologists the same question. Greg had worked with southern California tar pits in the past, so he provided additional information, saying that fossils had also been collected from natural asphalt seeps in Peru, Ecuador, Cuba, Trinidad, and Iran, but no one had ever heard of fossils of this sort from Venezuela. It made me wonder why. According to Greg, wherever long-duration natural asphalt seeps were present, fossils should also be present.

When I returned to Venezuela after the convention, I started to accumulate data. I had access to a lot of old petroleum exploration files and publications. These included maps showing the locations of more than 40 major natural asphalt seeps and 170 minor seeps throughout Venezuela. On occasion, Belkis, Ascanio, or other MBLUZ students accompanied me on field trips to locate and examine tar pits noted in the studies. I especially remember a series of tar pits near a Lagoven golf course, and I saw a golf ball stuck in one. The tar pits presented hazards and "traps" for golfers of an unusual nature. Belkis and I located several promising sites for more extensive exploration, and on one field trip, Greg McDonald, Ascanio, and I explored locations along the Sierra de Perijá mountain front while Greg was in Venezuela for another project. On September 27, 1997, Belkis and I were able to locate the Inciarte site based on old maps and by questioning local residents, but we didn't have time to explore the area that day. Many oil company employees knew about Inciarte through published literature.

About a month later, on October 24, I returned to the area with two LUZ biology students, Nicanor Cifuentes and Lisbeth Caceres. Ascanio would have normally been there, but he couldn't go on that occasion. The three of us explored only a part of Inciarte. I felt quite impressed by its size, and we found evidence of the asphalt mining operation that took place very early in the 20th century, including wooden railroad ties and pits full of liquid tar where some surface material had once been removed. We found it possible to navigate over much of the area if we watched our steps. However, in many places the seeps were active, producing messy liquid petroleum and natural gas. We saw the remains of modern animals imbedded in the asphalt, including insects, birds, dogs, and probably cattle. Grass, cacti, and small trees grew on the surface in many places.

Near the center of the area, I located some small bone and tooth fragments in what we later determined to be "spoil heaps" (small mounds of waste material), dating back to the mining operation. The fragments were weathered after many years of exposure.

In general, I viewed Inciarte, due its size, as holding more promise than any tar pit site I had seen up to then, but I didn't believe it would be a particularly simple process to collect the fossils of extinct Pleistocene fauna there. The deposits are extensive. Where would a person even start digging?

That same night (October 24), I started to clean the bone and tooth fragments by soaking them in gasoline. Parts of three teeth were present, and I noticed right away that two of the teeth were from a large carnivore, probably some sort of large cat. (A cat's first and only lower molar is distinctive.) I reconstructed the other tooth (a premolar) from the fragments, and on October 26, I did a quick comparison with the teeth of large, modern cats using information from my home library. None of the species seemed to match. Still later that night after a search through my other references, I located a September - 1984 publication by Tejada-Flores and Shaw in the *Journal of Vertebrate Paleontology* showing photos of the lower jaws of *Smilodon*—the Pleistocene saber-tooth cat—from Rancho La Brea. The Inciarte teeth were a very close match to those in the photos. I felt extremely excited and a little surprised that after believing it might be difficult to prove the presence of Pleistocene fossils at Inciarte, everything fell into place only two days after the initial discovery.

I think it's interesting to point out that the mining activities had occurred nearly 100 years earlier, but as far as I know, no one had ever mentioned fossils at Inciarte in the published literature. I believe the workers of that time must have encountered fossil bones as they dug the early pits, but they apparently didn't recognize the bones for what they represented.

I returned to the area with Ascanio on November 22, 1997. We explored more extensively, taking photos and making a few collections. By then, several people were aware of the discovery, including Greg McDonald. Others soon found out, such as Chris Shaw of the George C. Page Museum in Los Angeles, and Chris sounded very interested in the discovery when he learned that Inciarte was like Rancho La Brea had been a hundred years ago, only much larger. (This museum has more than a million catalogued tar pit specimens from La Brea alone.)

In the meantime, several other museum projects occupied much of my time. We visited Cerro Pintado five days later, making some important collections there. (This was a field trip in a Venezuelan Army helicopter to the top of Cerro Pintado that took more than four and a half years of planning.) Other projects soon became active again during the next year while we considered the impact of the Inciarte discovery. I imagined we would have had a few visitors to take a look, but I guess everyone else was too busy, as well.

John M. Moody

On September 12, 1998, I led another field trip to Inciarte along with Ascanio and Heberto Prieto, who was another LUZ biology student. While Ascanio and Heberto collected some more bones from the spoil heaps, I went exploring and taking photos again. Before long, I located a couple of large bone fragments imbedded in asphalt, and I immediately realized they were too large to be from a cow. They had to be from an extinct animal, perhaps a ground sloth. Later, Ascanio, Heberto, and I collected the bones on the surface, but as we did, we found more bones directly below the surface. On October 24, 1998 (exactly a year after my initial discovery), Ascanio and I returned with Henning Henningfeld, a petroleum geologist friend who worked at Shell. He had expressed an interested in seeing the location. Ascanio and I collected a large block of asphalt matrix from under where I found the large bone fragments the time before, and we discovered it to be full of bones of many sizes. One fossil we noticed right away was the jaw fragment from a very young *Eremotherium*, the giant ground sloth. We soon discovered that from the surface down to about 10 to 20 centimeters was very hard to dig in, but below this, the sand and asphalt mixture was rather pliable and soft.

At that point I decided we needed more specimens in order to get a variety of researchers interested in the site. Except for Greg, we received little response with regard to the discovery. From then on, we continued to dig two test pits at the same location, measuring the depths of the material as we removed it. We averaged a field trip to collect material about every two months, and in all, I made 16 more field trips to the area. It also helped early on when Sr. José González, a local farmer, invited us to park on his land. Afterward, I was able to drive my Jeep to within fifty yards of our primary collecting location. This allowed us to carry away a lot more bags of matrix and large specimens per trip. Greg McDonald made the first presentation on the Inciarte discoveries at a conference in Bolivia in May of 1999. Ascanio and I were the co-authors of the published summary.

The field work was messy, and the conditions could be stifling. I always used the same pair of jeans, the same shirt, and the same pair of gloves because after a trip, they were impossible to get clean. I had to scrub my arms using kerosene before taking a bath. It wasn't long before I bought a large beach umbrella and rigged three strong lines to the center pole to hold it upright with the help of stakes. This provided good shade over the work area.

Most of the larger bones were found to be incomplete or eroded in our test pits. Large fossils were often cracked and tended to come apart as we removed them, but it was little problem to fit the pieces of important fossils back together after we cleaned them. For smaller fossils, it turned out to be less damaging to extract them from lumps of asphalt matrix in screen baskets by soaking them in kerosene. It often took only 24 hours to process a sample of asphalt matrix, and when we examined the material from the screen baskets, we found more fossils than anything else. The preservation of small and delicate fossils was spectacular. Tiny bones were often complete. I even collected a coprolite from one sample.

This screening process resulted in a good deal of waste asphalt mixed with kerosene after we extracted the fossils, but I solved this problem by mixing the asphalt with gravel and using it to patch holes in the street in front of our house. It crusted over and worked like a charm once the kerosene evaporated, which happened pretty quickly under the strong, Maracaibo sun.

We were able to tentatively identify many of our fossils during the first two years with the help of Greg McDonald, and looking back, it was sort of a round-about process. Emails were still primitive at the university back then. After I cleaned a set of fossils and found ones I couldn't identify, I made scale drawings from different perspectives, numbering each specimen. (Photos didn't work well because the black surfaces didn't show details on developed film.) I then "snail-mailed" a set of drawings to Greg. In those days it took about three weeks for a regular letter mailed from Maracaibo to reach a destination in the US. When he received the letter, he sent me an email with the identifications of each numbered specimen, along with comments and words of encouragement. Greg also seemed pretty excited about what we were finding. I got to be reasonably good at drawing bones during this time, and I also learned a lot about the bones and teeth of many types of animals.

My final trip to Inciarte was on December 16, 2000. After two years of processing samples, we had found disarticulated remains representing more than 120 species and an untold number of individual specimens, including plants, insects, amphibians, reptiles, birds, and mammals. (Since 2001, the number of genera has increased to around 150, especially because of the number of birds identified.)

Plant remains mostly included pieces of wood, vine stems, and a few leaves, but I also collected seeds of several varieties. One of these was a hard-shelled seed with points on it, which in Texas I've heard called a "goat head."

We collected literally millions of insect parts, and at times we found insect bodies with folded wings still attached. I saw evidence of beetles, water bugs, weevils, and ants, to name a few briefly. A LUZ biology student, Rita Riveras, worked on a project to study fossil insect diversity at Inciarte in 2000.

With respect to other invertebrates, we collected a few crab claws.

We collected frog, lizard, snake, and turtle remains of several types, as well as caiman bones. The frog bones were of different sizes, so we likely had more than a single species. I saw the jaws of three or four small lizard species, and I even recognized iguana fossils. I observed the bones and shell sections from several turtle species of different sizes. The caiman bones were generally small. Based on only what I observed, we had at least 14 species of amphibians and reptiles in all, but there are probably more. As I understand it, Tito Barros and a student, Liz Lisett, later studied some of these.

The birds represent many sizes, with raptor-like birds and waterfowl the most notable. Ascanio and Dave Steadman presented the initial report on the Inciarte fossil birds in 2007. Later, in 2015, Ascanio, Dave, and another colleague, Jessica Oswald, reported at least 73 species of birds (and most these are from about two cubic meters of asphalt matrix in only one location). At least one fossil is from a hummingbird. Another seems to be from a condor, with about everything in between. We found the only fossil ever recorded of a puffbird, one of the local bird types we observed nearby on occasion. According to the researchers, Inciarte is the richest fossil site for avian diversity in the world.

Their report noted the presence of the blue-winged teal as a fossil among our collections. Interestingly enough, I recall Ascanio rescuing a live blue-winged teal from the Inciarte tar one day, which he took home, cleaned up, and nursed back to health until it could fly again. (It ended up as one potential victim that the tar pit never claimed as a future fossil.)

Mammals ranged in size from small rodents and insectivores (including several bats) to the giant ground sloths and *Haplomastodon* (an elephant), with a wide variety of sizes in between. Marisol Nuñez, another LUZ student, worked with Ascanio on the rodents. The fossils represent armadillo-like animals of four sizes up to glyptodonts. At least two sizes of marsupials (opossums) are represented as fossils. Some of the other animals include rabbits, llamas, deer, horses, toxodonts, and *Macrauchenia*—a strange, extinct, visual cross between a camel and a horse, only with a short, trunk-like snout. Carnivores are well represented, including saber-toothed cats, dire wolves, and foxes. There was some debate about a possible primate (monkey) tooth, but I never heard confirmation from an expert.

Once again, nearly everything came out of the two cubic meters of asphalt matrix, as previously noted. The Inciarte location measures roughly one kilometer long by half a kilometer wide, and if our test pits are representative of what might be present in other places below the surface, some people believe it might be the largest accumulation of Pleistocene fossils in South America—at least, up to now. (Asphalt deposits in eastern Venezuela may have more potential for fossils than Inciarte.) The age of the fossils from this particular spot at Inciarte was dated back to about 25,000 years before present, published in 2004.

A non-profit organization, The Foundation for Quaternary Paleontology of Venezuela, was organized after 2002 by Dave Orchard (a Houston-based petroleum geologist) in order to stimulate interest in working at Inciarte and at other locations in Venezuela. A few international researchers went on a field trip to Inciarte, sponsored by the foundation, to see the location. Later, the organization sponsored a meeting in Austin, Texas, through the help of the Alfred P. Sloan Foundation and the Jackson School of Geosciences, University of Texas at Austin. By this time many people were becoming interested in doing research on Venezuelan tar pits. I attended the meeting and was recognized for my earlier contributions.

At a banquet dinner for our gathering held in the front room of the Texas Memorial Museum on the campus of the University of Texas at Austin, Dave (representing the foundation) presented me with an award for my discovery and later work on Venezuelan tar pits. About forty people were in attendance. Belkis and Mary Ann were there beside me, as well as Ascanio, Angel, and others from the museum, along with Greg McDonald, Dave Steadman, Chris Shaw (expert on saber-tooth cats and on tar pits in general from Rancho La Brea), and other researchers and officials from across the US and Venezuela.

The actual award looked really sharp, and I still have it proudly on display at home. Dave Orchard had taken a reproduction skull of a saber-tooth cat and mounted it on a block of wood displaying an engraved plaque. After the presentation, he also announced that for future recipients, the award would from then on be known as the foundation's John M. Moody Award.

Unfortunately, the political environment in both Venezuela and the US wasn't favorable at the time, and if anything, it's now worse. The foundation never could stimulate the interests of researchers from the outside. Dave eventually announced his plans to dissolve the foundation for lack of interest. No other awards with my name on them were ever presented, as far as I'm aware.

Even so, it's difficult to keep paleontological researchers from working when they believe the work is valuable to science. A number of studies have been undertaken since then, mostly spearheaded by Ascanio Rincón (rodents, bats, carnivores, toxodonts, horses, birds, Xenarthra, and probably others of which I'm not aware), but the greatest part of Inciarte has never been explored. I have remained interested in seeing more work done there, and I hope it will happen someday. I see it as an extremely valuable location.

Because of his work at Inciarte, Ascanio was the perfect person to call upon when much older asphalt deposits containing fossils were discovered during oil pipeline construction near Maturín (eastern Venezuela). A number of international researchers are still interested in doing studies at Inciarte, but proper financial backing and better accommodations are needed. I understand that some work has continued. Even so, the remoteness of the Inciarte area and the climatic conditions make it difficult to properly extract fossils there. The area also needs to be protected from looting.

Over the years, I paid most of the expenses out of my own pocket for numerous field trips to Inciarte and to other locations while working at MBLUZ. I did it because I thought it was important, but without someone seriously willing to pay the necessary price for future research, it will probably never happen.

As I said earlier, Jorge Carrillo Briceño used the information when he wrote up a nice interview over the internet on my work at Inciarte. He published the interview in Spanish in his book *Bestias Prehistóricas de Venezuela, Colosos de la Edad de Hielo* (Universität Zürich, 2015). He also describes the Cerro Pintado expedition, where he published the only photo successfully captured by my camera inside the cave.

In addition, Marcelo Sánchez-Villagra wrote a nice paragraph about my work in the museum. The article is titled "A Short History of the Study of Venezuelan Vertebrate Fossils" published in *Urumaco & Venezuelan Paleontology*, (Marcelo R. Sánchez-Villagra, Orangel A. Aguilera, and Alfredo A. Carlini – Editors, Indiana University Press, 2010).

John M. Moody

An On-Going Life

My Love Affair with Books

Reading Skills

It has been said that books will eventually become obsolete as they are replaced by electronic readers. When I sell my novels in person at book events, I sometimes ask people, "Which do you prefer to read, an actually book in hand or a Kindle?" Nine times out of ten, they tell me, "I only read *real* books." They mostly enjoy the feel of turning the pages. Sorry, Kindle. Even so, this book will also be available in an electronic format to make the other 10 percent happy.

As I mentioned earlier, my first first-grade teacher gave me a book when my family moved from Dallas to Denison, but somewhere along the way, I fell behind when it came to reading well and rapidly. I remained the same way throughout much of my early education, but I started to improve during middle school. Still, I never became anything approaching a "speed reader," and even when I read now, I read rather slowly.

My mother recognized my reading problem early on, and she worked toward a solution. She believed I would read more if I read material I enjoyed. She bought me a comic book subscription. Once per month for a year or two, I received copies of Walt Disney's *Donald Duck* comic books, and I re-read them often.

I recall reading other things, too. I received copies of *Boy's Life* while I was a Boy Scout. I previously wrote about the time when a cousin gave me lots of comic books and copies of *Mad Magazine* after I successfully completed a treasure hunt, and I read and re-read those, as well. I remember one birthday when my sisters gave me some pretty interesting books as a gift. One of those was a book on archaeology, and looking back, I believe this became my initially inspiration for my novel *The Mighty Hand of Doom*. Then still later, I started receiving copies of *Mad Magazine* through a subscription. I can look back on these as some of the reasons I read as an adult and eventually became an author.

One evening while I attended middle school, my mother decided to experiment with some of her equipment for testing her remedial reading students, and she used me as a guinea pig. She discovered that my eyes didn't work correctly when it came to coordinating both of them from line to line of text. I guess she didn't consider it serious enough to do much about it—or nothing could be done about it at the time—but I've often wondered if maybe this is the reason I tend to read slowly.

On the northwest corner of Tone Avenue and Main Street in Denison, a convenience store once sat. This was the nearest place to where I grew up that sold paperback books, and while I attended middle school, I used to buy books there when I thought they might be interesting. And because I had to spend pretty good money on them (from as much as 49 to 95 cents), I made sure I read them from cover to cover. I found adventure stories, war stories, and other kinds of books. I not only improved my reading skills through these books, but they also inspired my sense of adventure.

I read books at the Denison Public Library, but because I didn't read rapidly, I preferred to own the books I read. I didn't have to worry about returning them when I wasn't finished. Even so, I recall certain library books I read. One of those was *The Scottish Chiefs*, by Jane Porter. Reading this book was a real challenge at my age at the time—perhaps early high school—but I did it. And I really enjoyed it. When the movie *Brave Heart* was released, I recalled this book in a big way.

School forces students to read, and I recall one teacher in middle school telling us we had to read and give oral book reports on 12 books during the school year, but these had to be from specific categories (fiction, non-fiction, biography, sports, etc.). That was probably the only book about sports I ever read.

When I went away to study in Golden, Colorado, I continued my book-buying habit. A little store a few blocks from where I lived sold paperbacks, and I bought quite a few of them to read in my room during cold nights. One book in particular was about the Marx Brothers, which made me even more of a fan of their movies.

As an adult in the Dallas area, I discovered Half-Price Books. I used to travel to the big store or to the various satellite stores while searching for reading material—often science fiction in those days. I amassed a pretty good collection. In fact, I still stop in at used book stores whenever I encounter one.

Still later, I had the idea I wanted to create a reference library. I decided I needed to have all sorts of books covering all sorts of subjects—whatever mankind would need in case some sort of great disaster struck, which might allow it to "rebuild." I used to carry with me a list in a notebook of the subjects I needed to search for. They included plenty of books on science and technology, medical references, food preservation, construction (even how to make bricks and pottery), and plenty of general subjects covering a little of everything. I once had in mind that my little library might serve as a nucleus for the survival of the species. This idea came to mind again when I wrote my novel *Into the Center of the Shadow*, which takes this idea to the extreme. I also mention my character named Chris Mitchell doing the same as I once did in *Intersecting Destinies*.

Then later, I returned to Venezuela for the third time and ended up packing all these books into boxes. I stayed 13 years that time, and when I returned to the US, I never lived in a place big enough to unpack them the proper way. Many of them are still in storage, but fortunately, the internet has made much of this knowledge easily accessible as long as a person can sort through all the junk—and until a general power failure plunges the world back into the Stone Age.

I still buy and read books, but my purchases have changed somewhat. I've also taken advantage of less costly books whenever I can find them, such as at garage sales, library book sales, on the internet, and of course, in used book stores like Half-Price Books whenever I'm near one. And unless it's a book from a fellow author I'm really looking forward to reading, the subject matter of the books I read usually deals with research for my own works. I gathered and read books on Greece for two years before I began to write *The Mighty Hand of Doom*. It was much the same with regard to Ireland when I wrote *Many Shades of Green*.

Early Writing

I've been writing for many years—especially during my years at schools—but my early works were nothing to brag about. One of the earliest works I produced where I received praise from a teacher was in middle school when I wrote a piece on the "Art of Torture," but I made it almost comical. The teacher liked it enough to read it to the rest of the class. Another time was in high school when a teacher wanted us to take part of Shakespeare's *Macbeth* and write it in another time period—much like the parallel between Shakespeare's *Romeo and Juliette* and Leonard Bernstein's *West Side Story*. The teacher told me my version was exactly what she hoped for.

For one class when we studied limericks, we had to each write one. I still recall mine, which I present for the first time in print below:

> There once was a man from Cape Horn,
> Who swallowed an ear of corn.
> When he stood in the sun,
> The popping begun,
> And he wished he had never been born.

I occasionally tried my hand at other poetry during middle school, high school, and college, and even now, I don't believe they were particularly bad. I wrote most of them in attempts to impress girls, but the girls I knew didn't seem especially impressed. I might still have a couple of them around as first drafts, but I usually gave away the only finished copies and never saw them again. I don't imagine they still exist anymore, being lost to the world forever.

I always preferred my poems to rhyme, so my finished ones always did. It's nice that poets I know today are expressing their feelings in free-style poetry, but it's simply not my thing.

In my novel, *Second Book of Marc*, from "The Mezet Trilogy," I wrote a couple of short songs that a group of women sing as they travel together through a dark tunnel, and I think they added a nice detail. The last poem I wrote for a book was for *Many Shades of Green*. In this novel, it is actually supposed to be a song. Fragments of it appear randomly in various parts of the book, but near the end of the story, Grace Kavanugh, my main female protagonist, sings the entire song. I think I did a pretty good job of expressing the fictional songwriter's feelings while at the same time making it rhyme. It is 13 stanzas long, and I wrote it in only two days.

Throughout much of my life, however, writing didn't play a big part of it. In school, I was more interested in math and science.

Scientific Writing

During my final years at the University of Texas at Arlington, I took a Natural History course as an elective. I briefly described the field trips for this class, but in another important way, this course actually changed my life. I learned early on from the professor how a person should take field notes. By the end of this course, I faithfully took notes each time I went into the field or even when I went on a trip out of town. I continued this practice for more than 25 years, the entire time I was active in paleontology as an adult. A few years later I began to use water-proof "Rite in the Rain" All-Weather Transit notebooks to take notes in the field, and after I returned home, I transcribed my notes into more readable words, including drawings, maps, and diagrams. I still have these notebooks and transcribed journals, and I look at them on occasion—such as when writing these stories. When I returned to Perijá in search of fossils in 1988 after being gone for years, I used my notes to find my way back to the most important fossil locations. And during other occasions, I don't know how many times I needed a bit of information and found it among my notes.

When I began to write my first book, *Journey from Mezet*—and especially when I wrote the rest of "The Mezet Trilogy"—I imagined my main character, Marc of Mezet, as a person much like me. He attempted to pass along information using the written word in a completely truthful, almost scientific manner. Even though the stories take place in the distant future, I saw this as a characteristic that doesn't change over time. Someone always views it as an important job to "tell it like it is."

Even though I usually wasn't the principal author for scientific studies with my name attached to them, I've felt proud to have participated in scientific work as a contributor.

Letters and Memos

After I had been working at Core Lab full time for two years, one of my bosses decided I would make a good project scheduler and report writer. After a few days of training, I was expected to co-ordinate incoming projects while at the same time take the results of laboratory tests and present them to the client in writing by way of a cover letter. Someone checked a few of them at first, but afterward, I was pretty much on my own. It was a stressful job, but it only lasted about a year and a half before a new boss changed the structure of the lab and made me a supervisor in charge of three lab departments. After this change, I didn't have to write as many letters.

Even so, I became famous for writing memos when I discovered some unsafe condition that no one seemed to view as important enough to correct. My wording usually got someone's attention.

The General Book of Knowledge

When I first started to work full-time and permanently at Core Lab, I felt surprised that no one ever seemed to use written instructions and procedures when performing laboratory tests. I imagine someone possessed written procedures somewhere, but I just never saw them. The older lab techs had been doing the same tests for many years; they probably had the procedures memorized. We usually used data sheets where we recorded the input data and the test measurements in order to calculate the final results, but when it came to what knob to turn and when to turn it, I saw nothing written down. The tests were normally taught by an older technician to a younger one through demonstration and supervision—sort of like from father to son (or daughter).

As noted earlier, I had already worked in the company during a summer while I was still at UTA, and during that time, they taught me to do some of the most common tests. However, when I was back to stay, they immediately placed me in one of the more complicated labs where we had to vary test procedures depending on conditions of temperature and pressure in the underground reservoir. So, what does this have to do with writing?

John M. Moody

I have already described a really nice, older fellow named Mark, who was in charge of this department, and the same as in other cases throughout the lab, he taught me how to run the tests through a "practical demonstration" method. These tests could be pretty complex, taking days to set up and perform; from test to test, I often feared I might forget some important detail or a vital step in the procedure if I didn't write everything down.

I began to accumulate my notes in a notebook, which I could take apart when I needed to add or change something. I included diagrams of the equipment, graphs we often used to determine data for later calculations, and most importantly, the step-by-step method to perform a particular type of test. My notes were quite detailed depending on how well I knew how to do the test and how important it was to get it right, keeping safety as a top priority.

Over several years, my notes grew to the point where I needed a second notebook—then a third, then a fourth. I started to organize them into volumes depending on the types of services. After a while, co-workers started to notice me using my notebooks, and they occasionally asked to look at them or to make copies of certain protocols. Around the lab, they started to call my collection "The General Book of Knowledge" or the "GBK," because the notebooks held a little of everything with respect to lab tests. Years later, the company began to write official operations manuals, but people still asked to look at my copies when in doubt.

When I left for Venezuela the first time to stay for only six weeks, I took with me photocopies of some of the analyses for the Maracaibo lab, leaving the originals in the care of a friend. Later, when I returned to Venezuela for the second time—remaining there for about three years—I carried with me full copies. Once again, however, I left the originals behind. After I returned to work in the Dallas lab again between 1984 and 1987, I discovered that some parts of the lab were still using my GBK on occasion. It's funny sometimes how a thing gets started.

Just for Fun

During my second time in Venezuela from 1981 to 1984, I corresponded with a friend I worked with in the company's Dallas office who had just been transferred to the office in Anaheim, California. About once a month I wrote something comical for him to read. I didn't save any of these, but I think he got a laugh out of them. In one I recall, I describe a battle taking place in our lab when competitors attack in an attempt to steal our operations manual. I wrote another on the back of a lottery ticket sheet, telling him he might already be a winner. This went on for about a year.

An Old Notebook

One day when I accompanied another of our managers in eastern Venezuela, he had to drive to an out-of-the-way location to check on some work being done there. One of the Venezuelan national oil companies had hired our company to clean out an old warehouse and dispose of everything inside. It contained oil well core samples and old company files dating back many years. When my companion parked near the building, I stepped out of the car to stretch my legs, and I walked around for a moment nearby while the manager spoke to his workers. I soon wandered over to examine a large pile of documents on the ground that was about to be burned in a bonfire, and I spotted a small, brown book. It looked like it had suffered a little damage on the outside. Surely, it had been wet once. Even so, I opened it and discovered hand-written notes in English.

The co-worker checking on the project finished up with his workers, so the time came to leave. I carried the notebook with me to study later. After all, it had already been thrown away and was about to be burned, so I figured no one would miss it.

A few days later when I had the chance to examine the notebook, I discovered it was a set of geologist's field notes from the early 1920s made in western Venezuela. In fact, it was practically an historical document with respect to Venezuelan geology because several well-known geologists had participated. It made me wonder what other documents might have been burned in the pile right after we left.

I ended up doing an extensive analysis on many aspects of the book, and the Venezuelan Geological Society later published my results in their journal. I placed the notebook in the MBLUZ library.

John M. Moody

If You Get Paid for It, You're a Professional

Through my regular petroleum services work and through the museum, I met Henning Henningfeld, a geologist from Germany who worked for Shell in Venezuela. Henning invited me to submit an article in English to his company's Venezuelan magazine (*Revista Shell*), and I thought it would be nice to promote the museum. I titled it "Views of the Past," and in it, I briefly covered several of the most important projects I had worked on as curator for the Paleontology Section. I was able to submit photos, as well, and when I saw it published in May of 1999, I felt pleased with the final result. To my delight, Shell paid me $100 for the article. It was the first time I ever got paid for writing a publication. By getting paid, I saw myself as a professional. Unfortunately, it took many years to get paid for writing anything else.

My Stories

Over the last few years, I've met people who asked where my ideas for novels come from. Fans sometimes ask, "How on earth did you come up with such a story?" Even a few of my fellow authors are interested in how creativity works, and they enjoy reading notes about my stories at the conclusions of my books, some of which describe how I first hatched an idea.

Throughout this book, I've already included where certain details of my stories originated. Even so, I haven't yet described how the plots came into being. At times, the simplest of thoughts led directly to an entire book plot. At other times, I worked on an idea for years, going back to it time after time, until I obtained the result I desired. In certain cases, I can't say a lot without giving too much away, but some readers might enjoy the following section.

Several years ago I attended a writer's conference sponsored by the newspaper *The Herald Democrat* and Austin College in Sherman, Texas. Many people present were just like me—independent, fiction authors attempting to discover their places in the universe. At the question and answer session following one event, several writers began to discuss how they used specialized computer programs to outline plots and characters, and I felt truly surprised to hear it. I never used (or use) anything of the sort. The nearest I came was to create timelines on MS Excel spreadsheets (after writing first drafts) to keep up with minor details such as days of the week and lunar phases. I kept everything else in my head. The way some others wrote sounded too artificial—and not much fun.

My books tend to evolve as I write them. When I start one, I normally have no idea what route it will take to reach the end. Sometimes I have an ending in mind when I begin, but this usually changes along the way, as well. Even when my conclusion is my fixed point to shoot for, I generally make up the rest of the story as I send my characters along their merry, tortuous paths to get there.

Journey from Mezet – This was my first try at writing a novel, and it became the first book of a trilogy when I wrote my next two books. However, each book is a stand-alone novel. I didn't want to do the same thing as so many writers do now days by writing a series where the reader is left hanging, forced into purchasing a copy of the next book to find out what happens. I view the practice as just a trick to sell additional books. While living in Venezuela. I most often couldn't find the next book of a series until years later—if ever. I never wanted this to be the case with mine. A person can pick up and read any book of my trilogy and have a good understanding of the setting or the plot to its conclusion without having access to the other books. (Of course, it is better to start my trilogy from the beginning and read the books in order because this gives the reader better insight and background for enjoying the later books.) I also imagined a reader being more willing to try one of my books if the person didn't feel obligated to buy two more in case he or she didn't like the first one.

I think of my trilogy as "future history." This was a term used by Robert A. Heinlein, and I always enjoyed reading his works while growing up. In fact, I wanted my stories to be like Heinlein's—as seen through the viewpoint of a single character, the storyteller, who is quite human with respect to his aspirations, his concerns, and his sense of duty.

I gave these books a setting following a great, global collapse of some sort, but the events of the past are so far removed, no one remembers how society reached its present situation. It's not dystopian, however. I imagined my created world as a Middle Ages type of society with a matching technological level—with a few notable exceptions. The weapons used are usually bows and arrows—once again, with a few exceptions.

The small village of Mezet, as I stated previously, is modeled after the small town of La Mesa among the mountains of southern Trujillo State, Venezuela. From the winding, mountain highway leading from La Puerta to Merida, I once took an excellent photo of some flat, cultivated fields hanging above an eroded valley, and it was this sort of place I tried to describe in my Mezet Trilogy at different moments of the village's history.

Before I started writing, I read and enjoyed the books by Debora Doyle and James McDonald (especially the Mageworld series). I attended high school in Denison with Debora, and our families were close friends with a lot of shared activities. Our families even traveled together on long trips on occasion.

When Debora moved on as I did after high school, I still visited with her family when I returned home, and sometimes I corresponded through the mail. On one of my trips home, Debora's mother had a copy of a book for me. Debora and James (her husband) had recently published it. I read it and liked it, and as soon as I could, I let them know. The same thing happened again on later trips. It was their writing that inspired me to try my hand at a story when I had what I believed to be an original idea.

My setting is a small village. A device resting on a mountaintop tells the villagers the next day's weather. It is a device left behind by "the ancient ones," and the people have become dependent on its service over the years to better take care of their crops. Then one day the apparatus is stolen. The village realizes it must get the device back; otherwise, its society will collapse. The leaders of the village choose four young men to search for their prized contraption, and afterward, the plan is to return with the information so the older men can recapture it—by force if necessary.

On one trip to the US, I bought my first laptop computer, along with an early version of MS Word. Before long while we lived in Maracaibo, we invited Belkis' mother from out of town to stay with us for a few days. On a weekend while the women caught up on news about people, places, and events they both knew and I didn't, I retired to the bedroom and opened my computer.

I tried to make a rough outline of my story and actually wrote the beginning of the book within a couple of days. Still, it wasn't long before I discarded my outline almost completely as the story began to evolve. I had a lot of fun writing this book, and once I finished it, I started thinking about the next one.

It took me a long time to get this book into print, and I describe this in greater detail in the author's notes of the second edition. After I first published *Journey from Mezet*, I quickly followed it with the other two. The second editions of this series came about when I promptly realized how much my writing had improved over the years with each book I wrote. Some readers may not realize how difficult it can be when self-publishing a book, but I was stuck with the quirks of the process and simply tried to do my best at the time. Even so, I heard from fans who enjoyed my stories. I eventually decided to re-edit them and fix some mistakes. I tried to leave the stories with the same flavor, but I cleaned up the sentences to make many of them more readable. I have since done the same thing with all my earlier novels.

Second Book of Marc – Although I began to think about this story soon after I wrote the first one of the series, I didn't begin to actually write this book for quite a while. I'm glad I hadn't published the first one at the time because as I wrote the second and third ones, I was able to add small details to the first one to tie it to the latter two.

The idea for a second book arose when I thought about contemporaries of my character, Marc of Mezet, expressing their approval of his first book and asking him for more. In the introduction of the second book, Marc explains to his readers that his first story is complete as it stands, and he can't tell them anything more. However, he thinks of another story to tell, and this becomes his second book—thus the title.

I show the village evolved to some degree following the conclusion of the first story, and a situation arises where Marc must once again take a journey to seek help from outside—and to save a friend. The tasks Marc first sees as pretty straightforward soon begin to escalate, and on many occasions, the story teller must do things against his better judgment due to circumstances. Marc once more has to depend on his skills with the bow and arrow to get him out of certain situations, sometimes in surprising ways.

At one point about halfway into the book, I placed my hero in a real fix. Then I had to stop writing for a couple of weeks as I pondered how he might get out of it in a believable way. Once more, it was a fun book to write, and I think I did a pretty good job creating a truly original story involving a likable main character in unique settings.

Marc's Final Journey – Even before I finished writing *Second Book of Marc*, I had developed the general story idea for the third book of the trilogy. I jumped right into it and finished it much more rapidly than the first two. Regardless of my first ideas, however, it is another book that tended to evolve as I wrote it. Because of my love for books, I made it into a book about books. It also has more of a science fiction flavor, although I still think of it as future history.

For this plot, Marc of Mezet is the oldest man of his village. As an old man, he now rests on his laurels, never imagining he will experience another adventure. He has become a learned man, and over the years, his village has done the same thing through the influences of Marc and his family. Marc writes his third book because he feels he must. Something has happened, and he wishes to share it with the world—but he does it is his own way by telling the story from the beginning.

As the story begins, word of his interest in books has spread, and promptly, he receives a formal invitation from the king of a neighboring land to pay him a visit. Rumors of an ancient library—one built by "the ancient ones"—in a difficult to reach location have reached the king, and he is calling a meeting to discuss the possibilities of seeking out these books. They need to discuss the feasibility of the project and if reaching the books will be worth the effort. And this is why the king has called upon Marc; he has some practical knowledge when it comes to ancient books. When Marc hears this information, he knows he can't stay home; he must get involved. And his involvement leads to an adventure far more "involved" than Marc ever imagines.

Before I leave the subject of the Mezet Trilogy, I wish to say that I know my books are not for everyone. Some readers are in too much of a hurry to finish a book in order to jump quickly to the next one. Maybe those people don't realize what I've tried to do. For anyone who decides to read my books, don't get into too much of a hurry to reach the end. You need to enjoy the journey getting there.

To add just a word about the covers for these three books, my long-time friend named Keith—the one who shares a passion for Thompson sub-machine guns and gangster movies—is also an artist. He showed me his work many times, and I always felt impressed. When the time came to first submit the covers for the Mezet Trilogy, I commissioned Keith to paint three pictures—selected scenes from each book. I still have the paintings, and when the time came to publish the second edition, I re-photographed them to use again.

For most of my other covers, I created the photos, often utilizing representative objects referred to in the story. On occasion, I created the actual objects, such as the necklace on the cover of *Many Shades of Green* or the puzzle pieces of *Brass Puzzle*. The only exception is the photo on the cover of *Snake Bluff Lodge*, which I took years ago on a family vacation.

Brass Puzzle – This was my first novel of its type, which has led me to my favorite mixture of genres—romance blended with mystery and adventure. Most of my books fall into this category.

If I remember correctly, I had just seen a film I enjoyed, and I wanted to create a modern novel along those lines with a touch of mystery involved. Most importantly, I wanted it to include a treasure hunt. I had my main protagonists in mind (Jim Hudson and Amy Stewart), but I pretty much made up everything as I went along. The actions I thought up and wrote led to natural responses, and so forth—action followed by reaction, but with twists thrown in. The Mezet Trilogy was like this to some extent, and while I had a general plot in mind for some of my later novels, much of the action in *Brass Puzzle* ended up fairly reactive and spontaneous.

When deciding on a setting, I looked at maps on the internet as I tried to locate the most remote region I could find in north Texas, but I needed a town for the antique shop at the beginning of the book. Gainesville, Texas, seemed like the perfect place. Then I wrote my story.

I ended up writing it in a certain way, but I felt something was missing. At that point, I extended the story slightly.

Once I had much of a first draft written, I drove Belkis and Mary Ann along some of the actual roads so I could see the locations in real life. I used this opportunity to collect details, which I added to my second draft.

I first published this book about two years after I published the Mezet Trilogy. Then I went back and reedited it for the second edition, fixing all sorts of problems I found, as well as making many of my sentences more pleasant with respect to reader enjoyment.

Searching for Jennifer – As soon as I finished *Brass Puzzle*, I started *Searching for Jennifer*. Even though this is the longest book I've ever written, I put it together in only about eight months. I've had many comments from people saying they enjoyed this plot. While writing it, two songs often came to mind; one was *I Know You're Out There Somewhere*, by Justin Hayward of The Moody Blues (The *Sur la mer* album, 1988 – Polygram Records) and *I Will Find You*, by Clannad, a theme from the film *Last of the Mohicans* (*Banba* album, 1993 – Atlantic Records).

The idea I had for this one arose as I wrote *Brass Puzzle*. I imagined a male author who began to write a book, but he falls in love with his female protagonist. In the book, George Summers, a reclusive novelist, becomes fascinated with his character named Jennifer. He begins to search for her everywhere he goes. Then I wondered what would happen if a group of criminals learns of his obsession. They hire an actress named Bridget Oliver—whom they model after the fictional character's written description—to take advantage of George. Their objective is George's late father's fabulous art collection.

Even so, their plan has a twist. While the George is in love with the actress without knowing what is going on, the actress begins to fall in love with the author, even though she knows she shouldn't. While the plot might sound improbable, I've set out the facts and circumstances so the story actually seems quite plausible.

I have a part where "Jennifer" goes through a training process. She must learn something about art from an older man named Dan, and I delighted in working out the details of the exchanges between these two characters.

At another point, some of the characters must travel to Denison, and while I thoroughly enjoyed writing this book from start to finish, I had the most fun using my home town as a setting for a small part of the story.

At this point, I wish to reveal something else; when I write my books, I usually follow a future calendar. I look for a time in the near future when my actions will take place. Then for my writing, I refer to days of the week, holidays, and weather conditions, even lunar phases on particular dates when necessary. I write my action sequences as if they are really occurring on a specific day at a certain time. I did this for *Searching for Jennifer*, and some weeks after I published it, I took a trip to downtown Denison on the correct date and time to see how well my imagination matched reality. I walked along the same route as my characters, and I found nothing I would have changed. Everything looked much like I thought it would. Naturally, if someone goes back to my locations years later, some things aren't the same. Buildings get torn down. Traffic lights are removed, school zones are eliminated, and the like. Even so, I use actual, public locations whenever I can.

Return to Nowhere – For this novel, I can't recall how I came up with the idea. I merely started with an initial modern scene I had in mind. A man named Paul on a rainy November day in rural Tennessee is collecting aluminum cans along a roadside when a young woman runs toward him across a field. She is dressed only in a white hospital gown. He helps her to cross a barbed-wire fence, but before he can figure out what's wrong, a couple of people drive up to take her away. They say they're from a private mental clinic, and the woman is a patient who has escaped. Even so, something the woman says causes Paul to have his doubts. His doubts become an obsession as he tries in every way he can think of to learn the truth. This book evolved *constantly* as I wrote it.

This novel grew long because it contains several subplots. One takes place in 1899 when a family is traveling by wagon in another part of Tennessee. This story later ties into the main plot. I've spaced this sub-plot out from the prologue through the early chapters in small parts. Then I mix the past events with present ones throughout the rest of the book. I was experimenting, but I think it works just fine.

As for another part of this book, I ended up using some of my actual Tennessee ancestors as characters—as I described near the beginning. The traveling family stops at the home of my great grandfather and great grandmother, and many of the details here are based on actual facts. I also use a tale passed along by Ganny, my grandmother, later in the story. I explain these details in the author's notes at the end of the book.

Intertwined with the modern story, I also included a subplot from the viewpoint of a woman named Marcie. She is the head of security at the clinic. When I began to write *Return to Nowhere*, I viewed Marcie as only a minor character, but the more I wrote, the better I liked her. She ends up playing a key role.

Into the Center of the Shadow – I drew upon a lot of ideas when writing this novel, including my day in Madrid, my time in Venezuela, my trip to the Guadeloupe Mountains during my years at the university, and my thoughts on preserving mankind's heritage. This plot involves Carlos Ocando, a researcher studying documents from the early Middle Ages, who has a chance meeting with a mysterious woman in Spain named "Lucia." In only one night, he finds he's in love with her. Promptly, she disappears, leaving behind a note telling him not to try to find her. She says if he does, it could get them both killed. It evolves from there along a rather twisted route.

In the meantime, I present a parallel chain of events in reverse chronological order going backward for hundreds of years, and this chain eventually merges with the main plot a little more than halfway through the book. I have heard other writers advise "Do something different," and this is what I did. Again, I think it works pretty well.

Some of the locations on the ground are actual places, but I also called upon pure imagination when describing a research facility in New Mexico. For this book, I did my own extensive research on a wide variety of subjects. My friend Angel Viloria wrote a book about the Sierra de Perijá, and this also inspired part of the plot. Once more, I had fun writing it, and I learned a lot in the process. I think I've said enough. If you like good adventure stories, you might consider it.

Many Shades of Green – I call this one my "half-Irish" romantic adventure; half of it takes place in Ireland. The title comes from the song I wrote, which plays an important part in the story. Once more, I undertook a couple of years of reading and studying photographs before I started to write. I wanted to do this one because of my Irish ancestors.

The story is about a woman, Grace Kavanagh, who is part Irish and living in Boston. She's a Celtic vocalist who doesn't see eye to eye with her manager, Jerry Raph, with regard to her future as a singer. Through a twist of fate, she gets to go to Ireland, and her young chauffeur in Boston, Lou Miller, is hired to look after her on her trip because she's not especially practical when it comes to travel. The story evolves into a mystery dating back to the time when Grace's mother, Eleanor Kavanagh, disappeared from her home near Castleisland, in County Kerry.

I especially enjoyed creating and writing the part about midway through the book when Grace walks alone to a bar at night and is called upon to sing. Lou, who is worried about her, follows without Grace knowing, and it's a good thing he does. This becomes a pivotal point of the story in several ways, which readers will simply have to read in order to find out why.

I searched for a location to fit my story's criteria and learned about Castleisland. I researched this town as much as I could, and after I published the book, I sent a copy to the town's public library. I did the same thing when I published the second edition. The librarians sounded pleased to receive them.

Intersecting Destinies – This story starts out in the office of a manufacturing company in Kansas City, Missouri. It simply starts with a man, Chris Mitchell, who works in the office, seeing a recently hired woman, "Amelia Church," for the first time. He immediately becomes interested in getting to know her. A parallel plot is also taking place, and part of this involves a group of men who wish to make sure a woman has died in the desert of northern Mexican while trying to cross illegally into Arizona. These two plots soon begin to merge.

I really can't say much more about this story without giving away too many details, but as the man in the office gets to know the newly-hired woman, he becomes deeper and deeper involved in a dangerous international plot. I drew upon my time in executive positions while working in company offices to write this one, and much of what I wrote about actually happens—although perhaps not on such a vast scale.

One of my favorite parts of this story involves a security guard named Darrell Ashburn. I wrote a scene from his point of view as he watches everyone else having fun at the company Christmas party. His actions shortly afterward become a turning point in the story.

When I let my sister Frances read an early draft, she said she loved it, especially the ending. She said she actually shed tears while reading the story toward the end. Authors like to hear such things.

Wherever the Wind Will Take Us – I had the idea for this book on August 29, 2013, while driving a short distance across town. I heard the song *Sailing*, both written and performed by Christopher

Cross. I decided to write a story about a man with a sailboat on the Caribbean. (I know the exact date because I immediately placed a note in my carry-around notebook, which I've been using off and on since Mary Ann gave it to me as a Christmas gift in 2012.) One thing led to another, and before long, I was doing research on sailboats and how to sail them. When I was in middle school, I thought it would be nice to own a large sailboat and sail around the world, sending picture post cards back to my mother for her collection from my ports of call.

I have part of the action taking place in Venezuela. By this time the country was politically and economically taking a turn for the worse, and I tried to reflect some of this as both background and plot.

Part of this story also takes place on the island of Trinidad. I used several locations I actually visited as settings.

In this story, Ginger Cardoso is basically a "kept woman" at the home of Kyros Sarkis. Kyros is a rich power player living on Venezuela's Margarita Island. Ginger realizes that women such as her have a short life expectancy when in Kyros' employ, so she is searching for a way to escape her expected fate. By chance, she meets Lee Snyder, who owns a sailboat. I can't say much more except both of them end up facing more danger and adventure than they imagined.

When writing this story, one of my favorite parts is when Lee falls off the boat without Ginger knowing he's gone. She must figure out how to return to search for him when she doesn't know much about how to sail his boat.

This book is one of Belkis' favorites. I think she mostly likes Lee, which makes me a little jealous.

Land on the Verge of Darkness – This book was another new venture for me. I wrote almost the entire story from the woman protagonist's point of view. Due to the nature of the story, I also had to create a factious town in central Texas called Fairfax.

The book starts out years earlier with an anthropologist named Roberto Castillo doing research on a remote tribe in eastern Peru. (While I used my experiences at the Boxi Mission in Venezuela as background, much of it comes from research.) Roberto is desperately trying to gather information for a publication, and he feels his time is limited because the community in question appears to be about to collapse. They have created a special ritual using a form of drug completely unknown to him, and he is trying to learn the secrets of this drug's manufacture, which the shaman guards closely. (I did research on drugs derived from native plants used by certain tribes.)

The main story involves a woman, Wendy Castillo, returning home after 12 years to sell her mother's home after she received word of her mother's death. Wendy is Roberto's daughter. Roberto has been dead for many years by this time. He was murdered.

Nearly the first person Wendy sees after she steps off the bus is the smart, handsome football player she had a crush on while in high school. In school, he hardly ever seemed to notice her, but 12 years later, he recognizes her right away. And she is no longer the shy girl she was in high school. Wendy is a worldly, attractive woman. She starts to wonder if maybe she should stay in town for a while to see what might develop. She soon learns that her mother didn't simply die; she was also murdered, much like her father. This book involves witchcraft and plenty of underhanded dealings.

I worked on the book for two years off and on before I finished it. I wrote about half of it before I decided it was moving too rapidly. Then I set it aside and worked on two other books before returning to it. By then, I had to go back into it and do a complete rewrite of some sections before I could move it forward. Even so, I kept changing my mind with regard to plot and ending, taking many more months than usual to complete it. In the end, I felt pretty happy with the final result.

Shards of Time – For years, I've wanted to write a mystery set in Denison, Texas, and I did it with this book. While some of the action takes place out of town, most of it occurs on Denison streets or among familiar landmarks. Locally, this has been my most popular book. I've previously described how I got the idea while hunting for fossils near Lake Texoma one day with Mary Ann.

For my plot, a girl named Scarlett Whitetower is hunting fossils with her father on Lake Texoma. He is a university paleontologist who has just retired to take care of his daughter after her mother dies. Scarlett wanders away for a few moments, and when she returns, she discovers her father has been murdered. His death places the girl under the care of a maiden aunt, making much of the girl's life afterward a living hell.

When the aunt dies years later, Scarlett, who has grown into a woman, decides to hire a private detective to see if he can determine who killed her father. It's a chillingly-frigid "cold case," but a young detective named Fitz Vaughn is sent up from Dallas by his boss to see what he can do.

Much of what I wrote comes from my experiences growing up around Lake Texoma, but I also drew heavily from what I learned at Texoma Rockhounds meetings and field trips, and from working as a paleontologist in Venezuela.

Woman in White, Cage of Black – This is another book with a long history. I started it and stopped it often, writing a little before setting it aside to write something more pressing. It took me about four years to finally complete and have published.

An early part of this book sounds like a typical urban legend. Les Melrose, my main male protagonist, is driving along a dark, rainy, foggy, mountainous road in Virginia when he manages to stop his car just in time to avoid hitting a woman who is walking in the middle of the road. She wears an antique-looking, white dress. He gives her a lift in his car down the mountain, but as they travel together, he notices plenty of odd characteristics. Even so, Les finds he likes her. It has something to do with her innocent personality.

He stops at a small, all-night convenience store along the way to buy her something she says she wants, but she prefers to remain in his car. He is only inside for a couple of moments, but when he returns to his car, she has disappeared, leaving only a wet spot on the seat of his car where she sat. This probably sounds typical up to here, right?

He feels devastated when he learns she's gone. He begins to investigate the next day. He soon learns through other evidence that the mysterious woman is a real person and not some phantom.

In the meantime, a woman Les knows named Vera is growing interested in him, and she works her way into helping him during his search for the mystery woman—even knowing he will probably no longer pay any attention to her if he ever locates the woman in the white dress.

This becomes one of my "darkest" novels, and some people might even find the subject matter offensive. Even so, I based much of it on facts and research.

Snake Bluff Lodge – In this book, a gentleman's club hires a group of women to travel to a remote lodge. They are to serve as the "entertainment" for three weeks during some sort of annual meeting. One of them is my main female protagonist, "Kayla Finley." Not everything is as it seems, however. I can't say much more about the plot without giving too much away.

The idea for this one comes from accounts and research about Bohemian Grove, a lodge for the elite in California. I merely drew upon the idea of a lodge for rich men in a remote location where they can do pretty much anything they want. In this case, however, a sinister agenda lies at the heart of the club's existence.

I wrote *Snake Bluff Lodge* about as rapidly as I've written any book, and I've received a lot of positive feedback from readers. This book contains a number of personal-favorite parts.

Fossil Excavation on Kanos IV – Presently, this book is still in the process of editing. Even so, I include it in my list because I expect to publish it at any time. While the book sellers classify my books of the Mezet Trilogy as science fiction, I view *Fossil Excavation on Kanos IV* as my only true science fiction novel so far. This book was actually the fourth book I ever wrote. I finished my first draft while still living in Venezuela, but after our family relocated to the US in 2001, I simply set it aside. I wanted to publish the Mezet books first, and afterward, I began to work on other projects.

I've tried to model this story after some of the "pre-Star-Wars" science fiction classics. As the title suggests, it also deals with paleontology.

For my plot, I have a team of paleontologists on a remote part of a planet that is still in the process of being colonized. Due to an equipment breakdown, most of the team travels to the nearest "town" to pick up supplies for the repair work. They leave behind only one of the team to watch things.

When they return, they find the man left behind has been killed. And it appears he's been murdered. However, I've written a number of twists to keep readers guessing, and the story soon escalates to greater and greater dangers for the team. I don't wish to give the rest of it away, but I used my experiences at the biology museum and a general knowledge of paleontology when writing this one, too.

The Mighty Hand of Doom – The basic idea for this novel came to me in a dream. Even so, I ended up modifying the plot heavily with many additions. Once more, I guess I did about two years of reading and research using maps before I began to write this one.

The plot involves a female, Greek tour guide named Daphne Nikolas who sets out to escort a group of international tourists all over Greece for three weeks. Early on, however, the woman experiences problems. Someone appears to be sabotaging her tour.

One of the tourists, an American named Walt Easton, soon recognizes her troubles. He has already started to like her since early in the tour, so he steps up to help. I can't give away much more, but I'll simply add that the problems turn deadly as the couple becomes more deeply involved with one another.

One of my favorite "scenes" of this book involves the tour bus out of control on a high mountain road. I searched for an exact location and designed the action around it. Once again, I had a lot of fun creating the minor characters, especially Rosemary, Kate, and Monty.

Just Another Tree in the Forest – I decided to include this latest one on the list. I began to write it soon after I thought up the idea on May 7, 2018. The first draft only took six weeks of actual writing time, but after I wrote for the first two weeks, I had to set it aside during the rest of 2018 and early 2019, finally finishing on March 2, 2019.

I classify this one as another romantic adventure, leaning more toward romance. The plot revolves around Loren, a 50-year-old widow. She initially feels disappointed with her life until Dan, a man she remembers from high school (who happens to be a widower) calls her out of the blue to invite her to dinner. As their relationship develops, Loren learns much more about Dan—and her late husband—than she ever expected. Again, I don't want to give too much away, but the story is full of emotions and surprises. It is my shortest book so far, but I don't feel it needs to be any longer.

The idea came from living and working in Houston for a while. I also drew upon a few memories of high school and college, even though none of the people are real, and none of the events actually took place.

The above lines and descriptions will give readers an idea of how I create my books. I hope to continue writing for as long as I am able. I'm really enjoying this part of my life. I already have a few projects in the works, but people will have to learn about those as they are released.

Final Thoughts

The Future

Then I worked in the petroleum industry, my company once sent me from Maracaibo to Dallas to attend a conference. The keynote speaker was a man named Monroe H. Waxman. Dr. Waxman had become famous for his research with a co-worker leading to the Waxman-Smits Equation, which has become a key ingredient of the well logging industry for determining how much oil might be extracted from a reservoir.

At the end of his speech, the event organizers presented Waxman with a "Lifetime Achievement Award." He graciously accepted the recognition, but when they allowed him to say a few words again, he basically told everyone "Thanks, but I still have years ahead of me. I'm not finished making contributions." Waxman lived for 25 years more, and after hearing what he said, I don't imagine he simply sat back and watched the rest of his life slip by.

I've often thought of Waxman while writing my memoirs. Even though I'm setting down these stories at this later stage of my life, this doesn't mean I'm finish. I may no longer go on any dangerous adventures, but I might have a few more stories (or books) to write. Even so, who knows? My main character from "The Mezet Trilogy," Marc of Mezet, is the oldest man of his village in my book *Marc's Final Journey*, but even so, he becomes wrapped up in some pretty dangerous adventures. Maybe I still have a few of those in store for me, too.

As I near the end of this book, if I can pass along any advice to others, it is this: live well, live as much as you can while you can, and live until you simply can't live anymore.

While organizing my memories, it also became obvious how knowledge learned during one phase of my life allowed advancements or revelations in others. For example, work experiences early in life taught me how to be successful in later jobs. Hunting for fossils with the Texoma Rockhounds as a boy led me to become a museum curator in Venezuela years later. And nearly everything I learned during my life has influenced me as a writer. As a finally bit of advice, while you live as much as you can, you should also learn as much as you can. Learn as much as you can no matter what you do. You might find this knowledge useful later.

Thanks for reading.

Acknowledgements

I wish to thank Frances Tucker, Esther Alford, Virginia Thompson, Cindy Reynolds, and Stella Thompson for their continued support. The Denison Public Library and Grayson College provided technical assistance. The small photo in the upper left corner of the front cover was taken by Keith White.

The Author's Round Table Society provides constant encouragement and collaboration. This diverse group of writers is now more than ever being recognized for their talents, and I'm pleased to now be numbered among its knights. I would especially like to thank James and Claudette Peercy (James is the author of *Without A Conscious* and *The Wall Outside*), Amber Jerome-Norrgard (*1:03 A.M.* and *Practical Life Advice*), Terri R. Malek (*My Path to Omega*), Natalie Clountz Bauman (*True Ghost Stories of Grayson County, Texas, Quantrill's Raiders in North Texas and Grayson County*), Thomas Fletcher Grooms (*Market Intelligence, The Original Work, The Collapse of Russia, a Time to Remember*) Rita Ownby Holcomb (*A Twist of Tobacco* series), William Jay Taylor (*The Father's Son, A Viking Saga*), Jackie Smith (*Cemetery Tours* series, *Trashy Romance Novel*), Alan Martin (*Fountain of the Gods, Dream Time*), and ChandaElaine Spurlock.

As always, I wish to thank my wife, Belkis, and my daughter, Mary Ann, for their continued patience and help. I love them very much.

Important Additional Note:

If you have read this far, there is something readers can do to help independent authors like me and like the authors listed above. If you liked this book or whatever other books you read (or even if you don't like them), please write a review on Amazon, on Goodreads, or on any other site where reviews might matter. It doesn't have to be an essay on why the scorpion fly doesn't really sting or how 8mm Mauser rifles with large trigger guards were made to fit hands wearing winter gloves. It can simply be a short note, even if it only says, "I liked it," or "The sexy character named Lee is someone I wish I could meet." This small act will help authors more than most people can imagine.

For one thing, it gives an author a little feedback, which helps any writer to improve his or her craft. Also, it's not just about the money for many authors (although the money surely helps in most cases); feedback encourages authors to keep going (showing writers that working on the dining room table for several months in hot temperatures without air conditioning to produce a novel a reader might consume in a couple of days is actually worth the trouble). Most importantly, when enough reviews are posted on some sponsored websites, the promoters begin to take notice and actively advertise the author's work. If you can do this, writers will be eternally grateful, and readers will also benefit. If you don't want to leave a review because you believe the website might be spying on you, at least tell your friends. This also helps. Thanks in advance.

John M. Moody
Denison, Texas

P.S. Here are some other references I found useful when writing my memoirs.

Butsch, Robert, "The 1957 Dallas Tornado," (updated August, 2018) http://1957dallastornado.net/

Cassel, Jonathon F., 1969, *Tarahumara Indians*, The Naylor Company, San Antonio, TX, 160 p. (1969)

"Eisenhower Birthplace History," Texas Historical Commission (2018) http://www.thc.texas.gov/historic-sites/eisenhower-birthplace/eisenhower-birthplace-history

Logsdon, David R., *Tennessee Antebellum Trail Guidebook*, Kettle Mills Press, Lyles, TN, 128 p. (1995)

Oden, Sue Barton, *Hold Us Not Boastful, A History of Thompson's Station, Tennessee, and its People*, Creative Designs, Thompson's Station, TN, 238 p. (1996)

The Division Historical Association (ed.), *Lightning, The History of the 78th Infantry Division*, Washington Infantry Journal Press, Washington, DC, 301 p. (1947)

The Walt Disney Family Museum, "Walt's Animation and Special Effects Master: Josh Meador," posted Oct. 11, 2017, https://www.waltdisney.org/blog/walts-animation-and-special-effects-master-josh-meador

United States Naval Aviation 1910-1970, NAVAIR 00-80P-1, US Government Printing Office, Washington, DC (1970)

Other Books by John M. Moody

(Romantic Adventure / Mystery Novels)

Brass Puzzle (Second Edition)
Searching for Jennifer (Second Edition)
Return to Nowhere (Second Edition)
Into the Center of the Shadow (Second Edition)
Many Shades of Green (Second Edition)
Intersecting Destinies
Wherever the Wind Will Take Us
Land on the Verge of Darkness
Shards of Time
Woman in White, Cage of Black
Snake Bluff Lodge
The Mighty Hand of Doom
Just Another Tree in the Forest (Coming Soon)

(The Mezet Trilogy - Future History / Adventure)

Journey from Mezet (Second Edition)
Second Book of Marc (Second Edition)
Marc's Final Journey (Second Edition)

(Science Fiction)

Fossil Excavation on Kanos IV (Coming Soon)

See them at
amazon.com/author/jmoody

Made in the USA
Coppell, TX
14 August 2023